MAPS FOR PSYCHOANALYTIC EXPLORATION

MAPS FOR PSYCHOANALYTIC EXPLORATION

Parthenope Bion Talamo

Italian edition edited by Anna Baruzzi
This translation edited by Chris Mawson
Translated by Shaun Whiteside

Karnac Books would like to thank the Melanie Klein Trust
for their generous support in the translation of this title.

LONDON AND NEW YORK

This book was originally published as *Mappe per l'esplorazione psicoanalitica*
© 2011 Edizioni Borla srl
Via delle Fornaci, 50 - 00165 Roma

First published 2015 by Karnac Books Ltd.

Published 2018 by Routledge
2 Park Square, Milton Park, Abingdon, Oxon OX14 4RN
711 Third Avenue, New York, NY 10017, USA

Routledge is an imprint of the Taylor & Francis Group, an informa business

Translation copyright © Shaun Whiteside 2015

The right of Parthenope Bion Talamo to be identified as the author of this work has been asserted in accordance with §§ 77 and 78 of the Copyright Design and Patents Act 1988.

All rights reserved. No part of this book may be reprinted or reproduced or utilised in any form or by any electronic, mechanical, or other means, now known or hereafter invented, including photocopying and recording, or in any information storage or retrieval system, without permission in writing from the publishers.

Notice:
Product or corporate names may be trademarks or registered trademarks, and are used only for identification and explanation without intent to infringe.

British Library Cataloguing in Publication Data

A C.I.P. for this book is available from the British Library

ISBN-13: 9781782201038 (pbk)

Typeset by V Publishing Solutions Pvt Ltd., Chennai, India

CONTENTS

PREFACE ix
Claudio Neri

FOREWORD xvii
by Chris Mawson

INTRODUCTION xxi
Anna Baruzzi

CHAPTER ONE
Why we can't call ourselves Bionians (1987): notes on the
   life and work of W. R. Bion 1

CHAPTER TWO
Psychoanalysis is a "poppy field" (1988): "vision" in analysis;
   a *divertissement* about the vertex 9

CHAPTER THREE
Ps $\rightleftharpoons$ D (1981) 17

CHAPTER FOUR
The role of the group with regard to the "unthinkability"
of nuclear war (1987)   21

CHAPTER FIVE
On "non-therapeutic" groups (1989): the use of the "task"
as a defence against anxieties   29

CHAPTER SIX
Warum Krieg? (1990): the Freud–Einstein correspondence
in the context of psychoanalytic social thought   39

CHAPTER SEVEN
Aggressiveness-bellicosity and belligerence (1991): passing
from the mental state to active behaviour   49

CHAPTER EIGHT
The creation of mental models (1992): basic and
ephemeral models   73

CHAPTER NINE
Experiences in Groups revisited (1992)   91

CHAPTER TEN
Some notes on the theories of structure and mental functioning
underlying *A Memoir of the Future* by W. R. Bion (1993):
festschrift for Francesco Corrao   103

CHAPTER ELEVEN
From free-floating attention to dream-work-α (1993)   117

CHAPTER TWELVE
Inside and outside the transference: more versions of the
same story (1995)—or: history *versus* geography?   131

CHAPTER THIRTEEN
The concept of the individual in the work of W. R. Bion,
with particular reference to *Cogitations* (1996)   143

CHAPTER FOURTEEN
The two sides of the caesura (1996)   159

CHAPTER FIFTEEN
Bion and the group: knowing, learning, teaching (1996)   167

CHAPTER SIXTEEN
Bion's contribution to psychoanalysis (1996)   179

CHAPTER SEVENTEEN
Bion: a Freudian innovator (1997)   197

CHAPTER EIGHTEEN
Dreams (1998)   211

CHAPTER NINETEEN
From formless to form (1998)   225

CHAPTER TWENTY
Laying low and saying (almost) nothing (1998)   239

REFERENCES   245

FURTHER READING   249

INDEX   253

PREFACE

Claudio Neri

> It is true that with regard to the history of science it is important to be able to attribute correctly to their authors the paternity of the concepts used, but it is also true that thinking dies if it is not re-fertilised and subsequently developed in the generation and the mind of each thinker. (Bion Talamo, Chapter Ten in this volume)

One of the numerous threads in this collection may be indicated in a single sentence: Parthenope seeks her father, and after many efforts and vicissitudes, she finds him along with the psychoanalyst. The pages in which Parthenope manages to connect the father of her earliest childhood with the "mythical psychoanalyst Bion" are very beautiful, as in this extract from Chapter Twenty in this volume:

> Some years ago, a friend of mine, Silvio Merciai, noticed that when I speak in public about W. R. Bion I tend to oscillate (in quite a disconcerting way). [I tend …] to refer to him as "Bion" and […] "my father". […] If I am thinking of him as I remember him personally—and when I was a child he was simply "Dad", and […] I tend to use a more familiar term, but if I am thinking of his theoretical or clinical writings, I tend to refer to him as "Bion", as people normally do in a scientific context.

Today [...] I will move from one use to the other. You have been warned!

Reading was a very important part of our family life, from the moment that my father read to us three children in the evening at the weekend, as Francesca [Parthenope's stepmother] did during the week.

The [...] quotation [that I want to mention today] comes from one of the stories of *Uncle Remus*. [More precisely it is] "The Wonderful Tar-Baby Story", which is part of the saga of the unending struggle between Brer Rabbit and Brer Fox, who was his sworn enemy. In this particular story, Brer Fox makes a sort of statue of tar mixed with turpentine and sets it in the road along which the rabbit will be passing. The tar-baby, of course, does not reply to Brer Rabbit's polite greeting—so Brer rabbit, punches, kicks and butts it with his head, to teach it a lesson in good manners, getting completely stuck in it, all four paws and his head too, while Brer Fox lies low, and the tar-baby goes on saying nothing. [...] I remember my father [when telling this story] misquoting it as "Brer Fox, he lay low and he said... Nothing".

I now tend to think of Bion as an analyst partaking a little of the characteristics of all three figures, the fox, the tar-baby and the rabbit.

For example, his comments on α-elements in *Cogitations* make it quite clear that there really were moments when he felt "stuck", like the rabbit, and that he was only able to get clear of the morass by thinking very deeply about his own emotional reactions to the atmosphere in the consulting room.

And as for the fox? Well, from my childhood memories of him, I can imagine my father "laying back" in the rocking-chair in his consulting room and just waiting to see and to feel his way through what was about to happen—although not with the malicious intentions of the story-tale fox.

The complex concept of working without memory or desire links up, in fact, with the idea of trying to purify your mind, letting what is inessential sediment somewhere and drain away, so that you could have the "laying low" without the sneaky or violent element [of the fox in the story].

The other points that arise in connection with "laying low" include simply sitting and waiting, with the negative capability involved in this stance, not striving after answers of any sort.

The effort that Parthenope makes is one that we should all make. How to use in clinical work some concepts elaborated by Bion, without being too subjugated by his myth. In other terms, how to think of the concepts proposed by Bion while expressing them with one's own images and words, one's own style and voice.

A second thread that goes to make up the fabric of the book corresponds to the reflection on the difficulty of thinking about nuclear war. In Chapter One, Parthenope aptly begins by stressing that the problem of thinking something is never separable from that of feeling, and giving a place to the emotions that accompany it:

> [...] The thoughts expressed [...] in a session [are not separable] from the emotional climate that is created and which underpins the formation of thoughts, which are then expressed verbally.

In Chapter Four, Parthenope Bion Talamo then interweaves the theme of how to think about atomic war with that of the relationship between the individual and the group:

> Holding a thought in one's own mind means to some extent making oneself responsible either for feeding that thought or for standing up to it, but if our mind has nothing in the internal or the external world to shore up the disaster provoked by the encounter between a frightening preconception and an equally frightening external reality, we give up thinking about it. Here the mechanisms so masterfully described by Hanna Segal: denial, separation, projection, linguistic mystification, which make it difficult even for the group to confront the reality of what a nuclear war would imply.
>
> It seems quite likely that the single individual cannot manage this mental situation in which he has to receive the thought of total destructiveness, in isolation, and has to entrust himself to the group, in the hope that this, with a function analogous that of the original breast, may contain "the scream" and render it thinkable. But to which group can he entrust himself, and what can the group do?

Parthenope Bion Talamo goes on to develop the problem of the difficulty of thinking some frightening thoughts, linking it to the concept of *Caesura*. This concept is introduced by Parthenope in only two lines, with great elegance, in Chapter Fourteen:

> The slamming of the door alone might be too abrupt a caesura. (At the end of a session it's better to have a patient who's irascible but full of thoughts).

The dramatic passage from intra-uterine life to that of the aerial extra-uterine environment is not only a caesura; simply leaving the atmosphere, the thoughts and feelings in which we are immersed in the course of the session and going into the world of everyday life can also be one.

Parthenope Bion Talamo then goes on to develop the concept of the caesura more broadly, and put it in relation with the difficulty of thinking:

> Even though I have not dwelt for long on the aspect of connection of the caesura, I maintain that it is clear from the clinical material presented that [some] patients use the interruptions with the intention of creating [not a separation, but] a connection. But these [attempted and abrupt connections] are [often] only pseudo-connections because each of them is a kind of shaky bridge over an abyss of anxiety, "Do not look down!"
>
> But if the analyst is lucky enough to be able to feel that the bridge has a dull and unconvincing sound, and that the patient can do so as well, or is helped to do so, it becomes possible to "look down" and see something of this abyss [...]. In this way the caesura/interruption may sometimes be transformed, through the reversal of perspective, into a [possible] caesura/connection with a subsequent evolutionary passage [in analytic work].

The reflection launched by Parthenope about the difficulty of thinking the effects of a nuclear war strikes me as important for many reasons; one of these is that her effort is continuous with that of many writers, philosophers, artists and poets who have attempted to match this task, and that of giving form and representation to the horror of colonialism, the terror of the First World War, to the loss of direction and orientation of the hyper-modern condition.

It is also an important reflection for analytic work. How many resistances and how much emotional turbulence must we confront when we try to look at the relationship with a certain patient in a new way, considering him in a different light from the one in which we have always viewed him? But the theme that has always struck me as most original is that of the geography of the mind, as in Chapter Twelve:

> I have convinced myself [...] that my way of working with patients might be [...] compared with the revelation of the topology (or geography, if we prefer) of the patient's mind, because it certainly does not follow a linear trajectory [...].
>
> The fact of trusting oneself very much to "free-floating attention" in the concentrated form of reverie favours the emergence of "self-selecting facts", and these quite rarely have connotations of any temporal (and hence causal) considerations. The reason for this is that the reverie is an instrument that is refined to pick up the movements of the primary process: this is the thought that must be picked up *in statu nascendi* and interpreted [in psychoanalytic work], not that of the secondary process, in which time and cause have their appropriate role.
>
> In reality, the idea of a map (perhaps with "hic sunt leones" and question marks along the lines of "inland sea?" in many of its parts).

Parthenope had talked to me about this idea a long time before I had an opportunity to read the text. Listening to her, I had imagined an actual map, with colours and more or less stable borders dividing different populations. "The evolved and refined idealists"—for example—might live in a territory on the top right, and bizarrely share a border only with "the inconclusive mad", whose chance of meeting them via "in contact with analysis and analyst" necessarily involved crossing their territory and entering into relations with them. And so on.

This idea of maps and different populations had struck me as a far more valid image than the hypothesis about the existence in the psyche of internal groups. Speaking about populations and their territories, in fact, draws the attention to general characteristics of functioning of the psyche, and avoids reconfiguring it as a package containing a quantity of "little men" brought together in a group. (For

Parthenope Bion Talamo's use of *internal group*, see Chapters Nine, Fifteen, and Twenty.)

I have put this model of maps and populations to the test in my clinical work. And in fact, reconfiguring patients' psyches—in this way—has turned out to be useful for me both in terms of reflection on my analytic work and in discussions with colleagues bringing me accounts of their clinical work. The maps that I sometimes drew during supervisions in fact succeeded in giving an immediate idea of the concurrence of different aspects of the functioning of the psyche of the person whose problems we were trying to understand. They also clearly showed how certain ways of functioning might be very remote and almost unrelated to one another, while others had borders in common. Last of all, the maps allowed us to make hypotheses about what happened if a population changed its seat and established new relationships with others, and so on.

A few years later, a colleague talked to me about a book by Philip Bromberg whose title *Standing in the Spaces* (1998–2001) was translated into Italian with the much less expressive *Clinica del trauma e della dissociazione* [Clinical treatment of trauma and dissociation].

My friend and colleague maintained—rightly—that one of the interesting ideas in the book consisted in the fact that in contemporary society it is illusory to speculate about working with patients with a view to integration. The goal that we can realistically set for ourselves is that of *standing in the spaces* between the various aspects of the self of the people who come to us for help. Our standing in spaces is a way of testifying to the possibility of some kind of bond between different states of the self.

I then read Bromberg's book. He expresses himself rather differently from the way my colleague had (creatively) done, suggesting that every form of integration and any condition of psychical wellbeing always imply the concurrence of different states of self:

> Psychological "integration" [...] does not lead to a single "real you" or a "true self". Rather, it is the ability to stand in the spaces between realities without losing any of them, the capacity to feel like one self while being many. (Bromberg, 1998–2001, p. 256)

One other important element in Bromberg's book corresponds to the attention that he devotes to border areas and/or areas of superimposition between various states of the self.

Bromberg's text reminded me of Parthenope's maps. I thought above all of the importance of the fact that the borders between the different territories might not be rigid "transitional areas".

So I started thinking in terms not of one transitional area, but of many: many, as many as the adjoining states of the self (Winnicott, 1953).

So an aspect of my clinical work changed. I have—always—worked more with patients about the quality of the border and transit areas (we might even speak—using Bion's concepts—of caesuras or linkings), and about how I was able to see them and about how the patient became aware of them. Reflection and observation about what happened in these areas of linking and borders enabled, for example, some of my patients to be less afraid of what at first seemed to them to be incomprehensible mood shifts, the appearance of strange feelings and fantasies, faint phenomena of depersonalisation, the difficulty of reaching feelings and states of mind which had, even recently, seemed to them to be within their reach.

FOREWORD

Chris Mawson

Parthenope Bion Talamo had a deep comprehension of her father's work, and particularly his later work, including the allusive and wide-ranging *Memoir of the Future*. Her understanding is evident in the papers and the talks that comprise this book, in which she conveys with clarity and directness her own ideas and those of her father. She understood that Wilfred Bion's overall project was, as she put it in her paper *Ps ⇌ D* (Chapter Three), "to make the emotions that permeate the abstract formulations of psychoanalytic theories come alive for the reader or the listener".[1]

Parthenope appreciated that Bion's model of the mind was, essentially, phenomenological and dramaturgical. He seems, she wrote, to have adopted a model, "... in which all the aspects of the personality in their chronological personifications are simultaneously present". This derives from Bion's description of the personality and its presentations variously as a drama, a palimpsest,[2] and analogous to the images

---

[1] (1981). Rivista di Psicoanalisi, 27: 626–628.
[2] Paper, parchment, or other writing-material prepared for writing on and wiping out again, like a slate.

viewed in a kaleidoscope. Insofar as the idea of a palimpsest is useful, the analogy to the human personality holds up particularly well if the reader considers a writing-surface which, when its contents have been erased, something remains nevertheless, mysteriously beneath whatever has been over-written upon it. The large canvases of the painter Gerhard Richter are a good example.[3]

In his 1966 paper, "Catastrophic Change", he had written that his description "could be seen as a dramatized, personified, socialized and pictorialized representation of the human personality". Parthenope describes how such a perspective adds a dimension to the standard tripartite model of ego, superego and id, expanding it in such a way as to reduce the explanatory usefulness of the concept of regression.

In her writing, and in her thoughtful responses to her questioners, Parthenope shows a consistent and rigorous curiosity into what she calls "the simultaneous presence of archaic and evolved aspects" of the mind—or, as she also put it, "the internal world as populated by a congregation of parts of the personality".

I will pick out just two further threads. The first is to do with psychoanalytic method. The second relates to a potential misuse and misunderstanding of Bion's work.

In relation to the former, Parthenoperesponded to a questioner who raised the issue of *narrative*.[4] She replied, associating to a recollection of one of Bion's *Cogitations*:

> "… the narration of a dream in which things apparently come in sequence is sometimes what the patient imposes on material that is not in fact sequential. But the narration forms a kind of mortar that sticks together the different little pieces. Sometimes I've told a patient that I had a sense that he was relating a dream as if it were a story, when in fact it was, let's say, three different scenes relating the same thing on different levels of the mind, or with regard to different aspects of the patient's life, and hence the narrative form was in fact, in a sense, a fake one. *But we tend to prefer narrative to*

---

[3] There is a film of Richter painting; he paints fairly detailed "under-paintings", which he contemplates in an evenly-suspended way for some time, and yet all but a tiny, almost imperceptible trace of this image will be hidden permanently by the subsequent layers of his painting.

[4] End of Chapter Eighteen, *Dreams*.

> *anything else.*[5] It is true that in the twentieth century this is changing, we are getting used to things that don't necessarily tell a story, so I am a little worried, it's too much! In short, I'm a bit doubtful about the influence of 'narratology' in psychoanalysis and in psychoanalytic interpretations because I have a sense that we are making a big mistake, that we are privileging, as if it were something important, something that is only a habit of our way of thinking".

Here Parthenope is reminding us of something remarkably difficult to hold onto—the central importance of *evenly-suspended attention*, in which sequence and cause are suspended in order to allow a state of mind receptive to the impressions and indications of non-sensuous, psychic reality to emerge and to evolve in the psychoanalytical situation. I like her neologism, "Narratology". It has the sound of a disease.

Parthenope, in the paper that forms the first chapter, "Why we can't call ourselves Bionians", stresses Bion's mental freedom, making a particular point that her father did *not* found a new and separate school of psychoanalysis, and that it makes no sense to speak of "Bionians". (I would add that it makes as much sense as speaking of followers of Hanna Segal as "Segalians"). Unfortunately her insistence on this has gone unheeded. She writes, at the end of her paper:

> To conclude, I would like to say that it is probably this quality of mental freedom that made Bion such a disconcerting person, and an academic who could not, by his very nature, "found a school"—we cannot call ourselves Bionians, because that would primarily mean being ourselves, being mentally free of our voyages of discovery—always, however, on the basis of personal iron discipline, because freedom and anarchy are not synonymous.

Finally, I want to draw attention to the following passage from Parthenope's text (Ch. 8). It is a clear description of the mental journey that she has undergone, and which informs all of the work contained in this book:

> In the course of working with these and other patients, and also in the course of a kind of continuous monitoring of my own mental activity, which it is perhaps not entirely improper to call

---

[5] My emphasis.

"self-analysis", I think I can acknowledge that I have constructed for my own professional use a model of mental functioning which, although based on classical models, does not precisely coincide with them. Or rather, I think it is necessary to have as instruments of analytic work some types of visualisation of the mental structure and mental events, and that these visualisations lead to the use of a specific and personal vocabulary. At this point I find myself face to face with Bion's advice that every analyst finds his own personal linguistic baggage: but now I know what lies behind that advice, what type of mental journey I have had to take to begin to understand it.

It was with delight that Francesca Bion heard from Oliver Rathbone of Karnac Books that Parthenope's writings, published already in Italian, had been translated into English for the first time and were almost ready for publication. I too am grateful to Oliver and to Karnac for making this possible, and for the generosity of the Melanie Klein Trust for their financial help and support. Parthenope's writings are a significant psychoanalytic contribution in their own right, as well as helping illuminate some of Bion's more difficult ideas.

INTRODUCTION

Anna Baruzzi

Parthenope has gone; her bright star was extinguished too soon.

I met Parthenope in the early seventies: I clearly remember our first meeting. She was living in Rome at the time with Luigi and Alessandra, her first daughter who was very young. Patricia hadn't been born yet. I remember that it was a meeting organised by other people for some reason involving her father Wilfred Bion. I remember that I went to that meeting with a certain reluctance, because I imagined that it would be very formal, and was only going out of duty.

It was early afternoon: I remember the immediate impression I had when I found myself face to face with an extraordinary person, and my curiosity was aroused by trying to understand why, as I completely forgot about the problem of her father and the reasons for our appointment.

It all made me very happy, as sometimes happens when we unexpectedly meet an interesting and unusual person.

I remember that we immediately started talking nineteen to the dozen, going off in all sorts of tangents; the sulks disappeared straight away, and I was invited to dinner, and our chitchat about things, some deep and very sad, continued without a break, as we went to the park with Alessandra and then to the kitchen while Parthenope prepared a roast dinner.

Parthenope was still thinking about starting analysis, which she then went on to do with Dr. Adda Corti.

I still look back with nostalgia at Parthenope's particular quality of being able to discourse quite naturally with her thoughts and imagination in areas of constructive dreaming (Parthenope was very committed to the anti-war movement), to be able to condense a large number of intense and sympathetic thoughts in essential times.

Parthenope had a very broad mind that she carried modestly and with great reserve: a genuine desire for knowledge, a rare intellectual honesty that instilled respect and was reflected in her clear, clear eyes that opened wide as she listened, like the eyes of a little child.

Talking to Parthenope brought the serenity transmitted by people who know how to be really in contact with the saddest events, with great suffering. Sometimes she would fall into a gloom, and her eyes darkened, as if she were carrying a very heavy burden: the burden of all human beings, her own particular burden, and the enormous one already borne by her father.

But she was also an authentically cheerful person, with a great sense of humour, with a silvery laugh which often, I noticed at the time, faded into a gloomy smile which I later came to think belonged to little Parthenope whose mother had died too soon.

Parthenope had a great capacity for contact with people, and understood them, so she had lots of friends all over the world and in Italy, where she had put down roots to an extraordinary degree. She very much liked having ideas that she stood up for like a warrior, but she was really interested in, and knew how to value, other people's ideas.

She would listen attentively, and then express a point of view of her own which was plainly full of respect; this meant that it was possible to remain in "loyal disagreement" with her. I remember the respect with which she approached her psychoanalytic training with the Società Psicoanalitica Italiana from the first discussions onwards; she had a completely non-cynical trepidation that always struck me.

So she had gradually succeeded, with great commitment, in being Parthenope, and also Bion's daughter.

I remember the work groups in which we took part in various circumstances, both with the SPI and without: she automatically knew how to present herself as one individual among others; even though she was very shy at first, she worked passionately and without arrogance. She was particularly affectionate and generous towards our group in Pollaiolo, because of the great esteem in which she held Francesco Corrao, and we owe her real gratitude for the pleasure of her presence.

Parthenope was a mature psychoanalyst, her experience acquired with great effort and richly deserved, and she could afford to express her original thoughts about her father's work more freely so her contribution became more and more precious and constructive. Her death has left great sadness in all of us.

This volume effectively brings together all of Parthenope Bion Talamo's published works. I have also included some less refined interventions for various occasions and seminars to which Parthenope was invited more and more often in Italy and abroad.

I hope readers will appreciate the variety of subjects addressed which, an unusual element in a psychoanalytic text by a single author, brings together and weaves into a single fabric essays on themes of technique and theory of dual analysis, a large paper on groups and the relationship between individual and group, to digress into themes that are particularly current today, such as the relationship between man and environment, and the unthinkability of nuclear war. The latter were subjects particularly dear to Parthenope, who had participated and continued to participate actively in pacifist initiatives; she was a member of International Psychoanalysts Against Nuclear Weapons (IPANW).

A tireless industriousness then brought Parthenope to collaborate on institutional initiatives one example of which is a major task performed with groups of workers with the Department of Social Medicine of Busto Arsizio, Valle Olona on the treatment of terminal illness. For obvious reasons of privacy and the fragmentary nature of the minutes of group meetings, it has not been possible to publish that experiment.

I have not included the presentations that Parthenope made of the writings of W. R. Bion, *Cogitations* and "Domesticating Wild Thoughts", and *Gruppo* by C. Neri. Another work that could not be included was the thesis for the PhD (pursued in Florence in 1974), of which Parthenope was very fond; the result of intense work think is extremely precious into the use of meta-mathematics in psychoanalytic meta-theorisation, with specific reference to the work of I. Matte Blanco (1980) and W. R. Bion (it can be found on the SPI site "Introvabili").

The thread that links all the essays in this collection is the profound and original reflection that Parthenope was doing into her father's work: sometimes called Dad, sometimes Wilfred Bion, and the constant preoccupation with being able to divulge his thoughts in the most accurate way. This work culminated in the organisation of the International Centennial Conference on the work of W. R. Bion—W. R. Bion: Past and Future, held in Turin in July 1997, and of which she was president.

It might seem that some texts are repetitive: in fact, some identical quotations are used to develop different thoughts in different directions.

This book contains, in condensed forms, reflections on subjects that we have debated, and which we have probed over the course of the last few years; I do not think that they are dated, but rather that they are particularly useful both for those who know Bion's thought and those who want to approach it. Bion is very well known today but not really very much read.

I find that, apart from the inclusion of personal memories and an outline of Bion's life, the quality of the text also makes Bion more accessible than many writings about his life.

I will allow myself some "word play": the affectionate familiarity, respectful but free, of Parthenope with W. R. Bion's thought offers an opportunity for detailed and fascinating reading.

CHAPTER ONE

Why we can't call ourselves Bionians (1987): notes on the life and work of W. R. Bion

Bion has the reputation of being a difficult writer—abstruse, tough, and, I would add, not easily reducible to a "short summary". In fact, it is practically impossible to speak of his work overall without misrepresenting it: so it seems to me that the simplest, and perhaps the wisest, approach is that of identifying at least some of the elements that make this work such uneasy reading, not least for the psychoanalysts who are the audience the Bion specifically had in mind as the addressees of his books.

To start with, we may make a first, crude (and falsifying) distinction between form and content: then, might difficulties of reading have arisen only because his style of writing was intentionally so concentrated as to appear practically spare? Or is there some difficulty inherent in the nature of the object under discussion?

I think that both these factors probably have a role to play, and I maintain that it is worth looking at them in greater detail, before moving on to some considerations of Bion's life in the light of his intellectual journey. From the first work published by Bion with his own signature—hence omitting articles in scientific journals that were published anonymously—which is a chapter in the contribution to a book edited by Emanuel Miller into shell-shock victims, published in 1940, we see two aspects of Bion's writing which will remain throughout the whole span of his creative life and which give, from the start, an idea of the stylistic difficulties of his work, that is, a need to write in a clear and concise way, and the preoccupation with the emotional effect that his words have been able to produce in the reader. The text of Bion's chapter begins as follows:

> The war of nerves is nothing new as a fact of human experience; what is new is that its existence has been recognised under an almost medical title. The subject is too vast and too theoretical for a book which is intended to be of immediate use, and this chapter will therefore be limited to the consideration of a few points that may be helpful in understanding practical suggestions made later. *If the style is dogmatic, this may be taken as a symptom of the need for compression and not as a claim to omniscience.* (Bion, 1940, p. 5)[1]

Without making any other comments, I should like to juxtapose with this quotation a phrase from a paper by Nissim Momigliano (1981) in which she describes her own reaction to a paper by Bion from 1967[2]

> ... the unusual style, absolutely unexpected for a scientific work. This author, almost unknown to me at the time, did not propose, but proclaimed in a curt, crisp and almost hermetic way ... (Momigliano, 1981, p. 546)

It may be said that a certain essentiality of writing, which obliged Bion to make quite a recherché and precise choice of terminology, was one of the constants in his work, and I think in the extreme economy of Bion's writing we may identify one of the reasons why it is so difficult to "sum up" Bion—is already a "brief summary" in itself. He seemed to write according to a sculptural rule of Michelangelo's, that of "taking away": having always set himself the problem of how to write to be better understood, Bion "lent an ear", so to speak, to the

---

[1] Author's italics.
[2] Notes on Memory and Desire (1967) was published in 1969 in Italian, Notas sobra la memoria y el deseo. *Revista de Psicoanàlisis*, XXVI, 3, 679–682 (translated from *The Psychoanalytic Forum*, 1967, II, 3).

possible reactions of his readers, to the emotional effect that his words could evoke. It is certainly no coincidence that in this short paper from 1940 there already appears a fragment of Tacitus in which the Roman historian describes the emotional effect on the barbarian hordes of the war chants of their bards, and the use made of the observations of the emotional reactions of the mass of warriors to make a decision about what to do. This attention devoted to the emotional reactions of the reader, which is naturally interwoven with the accurate choice of terminology, developed more and more with the passing years until it became the pressing need to write about psychoanalysis in such a way as to make the object of the analytic discourse *present* in all its concision.

In the last trilogy (*A Memoir of the Future*, 1975–1979), we can clearly see how for Bion the object of analytic discourse takes in not only the thoughts expressed, for example, in a session, but also the emotional climate created, and which underpins the formation of the thoughts, which are then expressed verbally. Certainly the desired stimulation of the reader's emotions, which are then "discussed" with him—hence the dialogue form of certain passages in these books—is one of the factors that make these last texts very unsettling to read. Until now, we have identified two elements that make it very difficult to read Bion calmly, and also to talk about his work over all—the essential writing and the evocation of emotions. This leads us to the second aspect of the problem—is it possible that there is something inherent in the very nature of the universe of discourse that Bion has chosen that makes it impossible to "place" him? And which also has a profoundly unsettling effect on his readers? I think so: I think the universe we are dealing with is a post-big-bang universe—a universe in expansion after the catastrophic changes that have occurred in various waves through the work of Freud, Klein, and Bion himself. We can no longer think in terms of a closed system; as Bion asserts a number of times, *we must not* think of psychoanalysis as a closed system, as a container of psychoanalytic knowledge, but rather as a spatial probe. Our problem is that we can only follow the probe, we can't know where it will go—we are always on the brink of the unknown, and this is an extremely disagreeable situation. We might say that the "mystic" Bion has "burst" the previous bounds of the analytic universe: so what happens next, and how do we go on practising psychoanalysis today?

Bion's advice to eliminate Memory and Desire, advice that has given rise to a great variety of misunderstandings,[3] is revealed not to be an esoteric asceticism, but something like a practical piece of advice very firmly rooted in professional experience; following this technique, we can see moment by moment the evolution of the session, the subtle movements and displacements of forces which "are" the psychoanalytic session.[4] It turns the experience psychoanalysis for the analyst—and, I think, also for the patients—something absolutely extraordinary and unique; certainly the initial price that is paid when we try to put this particular mental discipline into practice, which has a curious aesthetic quality, is to feel extremely lost and unsupported—where are the psychiatric nosology, the structures and defences, the ego, the self? Where can I anchor myself? The answer seems to be nowhere—if you anchor yourself, you stop travelling.

This mental attitude on the part of the analyst, which at first glance seems to be a long way away from Freud, is nothing but the evolution of free-floating attention through the maternal reverie, and is an emanation of a meta-psychological concept that underpins all of Bion's work, that of truth, in a meaning, however, very different from the more familiar religious one, in which the Truth is considered Absolute and Immutable. For Bion, on the other hand, the truth is in a continuous process of becoming, in evolution.—it is not a progressive approach towards the truth on our part, but the evolution of the truth itself.[5] This concept, in itself simple to set out, turns out to contrast starkly with the usual way of conceiving the truth. It also seems to be quite a difficult concept to link to practical life—not only in psychoanalysis, in sessions, where its use, working from this point of view, is often accompanied by an effect of "holy terror", but which also asks us how the perception of truth *as a process* can change the individual's way of life and daily thought—or perhaps it makes no difference?

I think, on the other hand, that it does make a difference, in an obvious way. Of course, it is a commonplace that the scientist is in constant

---

[3] See, for example, Cremerius (1985, p. 115): "… the others (for example Bion, 1976) say that analysis is aimed at attainment [*on the part of the patient*] of a state 'free of memory, desire or understanding'." The italicised text, which gives the complete sense of Cremerius's phrase, is the author's.
[4] Very illuminating with regard to the work of Betty Joseph and "psychic change".
[5] See *Attention and Interpretation*, Chapter Three.

search of the truth—but this is not the point. If I look at the development of Bion's work, and his life choices after the First World War, bearing in mind the concept of "ever-evolving truth", I think I identify a certain coherence which bears out the sense of restlessness—and which corresponds, incidentally, to Fornari's critique concerning the "break in continuity" that Bion often mentions in relation to the transformations in K.[6] My impression of Bion, as a person, was of someone who lived every intellectual experience so intensely as to get to the bottom of it, and to touch the boundaries of the mental space that that experience could give: at this point, simply, those boundaries which had been a goal became an obstacle to be overcome, a jetty to set off from for other shores, in a way similar to those in which the individual's first defences, being functional and useful, become an obstacle to subsequent growth: but Bion did not allow himself to be obstructed for long—he had a great sense of freedom.

In this light we may see how the experience of working with a great surgeon, turns into an interest in work that its not surgical at all, on the herd instincts in peace and war, how these interests then led Bion to undertake a course of psychotherapy with Hadfield at the Tavistock, to perform psychotherapy himself, to deal not only with formal groups (not intended to treat the individual in the group—publicly—or to discover the origins of the unease of the individual in the group, but rather to show that individual neuroses are a problem for the group, and that the group must learn to manage the disorder created by its own sick members) but also social aspects and social duties of the specialist in psychic matters—it is highly illuminating with regard to the work "Psychiatry at a time of crisis" along with the chapter of Miller's book quoted above.

In 1937 it appears that Bion had exhausted the possibilities of psychotherapy and began a course of analysis with Rickman: his first impact on the training committee of the British Society seems both like a good illustration of his own need to make things clear and the capacity of the British Society to "make room" for a personality who was perhaps, even then, a little awkward, and not at all inclined to compromise. On 3 May 1938, the name of Bion appears in the minutes of the training committee because he was not willing to sign the commitment not to use the

---

[6] See Fornari (1981, p. 655).

title of psychoanalyst, or that of not working as a psychotherapist if he were accepted as a candidate. On 5 July the Committee was informed the Bion had agreed to reformulate this commitment after a discussion with Glover, and had promised that he would not go on working for the Institute of Medical Psychology[7] after completing his analytic training. On 25 October Rickman informed the Training Committee that Bion had begun analysis with him, and the decision was made to treat Bion *as if* had been accepted as a candidate.

In reality, the course of Bion's training was not easy, not just because of his previous relations with the Tavistock, which were very unpopular, but also because he had to interrupt his analysis with Rickman, because of the war, and because they found themselves working together in Northfield, he was unable to resume it. In spite of the advice of the teaching committee to begin an analysis with Winnicott, Bion preferred to start with Klein in 1945. He was elected Associate Member in 1948 and a Member in 1951. Bion's move to California in 1968 responded not only to his need to live in a climate more tolerable than the one in London, but also the need to open up new mental spaces, of find new stimuli.

I would now like to turn my attention to Bion's work, to see if we can follow the evolution—perhaps only of a single concept—through the phases of conception, birth, development and abandonment, when the concept itself had become too tight and rigid a container for its author's thought; perhaps the concept that left a more visible trace is that of the grid.

This story also begins in the 1943 paper "Intra-group tensions in therapy" (originally published in *The Lancet*, it was then published as the first chapter of *Experiences in Groups*, 1961). Bion was trying to explain how he visualised the future organisation of the training wing of Northfield, a military hospital where Bion and Rickman had the task of managing patients "with nervous illnesses". I quote Bion's visualisation of "… the projected organisation of the training wing as if it were a framework enclosed within transparent walls. Into this space the patient would be admitted at one point, and the activities within that space would be so organised that he could move freely in any direction according to the resultant of his conflicting impulses. His movements

---

[7] This was the name of the Tavistock Clinic before the war. I am indebted to Miss P. King for this information.

as far as possible were not to be distorted by outside interference. As a result his behaviour could be trusted to give a fair indication of his effective will and aims, as opposed to the aims he himself proclaimed or that the psychiatrist wished him to have." I think that anyone familiar with the use of the grid to map the patient's movements during the sessions will recognise its precursor in this brief sketch. The actual grid appeared in 1963, and remained a valid working tool for a number of years.

The short paper "The Grid" dates from 1971, but its importance already seems to be diminishing from "Notes on memory and desire" (1967), and *Attention and Interpretation* (1970) seems to mark a kind of watershed, in which the rigidity of the grid is gradually abandoned in favour of the richer and more generative concept of ideas concerning the idea of seeking "configurations" in the session and the evolution of O.

We might also wonder on which plane in his strictly personal and family life Bion felt the same freedom of development. I have tried to work out whether there are traces of my memories of Bion, as a father and not as a psychoanalyst, because they might be able to shed some light: an episode immediately came to mind which struck me as entirely normal, even if in retrospective it made me think a great deal about Bion's ability to contain his own paternal anxieties in favour of other people's freedom.

I had to leave, having just turned eighteen, for a long period of study in Italy. The day before I left, my father told me he wanted to talk to me in his study. I went into the room: silence—he was writing, perhaps he hadn't even noticed that I was there. After a while, and without much enthusiasm, because I had expected something paternal in some way—which would have been logical—I said, "I'm here."

"Oh, yes—I just wanted to say two things to you before you left. Remember to go and see the contemporary paintings in the Pitti Palace as well," (meaning, don't forget that Italy, Italian culture, isn't just a thing of the past, it's alive and growing "and also, this is for when you get lost." "This" was a little map of Europe and Asia Minor.)

To conclude, I would like to say that it is probably this quality of mental freedom that made Bion such a disconcerting person, and an academic who could not, by his very nature, "found a school"—we cannot call ourselves Bionians, because that would primarily mean being ourselves, being mentally free of our voyages of discovery—always, however, on the basis of personal iron discipline, because freedom and anarchy are not synonymous.

CHAPTER TWO

Psychoanalysis is a "poppy field" (1988): "vision" in analysis; a *divertissement* about the vertex

When I was very young and went on long journeys on the London Underground every day, I always read the advertisements; among them was (and still is) a series of humorous "poems" singing the virtues of pure virgin wool. I remember them only vaguely, apart from the last line, which was always "There is no substitute for wool". The phrase came into my mind recently as something closely associated with psychoanalysis—perhaps only because those journeys took me to sessions? Could be, but there's also a more serious reason: for tonight I wanted to write an essay elucidating some particularly difficult aspects of Bion's work—or at least those which I find to be so—and thought about calling it something like "From the 'Grid' to the 'O'". But that would have required some quite ponderous, lengthy restructuring of Bion, which struck me as both presumptuous and fruitless—nothing can substitute for the personal reading of Bion, if you want to read and know him, of course, because he was perfectly capable of writing what he meant to say, and needs no exegesis. It might seem that this assertion sits badly with what I said a moment ago, namely that there are difficult aspects; but taking a closer look, it seems to me that these concern the *practical application* of Bion's ideas within the analytic session, particular with regard to the concept of absence of memory and desire in the analyst, and I would like to clarify some of my ideas about this problem, which in my view has a great deal to do with the "vertex", the point of view from which the analyst "sees" the session.

Because Bion's work "Notes on memory and desire" (1967) is very short, I quote it in full so that it can serve as a basis for the talk I should like to give about putting these ideas into practice:

> Memory is always misleading as a record of fact since it is distorted by the influence of unconscious forces. Desires interfere, by absence of mind when observation is essential, with the operation of judgement. Desires distort judgement by selection and suppression of material to be judged.
>
> Memory and Desire exercise and intensify those aspects of the mind that derive from sensuous experience. They thus promote capacity derived from sense impressions and designed to serve impressions of sense. They deal, respectively, with sense impressions of what is supposed to have happened and sense impressions of what has not yet happened.
>
> Psychoanalytic 'observation' is concerned neither with what has happened nor with what is going to happen, but with what is happening. Furthermore, it is not concerned with sense impressions or objects of sense. Any psychoanalyst knows depression, anxiety, fear, and other aspects of psychic reality, whether those aspects have been or can be successfully named or not. These are the psychoanalyst's real world. Of its reality he has no doubt. Yet anxiety, to take one example, has no shape, no smell, no taste; awareness of the sensuous accompaniments of emotional experience are a hindrance to the psychoanalyst's intuition of the reality with which he must be at one.
>
> Every session attended by the psychoanalyst must have no history and no future. What is 'known' about the patient is of no further consequence: it is either false or irrelevant. If it is 'known' by patient and analyst, it is obsolete. If it is 'known' by the one but not the other, a defence or grid category 2 element (1, 2) is operating. The only point of importance in any session is the unknown. Nothing must be allowed to distract from intuiting that.
>
> In any session, evolution takes place. Out of the darkness and formlessness something evolves. That evolution can bear a superficial resemblance to memory, but once it has been experienced, it can never be confounded with memory. It shares with dreams the

quality of being wholly present or unaccountably and suddenly absent. This evolution is what the psychoanalyst must be ready to interpret.

To do this, he needs to discipline his thoughts. First and foremost, as every psychoanalyst knows, he must have had as thorough an analysis as possible; nothing said here must be taken as casting doubt on that. Second, he must cultivate a watchful avoidance of memory. Notes should be confined to matters that can be recorded—the program of appointments is an obvious example.

Obey the following rules:

1. Memory: Do not remember past sessions. The greater the impulse to remember what has been said or done, the more the need to resist it. This impulse can present itself as a wish to remember something that has happened because it appears to have precipitated an emotional crisis: no crisis should be allowed to breach this rule. The supposed events must not be allowed to occupy the mind. Otherwise the evolution of the session will not be observed at the only time when it can be observed—while it is taking place.
2. Desires: The psychoanalyst can start by avoiding any desires for the approaching end of the session (or week, or term). Desires for results, "cure" or even understanding must not be allowed to proliferate.

These rules must be obeyed all the time and not simply during the sessions. In time the psychoanalyst will become more aware of the pressure of memories and desires and more skilled at eschewing them.

If this discipline is followed, there will be an increase of anxiety in the psychoanalyst at first, but it must not interfere with preservation of the rules. The procedure should be started at once and not abandoned on any pretext whatever.

The pattern of analysis will change. Roughly speaking, the patient will not appear to develop over a period of time, but each session will be complete in itself. `Progress' will be measured by the increased number and variety of moods, ideas, and attitudes seen in any given session. There will be less clogging of the sessions by the repetition of material that should have disappeared and, consequently, a quickened tempo within each session every session.

> The psychoanalyst should aim at achieving a state of mind so that at every session he feels he has not seen the patient before. If he feels he has, he is treating the wrong patient. This procedure is extremely penetrating. Therefore the psychoanalyst must aim at a steady exclusion of memory and desire and not be too disturbed if the results appear alarming at first. He will become used to it and he will have the consolation of building his psychoanalytic technique on a firm basis of intuiting evolution and NOT on the shifting sand of slight experience imperfectly remembered which rapidly gives way not to experience, but to neurologically certain decay of mental faculty. The evolving session is unmistakable, and the intuiting of it does not deteriorate. If given a chance, it starts early and decays late.
>
> The foregoing is a brief account distilled from putting the precepts advocated into practice. The theoretical implications can be worked out by each psychoanalyst for himself. His interpretations should gain in force and conviction—both for himself and his patient—because they derive from the emotional experience with a unique individual and not from generalized theories imperfectly "remembered". (Bion, 1967)

At this point I should like to make some comments directly about this paper, which was not, I would say, "received well" by the psychoanalytic community which, with a few exceptions, ignored it. It isn't difficult to understand, but I think that if one is used to working with the mental structure of an orthodox psychoanalyst, to take an example that we can all imagine, it must be very difficult to think that the Bion's mental attitude is *right* as an approach, or that it can really lead anywhere, or promote the psychoanalytic process. This work is supported by a way of thinking diametrically opposed to that of the medicalisation of psychoanalysis, in which the patient must be "made to have" certain experiences, or "brought to" a certain stage or result; this kind of fundamental philosophy which seeks to take a voyage of discovery into the patient's inner world, into the analytic relationship and at the same time inside the analyst himself, clearly provokes a great deal of hostility among these analysts, most of whom any case prefer the "medical attitude".

The first paragraph does not require a comment. In the second, Bion refers to a problem connected with the use of the grid, which he himself would develop in 1970, in the following terms: the grid can be used to categorised the patient's expressions insofar as they are "transformations", and in this way an idea can be made of what is happening; but this kind of understanding is based on a collection of memory and desire, and hence it is not opportune to use it during the session, but only afterwards, as a stimulus to the analyst's capacity to make conjectures. This is the invisible type of use of the Grid which structures the work silently, for example in the Total Transference Situation as described by Betty Joseph.

In the fifth paragraph, Bion uses the grid to announce, in a form of psychoanalytic shorthand, a complex concept which might be expanded like this (1977): box A2 contains an element -β saturated—in this case, an affirmation that the patient knows is wrong, but which he none the less considers useful in preventing the start of any development in his own personality which might form part of a process of catastrophic change. The patient knows the truth (albeit unconsciously), and tells the analyst the untruth, blocking the discourse and saturating it with a defence. That section of the work is about the rules to be followed in terms of one's own mental discipline, which truly requires a revolution in one's own way of thinking: how the analyst can reach a state of mind in which they feel they have in front of them a new and unknown person at each session. It isn't very easy, but perhaps training oneself not have to have desires about the patient's journey or the session and then to block nascent memories ... but what did Bion have in mind when he speaks of "intuiting the unknown"? And then, he must have had some preconception about the human being before him, and some types of criteria to finish the analysis.

Something can be said about the latter: starting from the reflections on this brief work I should like to examine them first:

Bion's experience of analysis (and also of lived life) was such that he always had an ear open for signals of anxiety and fear, however faint they might be, and no matter how much the patients themselves might invite him not to take them into account. In the clinical seminars "Brasilia 1975" a notable attention emerges concerning the unconscious anxieties of the patients about what might come out of themselves, certainly Freud's idea expressed in *Analysis Terminable and Interminable* (1937c), that the ego defends itself against the changes experienced in the analysis because it remains afraid of them, is very present in Bion's working mind. I have the impression that if he permitted himself to expect something in particular, it was that both the patient and the analyst would be afraid.

As regards the "end of analysis" in this essay there is a brief indication in the sense that we may expect a better integration articulated on the part of the patient. And "intuiting the unknown"—what type of idea, what type of technique, lies behind that phrase? That is the point where putting Bion's ideas into practice becomes difficult! I have a sense that the only people who might really know something about it are his pupils and supervisees, but because that is not my (or our) fate, we must approach the problem in a different way. Thinking about it, I remembered some extra-analytic lectures that Bion gave, which amused him and which I remember allowed him to find some felicitous expressions specifically concerning analytic observation. One of them comes from Conan Doyle's Sherlock Holmes stories, in which at one point he says to Watson: "… And then there's the business about the dog barking …" Watson replies: "But I didn't hear a dog barking!" "Exactly!"

That story came to mind the other day with regard to a dog that didn't "bark"—he arrived with a remarkable anticipation of his session, and I, unaware of the fact that he was waiting for the lift, came down from my study with a few chairs in my hand to give to the concierge, and on the ground floor I met the patient, with a rather startled expression on his face. I told him he could go up and make himself comfortable in the waiting room. In the session, the patient made no reference to that meeting, but instead spoke of how during the holidays he had "put in the fridge" his feelings of absence and loss about me. Then he told me that he had been vaguely relieved at the fact that at a party he had met only his ex-fiancée and not her current companion. Then he had left the party and spent all afternoon walking on his own, feeling rather empty. End of the communication. Silence. I had a sense that something was wrong—certainly, it didn't seem to me that there was anything to interpret in his communication. After a while I told him it seemed to me that inside that package in the fridge there were also feelings of jealousy and curiosity about me, less "acceptable" feelings that he hadn't been able to talk about.

Another author of detective stories that Bion liked was Chesterton, and he sometimes quoted a story in which the murderer leaves the scene of the crime undisturbed, dressed as a postman, while everyone present swears that "no one was there".

I have always understood this story as an indication that that which is present in the session can be so obvious as to escape the attention—it can be thought so normal that its significance becomes invisible. Something of the kind recently happened to me with a patient who started relating a dream at the beginning of the session—long, detailed, very rich in meanings but I couldn't keep my attention on what he was saying—not even for half a minute, I kept slipping into lacklustre and irrelevant thoughts. It was a very curious situation. Once the dream was over, the patient fell silent—not even an association. He fell asleep, waking up a few minutes before the end of the session to tell me that he had dreamed again during the session, but couldn't remember anything: "Doing analysis certainly is very difficult". This comment allowed me to tell him that I had a sense that he was unconsciously trying to make it difficult for me too. In fact it was quite obvious, but I hadn't "noticed" it before, just as I hadn't noticed the subterranean hostility that dictated such behaviour.

Kipling was an author who had always been well-liked in my family, albeit with some reservations about his bellicosity and his respect for the military and brute force, and a little book of literary criticism of two short stories by Kipling gave Bion another example of "reading" of the unknown: the critic simply pointed out that in a short story about the capture and training of elephants, Kipling had introduced a whole other topic, under the surface, concerning the art of creative writing—and that what Kipling said about that art was important, but the salient point was this: a double reading of the text, approaching it from another point of view.

The idea of a different picture that appears if we look from a different vertex is central in Bion's work—we can find it from 1963 onwards, and it also informs the "game" of $Ps \leftrightarrows D$. I have a sense that one of the benchmarks of the different vertex is the use of his own reactions as an indicator of the emotional state of the patient: sometimes he almost has to do violence to himself to turn mentally on his heels and look inside, it may seem as if he has to force the barrier of his own desire for peace and quiet, and not to know: these are probably the moments when he needs to seek clues in what he is not conscious of within himself, to bring into the light of day something that might have its roots in his own counter-transference, in short, this is the moment of "Analyse, analyse thyself" within the session.

Among other things the desire for peace and quiet is one of those desires that Bion recommends eliminating.

I was recently struck by my reading of a passage from *Remembrance of Things Past* in which Proust describes the way in which, from a more or less stiff-joined position of his own limbs, he can "deduce" in which bedroom he is sleeping: I think that this is quite a common experience, and that it is possible to draw an analogy, however jocular, of the problem that faces the analyst who must look at himself to understand something of the patient.

And the famous poppy-field? Is it going to turn up at long last, or was it just a joke?

No, it wasn't a joke, even if, in a small game of slightly mad free associations I even found myself thinking of the Italian singer Nilla Pizzi (and her song "Poppies and paper"), as well as more solemn figures like Sir Thomas Browne, who speaks in "Urn Burial" of the poppies of oblivion. But I had started out with a more serious consideration: Bion often uses visual images to illustrate what he means to say, and one of these is a reference to an impressionist painting of a poppy-field. I have no wish to go into Bion's discourse on the subject, but I would like to use the same type of image to explore another aspect of the problem of vision in analysis. If we think of Botticelli's *Primavera*, for example, and then about a scene by Monet—perhaps the four studies of Rouen Cathedral, or Westminster Bridge between 1900 and 1904, or Monet's own *Springtime*, we note that in the second the forms emerge from the juxtaposition of the masses of colour, and from their blurred edges rather than from drawn lines. It seems to me that it is always useful, in an analytic session, to allow one's own mind's eyes to unfocus slightly, not necessarily to follow the path presented by the patient, but to allow oneself to pick the masses of colour that stand out the most. To return to my second clinical vignette, I would say that the patient's linear discourse within the dream was less significant than the colour of drowsiness with which his way of speaking was suffused—that was the configuration of the session. There are no poppy-fields in my study, but seen from the couch it presents only white, rather bare walls: but these act for me as hilltop and hedges[1] and encourage the deep concentration that allows cumbersome thoughts to fall away so that the patient can penetrate the indeterminate spaces of analytic experience.

---

[1] This refers to a poem by Leopardi. [Tr.]

CHAPTER THREE

Ps ⇌ D (1981)

At this conference I would like to present a small "unpublished object" by Bion which seems to me to illuminate an aspect of his way of working and may render more explicit one of the problems in which he was very immersed, particularly towards the end of his life, namely how to enable the reader or listener to understand the emotions in which the abstract formulations of psychoanalytic theories are drenched.

This type of problem has always been present in Bion's work since *Second Thoughts*, in which he asserts that "the subject matter with which psychoanalysis deals cannot employ any form of communication which can cater for the requirements of a problem in the absence of the problem". This phrase seems to me to imply the desire was already present in Bion's mind to indicate to the reader the subject under discussion in such a way as to make it emotionally present; to discuss it straight away with an immediate awareness of its emotional aspect. It seems to me that this kind of preoccupation informed the choice of the atypical style of the trilogy *A Memoir of the Future*, a text, among other things, about which little has been said in this conference, and which is probably a part of his work that still needs to be very well digested, as Meotti has written (Meotti, 1981) before it becomes available to be forgotten, and is the chief reason for alternating these books of highly evocative fragments with others of critical comment and reflection.

But I consider that this problem has already been given another type of solution which is not purely literary on a very reduced scale, still not taking into account a whole vast range of human emotions, as in the last trilogy, but only the kind of emotion implicitly contained in the formula $Ps \rightleftharpoons D$.

In *The Kleinian Development*, Meltzer criticises this formula for its lack of connection with the emotions, but I consider the criticism to be unfounded. In *Elements of Psycho-Analysis* Bion speaks of the "operation" of $Ps \rightleftharpoons D$ and asserts that: "It may be considered as representing approximately (a) the reaction between what Melanie Klein described as the paranoid-schizoid and depressive positions"—what is called oscillation—"and (b) the reaction precipitated by what Poincaré (1902) described as the discovery of the selected fact. This selected fact is what the thinking individual notices as a fact that suddenly harmonises all the other scattered facts; it is one of them, but it allows the thinker to "see" the meaning that was not visible before.

In the same text, Bion tries to clarify, with relation to β elements, which "operation" this is, and on page 40 he says: "I do not claim the existence of a realisation that corresponds to the description that follows; it must be taken as a representation of an hypothesis that is necessary to give coherence to diverse clinical observations."

"The β elements are dispersed; this dispersal should be terminated by $Ps \rightleftharpoons D$, and a selected fact, unless ..." The problem of how to make explicit the emotions accompanying the operation of $Ps \rightleftharpoons D$ + the selected fact is something that continued to irritate or annoy Bion for a long time, and eventually he tried to give concrete form to the realisation that he mentions in the fragment quoted above, probably between 1967 and 1972. Put into words, these emotions are describable as sensations of persecution and frustration, followed by a moment in which understanding occurs, along with a coagulation of the depression (Meltzer considers that this coagulation of depression itself becomes an element of the net problem—rather as the synthesis of a Hegelian triad becomes the thesis of the triad of the higher level) (Meltzer, 1978).

This formula, on the other hand, which had its "reification", almost like a game which consisted in the presentation to the unaware interlocutor of a rectangle of perforated cardboard with a peg in each hole (see diagram): the coloured pegs represented the dispersed β elements and effectively produced a sense of frustration in the interlocutor. The selected fact, on the other hand, which had to be applied mentally to the dispersed elements, was the concept of the "triangle". At the moment when the interlocutor realised that each peg was part of a triangle, in such a way as to "organise" the dispersed elements, he had passed through an oscillation from the paranoid-schizoid position to the depressive one, and was fully aware of the emotions involved in that oscillation. It seems important to me to stress that Bion seemed to consider that this kind of oscillation, drenched in emotions, was at the root of human thought. I should like to conclude by saying simply that it seems to me that this was one of Bion's first attempts to identify the analytic object, emotion, and at the same time to discuss the object itself critically and theoretically. I have a sense that it was the same kind of concern with the difficulty of identifying the emotions that underlay Dr. Corti's suggestion that clinical vignettes should always be presented along with theoretical works.[1]

---

[1] Personal communication.

CHAPTER FOUR

The role of the group with regard to the "unthinkability" of nuclear war (1987)*

The problem of the existence on earth of nuclear weapons, and of governments which contemplate their use in some way, cannot be seen by a psychoanalyst as exclusively political, economic or social: it is imbued with unconscious thoughts and fantasies, and I consider that it is very important to try to carry these unconscious elements to the conscious level, with a view to mitigating their power. The concept of nuclear war is supported by a fairly complex tangle of fantasies of different kinds; they certainly include fantasies of omnipotence, of personal magical immunity; there are also apocalyptic, millenarian, "religious" aspects—which sometimes emerge publicly in the statements of American politicians. Today I should like to distinguish one of the aspects of this tangle, and attempt to examine it in rather greater detail: the so-called "unthinkability" of nuclear war."

Recently I happened to read a review of a book about the various concepts of civil defence current in different countries—the USA, the USSR, Switzerland and Great Britain—in which nuclear war was described as

---

*Paper for the seminar of the "Forum for the problems of peace and war", December 1987, Florence.

"unthinkable". Apparently the reviewer meant that nuclear war was to be considered unacceptable, given that he was talking about a series of preparations which implied that at least the governments of those four countries were thinking about war in some way, but I have a sense that there is a truth hidden behind that imprecise use of language, which deserves to be studied.

Paradoxically, the real problem with nuclear war, unlike all the wars of the past, is not how to do it, but how not to do it—because doing it would mean destroying the human race, and the whole planet, and many of us think that that *must not* happen. When I say *must not* I mean something in the discourse that seems to be a moral element—but it is a morality that is not connected with the justice or otherwise of a given religious doctrine, political system or simple physical supremacy, but with the survival of the species: its roots can be traced through the super-ego to the id and the instinctual needs of the libido.

And yet, countless individuals do not seem to think that the question of nuclear war exists in these terms, as if the individual ego were not aware of the moral imperative present in the id: one of the *consequences* of this curious "leap" (to whose mechanisms I will return later on) is the way of thinking for which a nuclear war might be a local war, to be won or lost—and yet circumscribed and "elsewhere"—we think of the Gulf or Afghanistan, the Americans in Europe, as possible (and acceptable) theatres of war. Why is it so difficult to take on board the idea that the age of nuclear war is something different, something never experienced before? I think the difficulties appear on more than one level, in the individual, in the group, and in the relationship between the individual and the group—in those moments in our own lives, that is, when we are not in harmony with our own group and it presents itself as an interlocutor, or when we are standing up to the group, still dependent on it, but in solitary opposition to it.

It seems that as individuals we cannot believe (I would say, to conceptualise, and hence to think) in such a total degree of destructiveness, even when we do our best to do so. One very concise example of this arose in the course of a television programme on the nuclear winter, which showed the slow devastation of a piece of forest irradiated during a period of several years by a tiny radio-active source: the ghostly forest was quite striking, but all around the clearing there were trees that were still intact, and further away from the centre others were still alive. It seems that we cannot bear to visualise destruction that is not in some way contained and withstood by life flourishing again. To take account of the real dimensions of a boundless danger, we have to shake off a certain mental torpor, which seems to us like a kind of mixture of disbelief and impotence, and we have to try to find the appropriate mental means and theoretical instruments. Only when we have confronted the problem on the individual plane will it be possible to understand more clearly what happens within the group, what can be the positive function of the group and what the dysfunctions that a group may face and, perhaps, how we may try to stand up to them. Certainly, these are quite complex arguments, and today I want to limit the detailed discourse to the role o the group with regard to the individual, making only brief nods to the aspects of internal group dynamics.

But what theoretical tools can we use? We face the practical problem of having to put the brakes on human aggressiveness, because our aggressiveness can now use weapons which could slide into total destruction without our will, in the absence of any boundary between aggressiveness and destruction: this is a *new* problem for humanity, one which until now it has been able to fight against, if not with impunity exactly, at least without the risk of self-annihilation. As a new problem, our baggage of social and historical knowledge, and philosophical theoretical instruments, does not seem to be of much help. We are in fact unprepared not only in the face of the nuclear problem as such, but also in the face of having to consider that unbridled aggressiveness turns quite easily into destructiveness. Even a quick glance at philosophical texts creates the impression that for the philosophers of the past war simply wasn't a problem, it was not seen as something that had to be avoided at all costs: Plato, Aristotle, Rousseau, Hume (1739), and even Hobbes speaks of it as a "natural" aspect of the human condition, indeed as a moving force behind social contract, or an event in which, sooner or later, states find themselves involved. Politics, on the practical level, and political philosophies on the theoretical level, are in a sense attempts to regulate and hold back the phenomenon of war, on the basis of a fundamental acceptance of its inevitability as an inherent aspect of social life. They all exalt courage in war as a necessary virtue and all of them take it as a given—so obvious that it can be taken for granted—that only the military class is involved in war and that the civilian population is relatively protected (even though a not particularly deep reading of the *Iliad* and *The Peloponnesian War* (Thucydides) shows how differently poets and historians saw the situation).

So we have at our disposal these concepts of regulating war once it has been waged, but find ourselves confronted with facts which mean that nuclear war cannot be waged, and the classical concepts are no longer sufficient. Perhaps the reviewer was correct after all, and nuclear war is unthinkable because we lack the instruments to think about it?

But in this century we have already had to confront the problem of how to think about the unthinkable, with the regard to the Nazi camps, and the concept of genocide, thoughts that didn't even distantly concern the classical philosophers: I consider that the psychoanalysts who have had either survivors of the camps or their children in analysis perhaps know more about this particular "unthinkable", either regarding the social aspects of "ignorance" of the existence of the camps on the part of the local population, or from the point of view of the enormous difficulty that the survivors had trying to think about their own experience and communicating it to their own children. The idea emerges very clearly from many psychoanalytic studies about the survivors and their family relations that we cannot bear the thought of the camps: but while saying this, there is an implicit trust or belief that in reality (if circumstances had been slightly different) the human mind is perfectly capable, as it is, of receiving and elaborating this idea: but if we render explicit this premise concealed within our discourse, we can see that it too might be, and it is worth exploring this possibility.

Psychoanalysis has not dwelt at length on the formation of healthy thought, since for historical reasons it has been more interested in problems to do with the emotions and with unhealthy thought, so much so that Laplanche and Pontalis's (1967) dictionary does not even have a heading dedicated to "thought" or "thinking", and that this aspect of the life of the mind is just treated *"en passant"* in relation to subjects such as schizophrenia. In spite of this, some theorisation of this human activity obviously underlies our work with all patients, not only with psychotics, because we need standards for good mental functioning and some ideas about the genesis of the activity of thinking. The theories to which I refer personally in my work, and which I use as a scenario in which to be able to visualise "the state of the art" in the thinking of each patient, all derive from the area of thought of Klein-Bion-Segal, and a philosopher might be able to discover a neo-Kantian flavour in them.

THE ROLE OF THE GROUP WITH REGARD TO THE "UNTHINKABILITY"   25

Above all, the genesis and development of thought are seen as functions of a two-person relationship, between child (infant) and mother. The mother is not yet conceived as a person by the infant, but reduced to a breast. It is suggested that at birth the baby has a preconception of the breast (instinctual? genetic? Something closer to the physical than the mental, perhaps), which will encounter in external reality a realisation, a breast, that will give it real milk. But there are occasions in which the breast is not immediately present to satisfy the instinctive need for nutrition, and the preconception of the infant is frustrated; if the child is mentally healthy and can tolerate a sense of frustration (and, however, if the mother is reasonably good, this state of frustration will not last for every long), the child will start to conceptualise a non-breast (which is the absent breast), and this is a painful thought, linked to painful physical sensations such as hunger, for which the non-breast is bad. The first thing that the newborn child does at this point is cry, to expel the bad thing, the non-breast, and "magically" the real, concrete breast appears. This repeated experience forms the basis for a mental situation in which thought is lived, experienced, as a positive activity, which really works with regard to the outside world, produces an effect, produces a significant link with another being. Fundamentally, it seems that our thought is oriented towards dealing with a good world, a world that will come to meet us if we ourselves make a little effort, a world which we instinctively "trust".

Even if it remains profoundly unconscious, this prototype of thought continues to be active throughout our lives; it is joined by new abilities for introjections, we learn to keep vanished objects patiently in our minds while they cannot be connected together, we learn to endure processes of separation and integration. The fundamental truth, however, remains as a mechanism of primitive thought, that the spontaneous reaction to a bad thought is to expel it, in the hope that something better may take its place.

The problem that the prisoners in the extermination camps had to face was that the expulsion of the thought of their own situation was not followed by relief, but by the confirmation, in external reality, of a situation of non-breast, of hunger, death, insanity, with nothing to mitigate that confirmation. When Primo Levi says of the drowned, "... and if we could sum up in an image all the evil of our time, I would choose that image, which is familiar to me: an emaciated man, his brow lowered and his back bent, with no trace of thought to be read on his face or in his eyes", he is speaking of the condition of man entirely alone, the one who does not, as Levi did, have someone to share his suffering with.[1]

My experience with patients who are the children of ex-deportees, particularly those whose mothers were in extermination camps, is that the parents passed on to their children their own lack of confidence in the possibility that life has meaning, that a meaning can be conferred on it, that the devastated zones can be circumscribed with something alive, that there was a less hostile world outside the camp: all of this is passed on unconsciously, and it is the result, I think, of this experience of the annihilation of thought that Levi mentions.

We may then suggest that both the thought of the concentration camp and that of a nuclear winter should correctly be considered unthinkable for the individual, and we can also have a better understanding of how the preventive destruction of groups opposed to the Nazi regime really played a fundamental role with regard to the problem of "knowing nothing" about the extermination camps: the single individuals had no support group that could contain that thought that was "unthinkable" for the individual. Holding a thought in one's own mind means to some extent making oneself responsible either for feeding that thought or for standing up to it, but if our mind has nothing in the internal or the external world to shore up the disaster provoked by the encounter between a frightening preconception and an equally frightening external reality, we give up thinking about it. Here the mechanisms so masterfully described by Hanna Segal: denial, separation, projection, linguistic mystification, which make it difficult even for the group to confront the reality of what a nuclear war would imply.

It seems quite likely that the single individual cannot manage this mental situation in which he has to receive the thought of total destructiveness, in isolation, and has to entrust himself to the group, in the hope that this, with a function analogous that of the original breast, may contain "the scream" and render it thinkable. But to which group can he entrust himself, and what can the group do?

If the individual becomes part of a group to which he does not delegate his own responsibility, he will be able to observe that there "advantages"

---

[1] Levi, P. (1959) *Survival in Auschwitz (If this is a man)*. First published in 1947 in Italian as *Se questo è un uomo*; English translation by Stuart Woolf published in 1959.

on the emotional level, because the good functioning of a group with a common task can effectively reassure the individual that what cannot be borne if faced alone, in a group is partly stripped of its devastating ferocity. This situation allows the ego-functions of the individual to develop and strengthen themselves. Of course the good functioning of the group depends on its managing to remain on the level of the sophisticated work group, and holding at bay the unconscious mechanisms connected to primitive fantasies hostile to thought. One of the means that the group of individuals wishing to think about the nuclear problem has at its own disposal to safeguard itself against the emergence of counter-productive behaviour is, rather paradoxically, practical powerlessness.

Perhaps one example will help to shed some light on this thought: the large institutional work groups can put up with the emergence of phenomena of psychotic thought which, rather than encouraging the development of thought at the level of the ego, favour either super-ego (moralistic) reactions or actions. I think that we can identify signs of this kind of behaviour in those military groups which attempt to persuade national parliaments that they can use "limitations" of nuclear weapons; this strikes me as a flight from thought, and signals the tendency on the part of the group not to take on board the real significance of nuclear war. It seems to me that the formation within civil society of groups that have neither political power nor military power can create a space for the elaboration of thoughts that are too painful and dangerous for the individual, whose capacity for thought can be severely compromised (left at the mercy of the super-ego and the id) if he remains isolated, but that they need a place in which they can be treated at the level of mature thought. This mature elaboration can lead to a real understanding of the risk that we run, fundamentally, at the level of the peoples of the earth, and hence, I think, to the elimination of the danger. It is not enough to ask a specialist group (Parliament, for example) of which we are not physically a part and which is not felt psychologically as an emanation of ourselves, to take on the task of elaborating a series of thoughts which integrate the intolerable thought, because all of us suffer as individuals beneath the weight of this thought—as many studies of adolescents have shown, the very presence of nuclear weapons damages the quality of mental life—and we also feel the need to protect our mental health.

To conclude this brief paper, I would like to sum up the salient points: as human beings we are all burdened with the impossibility of really understanding, with an emotional adherence to the thought, what a nuclear war means: this is a thought that the ego refuses to understand—it might be said that we are born too optimistic and too sane to be able to think it: at the same time we intuit the necessity to prevent a similar catastrophe occurring, and to do that we have to form groups which are mentally sufficiently strong and practically sufficiently weak to be able to think about the consequences of a nuclear war without going mad and without fleeing into action: groups which are capable of holding an appalling thought in mind and translating that thought into actions that oppose it: this is a new task for the social group, which has until now chiefly had to give room to thoughts which needed to be translated directly into action.

CHAPTER FIVE

On "non-therapeutic" groups (1989): the use of the "task" as a defence against anxieties

Introduction

The hypothesis that I should like to present and develop, which has arisen on the basis of some reflections on work made over recent years with three different groups, is that the assignment of a "task" to a group which meets to study group problems gets in the way of the very study that it is intended to facilitate.

The term "non-therapeutic group" might sound somewhat contradictory, and one might also think that it contains a faintly polemical tinge, but by using it I intend to stress the fact that the groups I wish to describe were not formed with the primary intent of providing help or relief to the individuals of which it is composed, but to try to understand how groups work as groups, certainly with the intention of bringing about modifications which should themselves be therapeutic—with regard to the group. I realise that this is a slightly artificial topic one would expect that the improvements which are therapeutic for the group are also therapeutic for the individual when he finds himself elsewhere, with other people or on his own.

In fact my interest in the psychodynamics of groups is currently directed almost exclusively at the group as an organism, as if it were an entity in itself, and it seems legitimate to me to make interpretations about the behaviour, whether verbal or acted out, of the group, using the concept of the transference, and also using a technique derived from individual psychoanalysis, improperly known as "use of one's own counter-transference". I say that the use of this term is improper because if the transference is unconscious by definition, reciprocally so is the analyst's counter-transference; the most that the analyst can do, with regard to this specific aspect of one's own work, is a kind of monitoring of his own conscious emotions or his own physical sensations, to form an idea of what the patient, or the group, is communicating through the use of projective identification. I think this kind of technique can be used both in the case of very small groups—in which it is perhaps less worrying for the analyst—and with larger groups, but I maintain that we should go rather cautiously, because interpretations can easily prompt very strong emotions in those assembled. In short, I maintain that the appropriate size for a group whose unconscious dynamics one wishes to study should be quite small—I would say no more than six people, even though at the moment I am working with an even smaller group, while the work that is done with a larger group has different characteristics. My experiment with groups of twelve or sixteen people was designed (from my point of view) to discovering what unconscious elements disturbed the pursuit of the institutional task that the group was supposed to accomplish, and how the same structural defences of the group hampered its operation. Having to confront this type of problem also produces a different mental attitude in the leader of the group, who was asked not only to investigate but also supply operational suggestions. In these two groups, which were "institutional" in the sense that they were composed by the consultants in one case and by the nurses in the other, of twelve departments of a local hospital, the perception of the group by its members as an "existing object in reality" was more in the background—but perhaps this lack of self-perception as a group was one of the problems that the group presented unconsciously, a symptom of its unease, even though it was certainly not the reason why I was brought in as an advisor.

The group-dynamic attitude of the work undertaken in the case of the smaller group was not obvious from the outset; in fact, the precise requirement of the components of the group that I deal with intra-group dynamics as such, became clear only after a while, when the members of the group (six general paediatricians—all women) had discovered that their attempts to collaborate on some study and research projects were unexpectedly obstructed by difficulties in the relationship between the members of the group itself. The larger group was also a social organism that was already established in advance of my arrival but since it was a regional hospital, much larger and more complex. In fact, a good part of the "hospital" organisation never joined the groups I dealt with, but it is present as a container of the parts, perhaps more in physical than in mental reality.

The development of the small group

Because the request for intervention in the group of paediatricians emerged from a perception of more or less this kind: "in spite of the friendship that binds us, we cannot work together to understand anything more about our relationships with our patients", it seemed logical, at contract stage, to think of forming a kind of Balint group.

We worked along these lines for about four months, with results that were also good on the level of the comprehension of unconscious interpersonal dynamics between doctors, patients, and family members. I had the impression that, generally speaking, there was a kind of subterranean perception of the existence of transferential and countertransferential problems, without the paediatricians having at their disposal the theoretical instruments necessary to think about these experiences and verbalise them. Also apparent were those elements that made me think of something like a group transference towards me, and one that was very rich and various, but I didn't speak during that phase, because the operation of the "working group" did not seem to grant an opening of that kind. The working group was so functional that it did not in fact present the problems that I was supposed to be clearing up, following the first long interruption for a holiday, the attitude of the group changed.

At the first meeting after the summer holiday, I was informed that there had been a monumental row among the six, and the request to deal as a group with interpersonal dynamics within the group as a problem in itself, worthy of respect, was made explicit. This marked the beginning of a new phase of work. One interesting change which, it immediately became apparent, was the disappearance of the expressions of gratitude with regard to the understanding of very difficult work situations, of appreciation of the possibility of thinking in new ways, etc., which to a great degree characterised the verbal level of the first phase, plentifully accompanied by signs indicating a certain suspicion of me as someone who was probably a secretly sick individual, who refused to be treated (curiously, *all* families brought into the group in the Balint phase had one member—rarely the "official" patient—who was "unsettling", "worrying", "who provided much to think about" for the doctor involved). There had also been many elements in the material that made one think of a strong current of envious hostility towards me.

The group that thinks about itself

When the lid was taken off the Balint group, it was revealed that it constituted a real and actual defensive screen with regard to the seething cauldron below. In a relatively few sessions it was possible to start investigating a group religion, a religious-dependent attitude towards me, with all the doubts of the case and, that is, with which sort of god they were dealing with, and to coincide with that, a series of "pairings" has been identified between different members.

The group seemed to hinge, in spite of itself, on one of its members (A), who had a privileged relationship with one of the others (B) (not least in terms of habit, because they had been friends for at least fifteen years, while the other members (C, D, E, and F) had been united around this nucleus—at least that was my impression). In a recent session (from which B was missing) it emerged that the couple A–B had lived as a couple that could argue and bear the trouble of doing so, while the others were not allowed to do this. The absence of B, the one who mediated all the tensions, brought out the aggressiveness in all the members present. This led D to assert that A "gave the others things to do", something which A took very badly, as if she felt she was being accused of all kinds of abominations. In the subsequent discussion, which was often quite animated, two levels of relationship between the members of the group came to light. A was given certain functions as the boss, not least with regard to other groups with which this group has relationships (in the sense that she implements the group's "foreign policies"), and she accepted these even though the image of the group as egalitarian was still maintained. I thought I spotted in this contradiction, which became quite evident, the presence of unconscious expectations on the part of A with regard to C and D, as pairs of adults, first as parents, with extremely primitive projective associations, probably of the kind mentioned by Bion in *A Theory of Thinking* (1962), when he asserts that communication originally occurred through realistic projective identification, which *also* develops as part of the individual's social ability.

At the same time, more sophisticated sides of the same members create a situation in which A is portrayed as the head of the work group: but the leadership qualities required by this situation are experienced by A as contradictory, irreconcilable and indeed quite harmful, when they are unconsciously confronted with the expectations of a new-born child who "predicts" the existence of a breast, the existence of a pair of parents capable of spotting the primordial projective identifications with regard to C and D.

I think that this gap in levels is partly responsible for the aggressiveness unleashed within the group, intensified as it has been by the absence of B, who could probably perform a maternal role towards A, which did not conflict too much with the demands of leadership.

With this new set of investigations within the group, it was at last possible to detect the unconscious dynamics that hindered interpersonal relations, while on the other hand it was truly remarkable how group dynamics had been hidden by the use of the Balint group—which was itself a good research and study group for relations between paediatricians and users, but not at all appropriate for the understanding of the unconscious problems of the group itself as an entity.

Large groups

The opportunity for my encounter with large groups was provided by the decision, by a local hospital, to undertake research designed to improve the treatment of patients in the terminal phase. It was considered desirable and possible to create a structure of permanent training adapted to this purpose within the hospital. In order to be able to exploit the experience of the different hierarchical levels of the hospital staff, and identify their needs more accurately, the decision was made to approach representatives on all levels, and the first phase of research consisted in the training of homogeneous groups of colleagues for the discussion of the specific problems arising during the treatment of terminal patients.

The groups approached were formed of:

a. Consultants
b. Assistant and deputy physicians
c. Ward sisters
d. Nurses
e. District staff.

The group of consultants met a total of thirteen times, twice to set out the plan of work, 10 times to take the work forward, and once for a summing-up.

In practice, I found myself leading the group of consultants and that of the nurses, while a colleague dealt with the other groups, and research organisation carried out an investigation into patients and family members, with individual interviews, including some on the volunteers.

In theory, twelve hospital departments were involved, but not all the consultants were always present, either through a lack of interest or a feeling of non-involvement, or for reasons of professional commitments, some of them abroad, while in the nurses" group there was often more than one nurse per department present in the group, which made for sixteen members or more.

These groups were intended to be work groups, with the task of examining a case that had been particularly disturbing, or striking for other reasons, with a view to seeing (a) how the treatment of terminal patients were currently structured and (b) what proposals for improvement could arise out of discussions. In fact the work of the groups was very frequently interrupted by: personal memories of the death of a family members; expressions of anxiety about death and the elaboration of a series of defences against them; requests for personalised psychological treatment for the hospital staff, particularly at a nursing level.

Even though the discussions that took place in the groups revealed great unease about the problem of the treatment of terminal patients, both on the personal and the interpersonal levels, it remains likely that any initiative taken to improve treatment may prompt not only enthusiasm but also resistance and objections. One reason for thinking this is the lack within the discourse of each group of a characterisation of the other hierarchical groups, as if there were not an overall image of the hospital sufficiently tolerable to make one think that inter-hierarchical relationships could realistically be influenced—the unconscious images of "others" were all somewhat persecutory. I therefore think that the other levels of the hospital staff are not currently seen as real interlocutors. This will certainly be one of the aspects that we will have to deal with in the next phase of the research, which will consist in enlarged group meetings made up of some members from each of the original groups, which I hope will reveal more clearly the fantasies about colleagues on different hierarchical levels.

One very interesting aspect of the mental structure of the hospital that has emerged is the fact that it is structured in small groups, whose members are constantly changing, in the relationship between the patient and the hospital structure. Of course it is not in fact the hospital structure that deals with a terminal patient, but a series of individuals whose functions and degrees of contact with each individual patient could usefully be evaluated in detail. Similarly, it is difficult to consider the "patient" realistically as a single individual, rather than as the emergent nexus in a network of family relations which is why, in daily practice, the members of the hospital staff find their counterpart in a small group of individuals who are probably all disturbed, anxious and in difficulties with the management of their emotions, which can be contradictory and complex.

This consideration naturally leads us to examine the relationships between the family group and the hospital staff (as they have emerged in discussions so far), particularly at the crucial moment which is the decision about whether or not to tell the truth, and in some cases to whom, when dealing with fatal diagnoses and prognoses. In the course of the discussion with the group of medical consultants, different clinical cases were raised, which indicated how difficult it is for the patient, or his families, to accept being told the truth. Rather than being a justification for the use of half-truths which lead towards lies and fake reassurance, this observation seems to indicate that a great deal of attention needs to be paid to the ways in which these truths are communicated.

It should also be said that in those departments in which the demands of the type of more or less radical surgical intervention make it impossible to hide the truth from the patients, particular counter-indications have not been signalled with regard to clearly informing both the patients and their relatives.

It was precisely the emergence of this aspect of the hospital work that revealed the extent of disturbance in institutional functionality caused by the presence of unconscious anxieties and defences with regard to the subject's own death.

While this theme was not touched upon in the group in the terms in which I have portrayed it here, because this was a "work" group, and interpretations did not in fact fall within our mandate, either as regards terms of individual psychology or in terms of group dynamics, we attempted to obviate this obstacle with a demonstrative "action". A pilot project developed in one of the departments, to test the possibilities of a different modality of communication of diagnoses, based on a model of interactions between small groups (for example the consultant a deputy or an assistant, the ward sister or a professional nurse on the side of the hospital, and the patient with relatives or friends on the other) seemed to give good results on the level of the effectiveness of communication and the containment of anxiety for everybody. When these results were referred to the group by the consultant, who had put into practice this suggestion which had emerged during a meeting about a month previously, some members of the group who had until that point appeared very sceptical about the usefulness of the programme as a whole, began to be a little more convinced in their participation. Furthermore, the group as a whole "took heart" with regard to the possibility of being useful, albeit with the disadvantage that this sense of greater effectiveness might also prove to be bound up with a specific given situation, and not as an acquisition by the group.

This last consideration leads me to think that, in both the study of group dynamics and in psychoanalysis there are no learned theories or interpretations, only the facts that convince those involved of the reality of the psychical life. One other observation that we have made is that while it was clear enough that part of the difficulties encountered in the treatment of terminal patients could be attributed to the group dynamics of groups made up of *departments*, because the two groups I worked with were not vertically structured, it was impossible to see exactly what was happening in each department, which meant that it was seldom discussed and only from the point of view of the consultants or nurses, with no meetings with other hierarchical levels. At the same time, concentrating on the relationship with patients partly obscured the problems deriving from interpersonal and inter-group relationships. It was the change of attitude that took place in the group of paediatricians that enabled the emergence of fantasies deriving from basic assumptions.

Final considerations

In essence I cannot help observing that the assignment of a task to a group, forcing it to become a work group, makes the understanding of underlying dynamics and the elucidation of multiple (and sometimes contradictory) levels of communication more difficult. Conversely, I think that the task can be used to hold at bay very deep anxieties of psychotic disintegration both in the group and in the individual. Even if the group is almost aware of being disturbed by small eruptions from the inner world, defences against the study (which involve the clearer expression) of these "accidents" is rooted in efficiency surrounding the assigned task and the traditional way in which it is pursued. I have a sense that this situation may weigh heavily against institutional reforms, in spite of the presence and activity of some of the individuals and groups who desire them.

CHAPTER SIX

Warum Krieg? (1990): the Freud-Einstein correspondence in the context of psychoanalytic social thought

Introduction

The so-called "correspondence" between Freud and Einstein, which in fact consists of only two letters, is in many ways an anomaly in Freud's work, not only because of its genesis and its contents, but also because of Freud's attitude towards it. It is a work with two contexts, the historical context of the age and that of Freud's work as a whole, the latter located within a broader psychoanalytic contest; and yet it seems curiously remote from any physical or mental setting. Nor does Einstein's letter make reference to the political events of the day, even though they may have been the background to his choice of theme.

In 1931 the Permanent Committee for Culture and the Arts of the League of Nations invited the International Institute of Intellectual Cooperation to organise the epistolary exchanges between representative intellectuals "on themes calculated to serve the common interests of the League of Nations and of intellectual life" (Freud, 1933b, p. 197), and to publish the letters. Among the first to receive the invitation was Einstein, who put forward Freud's name. So here we find a first anomaly, in the sense that this letter does not seem to emerge from a spontaneous need of Freud's to write on the subject; in fact Freud says that he was taken by surprise by the contents of Einstein's letter, because he expected him to write on some other subject, in this case the upbringing of children, and not about something that he called "a practical problem, a concern for statesmen" (Freud, 1933b, p. 203).

A second element that strikes me as anomalous is the fact that there seems to be a total detachment from the political reality of the moment, to which not the slightest reference is made. It is perhaps worth bearing in mind that Freud received Einstein's letter at the beginning of August 1932, and finished his own reply a month later. But the first seven months of 1932 were dense with political events and threatening signals: the disarmament conference in Geneva opened in February, while only four years previously a referendum against the construction of new battleships had failed in Germany. On 9 July the Lausanne conference on reparation payments for war damage on the part of Germany came to an end, ending with the agreement to pay three billion marks. Contextually, Austria decided to forego *Anschluss* with Germany until 1952, in exchange for loans from the League of Nations, in spite of the fact that this contradicted the part of public opinion (Austrian and German) which had been favourable, only a year before, to the creation of a customs union between Germany and Austria, which had foundered on opposition by other European powers. The year 1932 also saw the rapid rise of the Nazi party in Germany, which won the April elections in Prussia, Bavaria, Wurttemberg, and Hamburg, while in the late July elections it had 230 seats.

None of this is mentioned in Freud's letter; and yet Freud was not cut off from his own environment and the political concerns of the moment, as we may indeed deduce from certain statements by Ernest Jones who notes, with regard to 1931, that events abroad were about to exert pressure on Freud's life, and on the psychoanalytic moment in general, starting with the world economic crisis that began with the collapse of the Viennese Kreditanstalt, which led to disastrous political consequences both for Germany and for Austria. In that same year, Freud declared his public support for the Pan-European movement of Count Coudenhove Kalergi, proposing (without success) his candidacy for the Nobel Peace Prize.

The following year, the first year of the correspondence, Freud signed an appeal distributed to the members of the medical profession by Henri Barbusse against the possibility of a new world war, an appeal which concluded with this sentence: "As guardians of the people's health we raise our voice in a warning against a new interminable carnage into which the nations are being driven, the consequences of which are unforeseeable."

Even on the strictly personal plane, however, we find Freud writing to Arnold Zweig, on 18 August (1927–1939), a letter full of worries and concerns about the fate both of Zweig and of Einstein, who had recently been forced to seek refuge in Leiden.

I would like to go on to discuss at greater length this curious "Ivory Tower" effect produced by Freud's text, saying for now only that it seems to me to be connected with a more general tendency on the part of the author to doubt that psychoanalysis can have any type of interrelation with the social world and real politics. However this position, which already appears at the end of *"Civilised" Sexual Morality and Modern Nervous Illness* (Freud, 1908d) in fact conflicts with this conceptualisation, which is also present from the very first Freudian writings, of the interaction between society and the individual as a source of neurotic distress, and that this is in a sense the price that human beings pay for the evolution of culture. It already appears in a letter to Fleiss dated 31/5/1897, in which it is the core idea which will lead on to *Civilisation and its Discontents* (1930a), and which is also expressed in the correspondence: "Civilisation consists in a progressive renunciation" (Jones, 1955, p. 335). Dating from 1905 is the assertion that "we are obliged to pay as much attention in our case histories to the purely human and social circumstances of our patients as to the somatic data and the symptoms of the disorder". Many Freudian writings, in fact, give an idea of the social dimension of early psychoanalysis considered under the aspect of the source of change in the individual in relation to society.

It is also interesting to see how the position of partial nonintervention and political non-prescription which was to a large extent characteristic of Freud contrasts with the position of Money-Kyrle (1931), for example, or the Viennese analysts of the second generation who recognised themselves in the ideas of Fenichel (Edith Jacobson, Annie Reich, Kate Friedlander, George Gero, Barbara Lantos, Edith Gyomroy, Berta Bornstein), who were convinced that psychoanalysis had to be committed on the social level, passing through a theorisation of Marxist or at least socialist psychoanalysis. This stance must have constituted an area of disagreement with other Viennese analysts, and the development of a "social" psychoanalysis in fact appeared in Berlin during the 1920s, with the foundation of the Berlin Institute by Eitingon and other colleagues, which was intended to provide psychoanalytic therapies for the less affluent. Freud had things to say about this which suggest that he had a positive view of the activities of the Berlin group. After all, Eitingon, at the suggestion of Freud himself, had been co-opted in 1919 as a member of the small committee which was to preserve psychoanalysis after Freud's death.

Echoes of this kind of social commitment appear in the constitution of the London Clinic of Psychoanalysis, formalised in 1924 (and subsequently that of the Hampstead Wartime Nursery in 1940, through the actions of Anna Freud, which would then develop through a training structure introduced in 1958 to become The Hampstead Clinic, based at 20 Maresfield Gardens in 1951).

Jacoby (1983) says that the establishment of the Berlin Institute occurred in the wake of Freud, presented at the fifth congress of the International Psychoanalytic Association in Budapest in 1918, at which Freud in fact asserted the need for the state to take charge of psychotherapeutic clinics in which the noble metal of psychoanalysis could be fused and alloyed with the copper of other forms of intervention. He also adds that it is very likely that the first step in this direction will be private philanthropic clinics.

Certainly, however, being able to document how Freud had a social sensibility towards that part of the population, which was surely burdened with neuroses to a considerable degree, which could not afford the cost of genuine psychoanalysis, is not enough to understand Freud's opinion on the function of psychoanalysis within society, about what its social role might be. On the other hand there are many Freudian quotations about the role and function of psychoanalysis within medicine or science. For example under the definition for an encyclopaedia or in the work *The Question of a Weltanschauung*, it is not too difficult to detect, albeit in rather generic terms, what Freud's opinion was about the role of psychoanalysis in society, through to the text by Freud (1933a) in which he expresses the idea that psychoanalysis is not very useful to a large stratum of society as a therapy as the basis for a reform of the upbringing (in a broad sense) of children.

I think that this certain vagueness of the social role of psychoanalysis underlies the curious detachment of the emotional reality which characterises the letter to Einstein, because Freud seems to feel not only that his interlocutor has said practically everything there was to say on the subject ("taken the wind out of my sails", as he puts it), but also that in reality there is no role for the psychoanalyst in this debate, except in the perhaps not very congenial garb of the philanthropist.

I think that the attitude of dissatisfaction with his own work which emerges from Freud's comments on this very letter clearly documents his sense of detachment and unease. He describes it as a boring and sterile discussion, and one which in fact brings nothing new of importance, for example, to the discussion of the relationship between law and power in *Civilisation and its Discontents*. In a sense he refers to earlier works not least for what he says in them about the life and death drives, and then even apologises to his correspondent for talking about his own theories! Even in this part of the text, the last part, in which he discusses his own pacifism, he seems content to leave the investigation on an entirely superficial level, basing his discussion on the concept of the development of culture as an organic process, but concluding it with a phrase that in fact denies any psychological dialectic: "With pacifists like us it is not merely an intellectual and affective repulsion, but a constitutional intolerance, an idiosyncrasy in its most drastic form" (Freud, 1933b, p. 215). His fear, expressed in the last phrase, of having disappointed his correspondent, may not be out of place. The implications of this state of mind, that of not feeling properly at ease with the task assigned to him, are many and significant not least for what will become the current developments of psychoanalysis.

It is worth noting that another Freudian text that caused its author some vexation with regard to his previous work, was *The Future of an Illusion* (1927c), of which he said to Ferenczi: "Now it already seems to me childish; fundamentally I think otherwise; I regard it as weak analytically and inadequate as a self-confession" (Jones, 1955, p. 138). Another text that would also give him qualms was *Moses and Monotheism* (1939a), although it seems that he was only concerned about the work's social impact. But it may be argued that before 1930 Freud did not consider that he had applied psychoanalysis as such to society, particularly if the facts just described are summed up in the considerations expressed in the following words:

> If the development of civilization has such a far-reaching similarity to the development of the individual and if it employs the same methods, may we not be justified in reaching the diagnosis that, under the influence of cultural urges, some civilizations, or some epochs of civilization—possibly the whole of mankind—have become "neurotic"? (Freud, 1930a, p. 144)

And even though Freud maintained that sociology could not be anything but psychology applied to society, it does not appear in the letter to Einstein that he felt he had succeeded in that intention.

Perhaps in that case we may suggest that Freud's lack of love for this brief piece of writing comes from feeling stripped of his own professionalism on the subject, and thus deprived of weapons to confront it. It is apparent from a reading of the text that Freud in fact felt that he almost had no theoretical tools with which to confront the direct question posed to him by Einstein, about whether humanity can avoid a war. One later indication of this state of mind, apart from the repetitiveness of the discourse with regard to the relationship between law and violence can be the reference that he makes to the Platonic idea of an elite that must be educated to guide society in a wise manner.

This discourse strikes me as very lacking in psychology, above all when compared to the extraordinary perception that Freud had of the individuality of every human being. It is true that Freud seemed to feel that mass psychology had qualities that distinguished it to a great extent from the psychology of the individual, but Freud's chosen way out of the dilemma that Einstein inflicted on him made no use of his own previous work on mass psychology, and is fundamentally a philosophical way, and one using an idealistic philosophy that has nothing to do either with unconscious thought or with the reality of mass psychology.

Apart from the fact that the theoretical instruments used by Freud are weak compared to the non-psychoanalytic ideas that he had at his disposal, the one most striking is that he did not even use any kind of psychoanalytic mind-set to confront the problem.

By this I mean that Freud often put himself outside the group while speaking about it, and in fact he does not even speak about groups, as it is translated into English, but about masses, perhaps an even more alienating concept. Emblematic of this mind set is the phrase in "Group psychology and the analysis of the ego", of all the Freudian texts on society the one which most fully merges the psychology of the individual with that of the ensemble of individuals, in which he claims: "The psychology of such a group, as we know it from the descriptions to which we have so often referred ..." (Freud, 1921c, p. 122). I think that this Freudian position, applying psychoanalytic discoveries to pre-formed groups in society "on paper", so to speak, without throwing oneself into the mix of the group itself, explains much of the sense of detachment, of "Turris Eburnea" which emanates from some of Freud's "sociological" texts, unlike the passionate empathy that arises with reference to practically the whole of the clinical or actually meta-psychological part of his work. From this point of view it is very instructive to make a comparison between the style of the correspondence and the infinitely more personal style of the two letters about war, which date from the First World War, in which Freud was present in the first person, with his own anxieties and his own curiosity about them.

In these two short papers one is aware of the presence of the psychoanalyst at work with regard to the group: he feels part of the group, something that emerges from the very first phrase: "In the confusion of wartime in which we are caught up ...". The second paragraph begins with a reference to the social situation of Freud himself, that of a non-combatant who feels "bewildered in his orientation, and inhibited in his powers and activities" (Freud, 1915c, p. 275). What Freud does is study his own reactions to the situation, question himself about it and start a chain of reasonings and considerations that always refer to the perceptions of Freud himself. This procedure is much more similar to that of the psychoanalytic clinic, and a long way from the "cold" application of theories to a theoretical group. The way in which Freud deals, in the two works, with the same historic material, the one about the Greek Amphictyonic Council, reveals in the first case an emotive involvement which is entirely absent from the second.

I think there is little point, and I would be committing a sin of presumption, if I set about looking for the psychological causes of this very radical change in Freud's way of thinking between one text and the other, this total renunciation of the psychoanalytic mind-set. In reality I would follow the same procedure, more philosophical than scientific, as Freud, if science means asking questions of nature in all its forms to be able to listen to the answers, continuously interrupting critically with one's own investigative instruments, because whatever hypothesis I might be able to make, there would never be the chance of checking it. However, it is precisely the difference between the two texts by Freud that brings out the difficulty which we all face when we leave our strictly psychoanalytic context, remaining analysts for ever, without, for example, becoming sociologists, historians or philosophers.

The problem becomes painfully contemporary for anyone who wants to deal with the same body of investigations that troubled Freud in 1915, which is to say war in general, but more specifically for us, the prevention of nuclear war. The advantage (only from the scientific point of view, of course) that Freud had in 1915 was to be in the middle of a war and to be able to question the surrounding reality, using amongst other things the perception of his own reactions as a given, while he was not in fact in the same situation in 1932. Luckily we too, now, are not in the middle of a war, but we want in some way to work to ensure that a war doesn't happen. We are, that is, in a situation more like Freud's in 1932 than in 1915.

I have wondered whether the development of psychoanalysis after Freud supplied us with other heuristic instruments that might the problem simpler: I think the answer is that there are indeed instruments, but the problem of applying them in a field that is not clinical psychoanalysis remains intact. For example the one that distinguishes Bion's theory of groups, in my opinion, from more descriptive theories like the Freudian is the fact that it is based not only on the concept of projective identification but also on the concept of transference, and on the interactive use of transference with the group, as a tool for understanding this, as we all do every day, to read the signals which tell us what the group's expectations are, and also how to live up to them. Not very differently from what happens in an individual psychoanalysis, it might be said that to understand a group we should use our somatic or emotional reactions not to collude spontaneously with the group, or with the patient, but to understand what is happening.

Recently I happened to have the experience of trying to "apply" Bion's theories to groups not to a group of living, present people, but to the theoretical problem of moving from the bellicose state of mind of a group (the equivalent in the group of aggressiveness in the individual) to bellicose action. In the course of this study, I found myself making a sort of detour around the Protestant hymns that I know from my school-days with a view to exemplifying a spontaneous system of control of belligerence that society tries to put into action, by subsuming it under the aegis and control of the church. I would say that the pursuit of this part of the work allowed me to understand that, for any "sociological" investigation using psychoanalytic theories to be "alive", a minimum but necessary condition must be that there is also a space in the mind of the analyst in which he is identified with the group he is speaking about, which means that he can use his own transferential reactions towards the group. Perhaps the conclusion, obvious though it might be, is that in the first place the analyst cannot analyse anything that is not in some way present for him, and that secondly, he can never at the same time disregard his own reactions from his self-analysis.

And yet, even if this seems to be the case, and is an obvious conclusion that one could not help but make, given the inter-relational nature between the known and the unknown of psychoanalysis itself, does not seem in itself to resolve the difficulties that we all face when it comes to using our theoretical and technical knowledge to understand society. I do not think it is fundamentally incorrect or methodologically inconsistent to "apply psychoanalysis to society", in spite of the methodological position of opposition for this use of psychoanalysis, which derives from the fact that the world is (luckily) not an analyst's consulting room, as well as acknowledging the seriousness of this attitude.

I do think, however, that these motives for opposition which derive from psychoanalytic practice can be overcome either in direct work with groups of individuals interested in working on group *dynamics*, rather than their own difficulties, or in the study of their own transferential reactions, and also those of the patients in analysis with regard to society.

It seems to me that, given that the methodological difficulties are insuperable, the reluctance that we feel to act as psychoanalysts, psychotherapists, or psychologists with regard to social problems, using our specific technical instruments, derives rather from our inner world. In fact I think that we all have unconscious ties to the society we live in, and aversions towards it, and society is charged with a multitude of extraordinarily rich and varied roles.

The study of these adhesions can be highly profitable for the understanding of the "states of mind" of society as a whole.

But at least part of the difficulties that we become aware of when we begin to think in psychoanalytical terms about the society around us comes from our own resistances with regard to the troubling of our universe. Emotionally speaking, we can to a greater or lesser extent bear ourselves and our patients being disturbed while we work, but this takes place within a truly restricted ambit, and we imagine that we can contain the waves of disturbance within our consulting room. But perhaps we cannot bear the idea of disturbing a larger entity to whose continued existence, to whose "status quo" we think, rightly or wrongly, that we owe our continued existence. To be able to work as psychoanalysts within and for society, we must also begin to come to terms with our unconscious projections about society. Bion says that the group *hates* being subjected to study and scrutiny, and perhaps we are all aware of that very "hatred" not least inside us, as members of the group, and we try to avoid paying for it.

Einstein and Freud's *Why War?* (1933b) poses a question to which we do not know the answer, and nor do we know if it will ever be possible to provide an exhaustive answer, there are so many factors at play. But I think that the study of the unconscious aspects of the aggressiveness of the individual and the bellicosity of social groups, starting with the many visible manifestations of these sentiments (racism, the supporting of sports and the role of the army in peace time are some of these) can be legitimate and appropriate areas of study for professionals in the field of psychology. Social applications of psychoanalysis remain a relatively unexplored area, and I consider that it is possible to explore it without neglecting the specific state of mind of psychotherapy and the psychoanalytic tradition that it has always contained, as an implicit characteristic a kind of challenge to the status quo.

CHAPTER SEVEN

Aggressiveness-bellicosity and belligerence (1991): passing from the mental state to active behaviour

Borrowing from Hobbes the idea of the state or the nation as a single organism, this idea can also be transferred to the mental plane, and to speak of a state or a nation as an entity that "thinks" this or that. Acting in this way, it is then possible to take on some concepts from psychoanalysis and apply them to the state as if it were an individual, using them as heuristic instruments. The concepts that might be fruitful in the context of this study are those of the super-ego, the ego and the id, the concept of mental conflict, of repression and of intra-psychical envy.

But it is also useful in this context to think of the state as a set of groups and apply to these Bion's group theory. In our common terms, we move with agility and without placing much weight on the event, between these two levels of conceptualisation of the state; no one is surprised if the television announcer says something along these lines: "The Soviet Union has recognised the new Romanian government, while on the internal political front the Latvians are claiming greater independence." In this single phrase, which I have invented as an example, the hypothetical journalist moves calmly from anthropomorphising the state to considering it as a set of groups, identified by nationality, and in conflict both among themselves and with the representative of central power.

In this essay I would like above all to develop the thesis that bellicosity is an emotive state belonging to the social group and not to the individual; the equivalent of bellicosity in the individual is aggressiveness. It may seem a little artificial to make a distinction of this kind, given that we all live in a group, but I see bellicosity and aggressiveness as two distinct qualities concerning different mental contexts, although there are channels of communication between them: the bellicosity of the group appeals to the aggressiveness of the individual, and is fed by it. Similarly, bellicosity as a mental quality seems to belong to the universe of discourse that sees the state as a set of groups, while it is easily modified and becomes a condition of belligerence when the state is understood, and behaves, as a single organism.

Secondly, I would like to try to understand the attitude of modern states towards bellicosity, and which systems they have adopted to manage it: is it a quality that is sought after and developed within society, or an awkward element of our group life that we try to keep under control? I think it is important to try to give an answer to these questions with a view to advancing the discourse about the problem of how to avoid a bellicose emotional state turning disastrously to an actual state of waged war. The advent of nuclear arms makes a war of this kind too dangerous for the whole of humanity, which makes it more and more urgent for us to understand the mental unconscious mental mechanisms that might encourage an outbreak of hostility, with a view to intervening appropriately to prevent a passage to hostility.

Concepts and theories of psychoanalysis and group psychoanalysis: their application to civil society

While I do not think that much needs to be said about the triadic division of the personality put forward by Freud into ego, super-ego (the judging authority which represents the parents, almost exclusively severe for Freud, while for Klein and the post-Kleinians it may have more friendly characteristics) and the id, and also the concept of repression is in general use, perhaps that of intra-psychical envy and Bion's group theory are less well known, and it is worth making a brief digression to illustrate the salient points of these theories, which I would like to use.

Intra-psychical envy is an emotion that can arise in conditions of serious mental unease, when different parts of the personality have very poor relationships with each other; the individual finds himself making gestures or having behaviours (including some that are merely mental) which are self-destructive, not least in the sense of unleashing denigrating or contemptuous attacks on one's own best qualities. This envy tends above all to damage one's own good qualities or one's own resources, and however clear it might be there might be many other elements in play, it is perhaps not too fantastical to put it forwards as an active element, not least in the choice of a government to throw one's own country to the wall.

In broad terms, Bion's theory, based primarily on the observation of small groups of people, asserts that the attempts of human beings brought together in a group to develop a creative behaviour (in whatever field) can be disturbed and even completely interrupted by the emergence of unconscious thoughts and emotions rooted in unconscious fantasies concerning the "true" motives for which the group has met. These fantasies fall under three main headings: "religious", in which the fantasy of depending totally on an absolute boss is dominant; "pairing", according to which it is claimed that the group met with the sole purpose of reproduction—this latter fundamental assumption blurs into the religious one when the product of pairing, whether of individuals or ideas, is seen as a Messiah still to come; "fight/flight", a basic fantasy according to which the group has met solely to deal with its own conservation, and this depends exclusively on behaviour either of mass-attack on or flight from the enemy.

It is this third basic assumption that most concerns us, because it seems to me to be a concept whose use can be quite illuminating concerning the presence of bellicosity in modern society. Bion effectively broadens his own discourse about the scope of the small group from which it arose, turning it almost into a sociological theory, and suggests that some social institutions are developed with a view to containing and, where possible, overcoming the very strong emotional drives that emerge from the proto-mental system (the breeding ground of basic assumptions, perhaps comparable to the Jungian Collective Unconscious) that underpins the life of the group. In particular, he considers the religions that belong more or less to the state as specialised work groups with the task of keeping under control the tendency to dependence, channelling it, removing it from the danger of becoming a dependence on a real human being, and making it visible and socially acceptable. Similarly, the aristocracy (or the "Jet-Set") has the function of a specialised group dealing with pairing and reproduction, while the army channels the impulses and drives to violence (characteristics which accompany the basic fight/flight assumption) to keep them under control.

According to Bion's thesis (somewhat paradoxical, at first sight), if the army finds itself having to rally to combat, if a war has broken out, [1] the army has failed in its real institution task—the unconscious one—which is to prevent the explosion of an active conflict. From this point of view, I think we may consider the army of the Swiss Confederation as a true model of efficiency, and its success may depend in part on the capillary diffusion of military service throughout the whole of the population as a permanent obligation. The Swiss army seems to work well in the collective imagination as a place where violence is to be deposited.

Bion himself warns that in civil society there are so many nuances and displacements that it is rare for the theoretical subdivisions set out above to be easily visible, or that there are examples of one or other basic assumption "in its pure state", so to speak. One of the reasons for this is the specialist groups themselves, church, army and aristocracy, are disturbed in their task of keeping under control their "own" basic assumption of the emergence of behaviours dictated by one of the others. For example sometimes, in the story of the Christian church, the church found itself managing its own belligerent behaviours, without keeping bellicose behaviours under control. This is a topic to which I shall return.

The task of the specialised work group is, fundamentally, that of thinking, and a sociological study by Franco De Masi (1989) into small creative groups, which does not in any way use Bion's theory, gives a series of quite interesting pictures of the working and the structures of different small specialised work groups operating in very different fields, which go from the Stazione Zoologica in Naples to the Vienna Circle of philosophers, to the Manhattan Project. This study clarifies the effective working of the work group, while the study of Reeves and Gould (1987) into Joachim of Fiore and the *myth* of the eternal gospel illustrates the way in which the magnificence of unconscious feelings of waiting for a Messiah (or a Messianic idea) can have a very disturbing effect on intellectual work. This study traces, in the culture of the nineteenth and early twentieth centuries, the ramifications both of Joachimism and, more significantly, the *conviction* that Joachim of

Fiore had written a text entitled *The Eternal Gospel*. This text would have been a new gospel, that of the Holy Spirit, and was understood by nineteenth-century scholars, not only in a strictly religious sense, but also as the precursor of a revolutionary era. The historiographic research by Leroux and Sand's group into Joachimite ideas is the activity of a specialised work group (and it is interesting to see how other intellectuals influenced by their writings, such as Marx and Mazzini, accept their version of historical facts without subjecting them to deeper, critical scrutiny). In substance, the whole group wished so intensely to see the Middle Ages as a revolutionary era and a precursor that would ratify their radicalism so that the historical data which they had at their disposal (and which would at least partially have denied that ancient paternity) could not be thoroughly used. Even Renan himself, who was part of Leroux's group, and whose studies dared to be more rigorous, so much so that he was able to wonder whether Joachim's text on the Eternal Gospel had ever existed, had to take a considerable amount of trouble to free himself from the unconscious trammels of the group.

I think that civil society can be usefully considered as a set of work groups either intersecting in different ways or in tense relations with one another. Because societies are made up of human beings, who often act on the basis of feelings and thoughts that have barely been understood or tested, as if they were governed by such unconscious thoughts rather than being in control of them, it is correct to use the psychological knowledge that we have, incomplete and susceptible to improvements though it might be, to understand undercurrents of fantasies and emotions which too often seem to exert control over our thoughts.

If society as a whole has appointed specialised work groups to manage the disturbance caused by the basic assumptions of dependence, pairing and fight/flight, which is the work group *par excellence* that these specialised groups are intended to protect? It seems to me to be both too vague and too simple to assert that society is trying to protect itself, even if it is correct to do so: however, I think that we may see the state government as the entity that acts as a specialised work group; it is the thinking authority of the state that can be considered as its "ego", to return to *Leviathan*. It is easy to see it as a government whose tasks include both the preservation and the conversation of the *Res Publica* which develops it and its evolution can be subject to tensions and drives issuing from different social groups that "become spokespeople", so to speak, for the unconscious fantasies that arise from the proto-mental system.

Governments feel threatened and expend a great deal of energy when they try to run for shelter and defend themselves from unconscious psychological pressures: they try to channel the unconscious fantasies of the group in very precise directions towards the childhood of the citizens. They do not only use the institution of the army to keep the bellicosity of subjects or citizens under control, seen primarily as a threat to stability, and the peaceful cohabitation within the same society,[1] but the school is also used to this end, and in some circumstances so is the state religion, as we shall see below.

The characteristics of the bellicosity of the group

In the tangle of human nature, a thread of aggressiveness is inextricably interwoven with everything else; as I said before, the bellicosity of the group appeals to the aggressiveness of the individual, and feeds on it. But they are not exactly the same thing, and nor does the difference in quality lie exclusively in quantitative difference. Just as we can consider that a hypothetical new-born human without any trace of aggressiveness in its own character would not survive for long, because it would not be capable of "attaching" itself to the breast, or to claim the next feed, it becomes more and more difficult to ascribe anything positive to the results of bellicosity, which are only ever death and destruction. This difference in result between the two mental states seems to imply that while aggressiveness can be used by the individual towards the ends of his own survival, bellicosity is not so malleable, and is in fact a mental characteristic of the group that the group itself fears precisely because of its uncontrollable pervasiveness.

To counter this idea one might object that, after all, there are also those who *win* wars, and who may be able to enjoy territorial enlargements: but how many times could the same ends have been achieved with peaceful means, without giving rise to war? Isnenghi (1989,

---

[1]The suspicion with which the army is looked upon by civilians has been well documented over the last two centuries: (q.v. Isnenghi) we need only think of the fact that British officers are *forbidden* leave the barracks on leave in uniform, they are seen in such a bad light by the population. One might think that the hatred and fear provoked by bellicosity have been transferred to those who are supposed to contain that unconscious mental state and prevent its spread.

p. 28) asserts that Giolitti had "... a parallel, unofficial diplomatic initiative which might lead Austria to concede to Italy, just to keep it out of the war, 'some' of what Italy will then effectively end up having in exchange for three and a half years of war and over half a million dead." If we look in broad lines at the history of Europe over the last century and a half, we have a sense that some recent wars were strongly desired by relatively few individuals who in turn influenced the masses, or alternatively the halls of power, to awaken in them the bellicose state of mind, which then leads to an actual waging of war. Among these we might number Garibaldi, D'Annunzio, Mussolini, and Hitler. One might also think that most of the wars which have occurred on European territory over the same period of time did not have the lasting territorial effects yearned for and desired by their fomenters.

I do not want to give the impression of wanting to propound a teleological or moralistic argument, in which the individual's aggressiveness is deemed to be "good" and the group's bellicosity "bad" on the basis of the results achieved. What I am trying to illuminate is the fact that bellicosity is a mental state, and also a proto-mental state, which participates in the general characteristics of this latter class, which include unavailability for the development of thought. A group in the mental state of fight/flight is a group that has renounced the use of thought unless it is targeted either at attacking the enemy or escaping them, because it is a group that forms around the psychological need to preserve one's own existence.

The aggressiveness of the individual, on the other hand, is an emotional state that favours, or at least permits, a certain relationality either with other individuals or with internal objects, and consequently it is mitigable and modifiable by means of thought; it may also stimulate thought, while proto-mental states stimulate action more than others.

The emergence in a group of a proto-mental state produces an effect of "stupidification" of the individual members, and also of homogenisation of their reactions; it is a situation in which it is quite difficult to think autonomously, while the group, by contrast, is easily manipulated. In the text by Isnenghi quoted above there are many examples of manipulating arguments designed to provoke the crowd to action, not to thought:

> "Comrades, the time for talking has passed, and it is now time to do: it is no longer a time for forgiveness, but for actions, and Roman actions. If it is considered a crime to incite citizens to violence,

I boast of that crime, I will take it on my own shoulders ...".
(Isnenghi, 1989, p. 27)

If Isnenghi can comment that: "... while there is certainly a D'Annunzian Italy, ready to follow the master along the ways of hypnotism and verbal autosuggestion, there are doubts about whether there is a Battistian Italy: inclined, that is, to maintain an analytic attitude towards their own feelings and to give reasons for their own choices". This phenomenon may be considered in psychological terms with the availability of the group to remain in a proto-mental state of bellicosity, for the reproach, easily manoeuvrable as such and hostile to any event, including thought, which could alter that mental state.

To sum up, we might say that the characteristics that the emergence of bellicosity confers on the group are those of becoming more susceptible to emotional manipulations and, as a corollary, less permeable to reason and thought.

Visible traces of bellicosity in society

We can consider bellicosity as an unconscious mental state of the social group, which can become active and become consciously warmongering. At this point society runs the risk of passing to practical activity, that is, going into war—it is here that the possible passage to belligerence occurs. We may compare the potentiality of bellicosity to the situation in which, in the body of the individual, there is always a bit of adrenalin in circulation: this can be intentionally augmented by the intervention of a second person who, simply by saying some things, makes his interlocutor angry, and the increment of adrenalin can go on to have an effect on that person's activity. In the same way there are always sex hormones and pheromones in circulation, whose influences change according to the quantities and qualities of the substances themselves. Bion, as we have already seen, theorised these states of potential "alert" on a more properly psychological plain in terms of the existence of a proto-mental system of the group which can be expressed from one moment to the next in different "basic assumptions" which are the unconscious convictions common to members of the group at that moment on the basis of which the group acts in reality.

I maintain that civil, thinking society has some perception of the danger of uncontrollable and violent behaviours which can spring from a group prey to the basic fight/flight assumption, and that it tries to protect itself from the eventualities of an explosion of those sentiments through different systems of containment or channelling of unconscious feelings. In my view, however, derivatives of the mental state of bellicosity (which for ease of argument I am for the time being allowing to coincide with the basic fight/flight assumption) are traceable in modern society. The social group finds itself having to confront phenomena within itself which are always connected at root with bellicosity, even if those derivatives are called "racism", "parochialism", or "sports supporting". It is possible that these phenomena become increasingly virulent as we move away from the likelihood of war.

The degeneration of sports hooliganism into real and actual assaults by one group against another—we might take as our example the Heysel Stadium episode, because it also stresses the nationalistic element, and the similarity with a war becomes clearer as a result—may be usefully seen as a relatively controlled explosion of unconscious feelings of bellicosity that society channels in a non-warlike direction, but which "allows" a certain release of the violence of those feelings. The fact that violent hooliganism seems principally connected to sports played in teams (I have never heard of the existence of sports supporters around golf courses or tennis courts, for example, or athletics events), as well as something that might almost be configured as a certain unconscious connivance in violent events (the stadiums or the trains that transport the supporters are not adequately controlled, and during the search for the guilty they seem to vanish into thin air) might also make us think that we are in the presence of events that are rooted in the unconscious mentality of the group which sees the football or basketball team as its own tribal or national army.

On the other hand it is also true that there are some countries, England in particular, where bellicosity seems to be a constant national characteristic and also a social value, starting with the personification of the nation as a "bulldog", which is commonly accepted. This observation introduces a note of ambiguity into the argument. Does this mean that bellicosity is a prized quality? Is the army really a machine intended for use only to fight against external enemies?

Unconscious systems for the control of bellicosity

Perhaps at this point it would be useful to return to the Hobbesian concept of *Leviathan*, and consider the state as a single unit. But Freudian discoveries show us that even the human individual is not "all of a piece" (or, if an individual comes close to having this characteristic, they are a very sick person). Rather the common experience is rather that of having a multifaceted personality, with different characteristics, with contrasting emotions, sometimes in conflict with one another even on the conscious plane. There are also unconscious conflicts between opposing feelings, or between repressed unconscious desires and the sphere of thought and conscious emotions. Among those thoughts and emotions which are less acceptable to the civilised ego, we should also number aggressiveness, and there are two primitive ways in which the individual can try to get rid of them: above all there is a divide with regard to aggressiveness, it is separated from other feelings, and then, according to the disposition of the individual, either it comes directly towards internal objects, the internal world (and in this situation a psychosomatic illness may develop), or else the aggressiveness is deflected towards the external world, in this way protecting the individual from himself, but damaging others.

So it is possible that what seems to be a quest for bellicosity on the social plane, encouraging its development, is in reality a system that society uses to protect itself against a situation of civil war, or at least of social agitation, comparable to the psychosomatic illness of the individual: we may read the history of social and political events in France between 1853 and 1870 as a sequence of attempts to suppress disorders and internal revolts by directing violence outwards.

But this is only one possible reading of the phenomenon of that bellicosity which seems to be loved and nurtured in the bosom not only of the state but also of the church, and perhaps another may be made in terms of interaction between social groups and the superimposition of their functions.

We have already seen how Bion hypothesised that the hidden, or unconscious function of the army was that of channelling the aggressiveness of the individual into a situation in which the bellicosity of the group was placed under a rigid hierarchical control which favoured repression above all, and then, when that repression was doomed to fail, the outward expression, towards other countries, of the same bellicosity, with the aim of protecting civil society against ill-advised eruptions of violence. Perhaps it is not out of place to think that the church too, above all, where it is institutionally an instrument of the state, may have an important role in taking on and internalising social violence and directing it in a way that is not harmful, or at least is harmful only to foreign countries. It is also reasonable to think that, along with this social function which sometimes falls to the Anglican Church, for example, the efficient functioning of the church as a specialised work group to check basic assumption dependency is disturbed by the eruption of social violence, which is why the church has to deal with it in some way, perhaps by organising a crusade.

In this context of intersections of social functions, it is worth noting that the Anglican Church is at the service of the state, and lives under the tutelage of the crown: the head of the Anglican Church is the king or queen of England, while the bishops are chosen with the blessing of the Home Office, and these two facts would be enough to explain how it is that the Anglican Church at least is consciously considered by the government as an actual instrument.[2]

So perhaps it should not surprise us that the curators of a collection of hymns, published for the first time in 1925, should have the specific intention of making "a collection of hymns that should be national in character; and a hope was expressed in the Preface that the book might be of use to those who bear the responsibility of our national education". This is a good illustration of the overlap between religion, state and public education in Great Britain. This collection is still widely used in Anglican churches, in whose rite choral singing, in which all the faithful take part, is an important element, and is also used in the schools of the United Kingdom, where the day often begins with an assembly of the whole school featuring a reading from the Bible, the singing of hymns and the saying of prayers. So widespread is it that it might be useful to take a look at the expanded 1962 edition.

In examining this text, I have taken into account not so much the statistical frequency with which a clearly bellicose terminology appears in the hymns, but more their capacity for "psychical penetration", that is, their capacity to imprint themselves in the memory even at a distance of thirty years, given the ease with which hymns that are decidedly more poetically beautiful and imbued with feelings such as the

---

[2] Even though it seems important that not too much publicity should be given to this state of affairs, because it seems to upset the faithful, as we can tell from the angry words of a perspicacious English poet in 1795: "... indignation on hearing sermons in which the poor are addressed in a manner which evidently shows the design of making religion an engine of government" A. L. Barbauld, quoted in Lonsdale (1989).

meekness, patience, faith, hope and charity of Christian teaching have been entirely forgotten along with their tunes.

There are two main classes of hymns which use a bellicose language: the first refers to the militant church, a concept shared with the Roman Catholic Church, which is why the terminology probably sounds familiar in spite of the difference in belief; hence I consider that we may use as our examples the battle song (sic!) of Julia Ward Howe and the very famous "Onward Christian Soldiers", which is very popular with children, particularly because of its march music.

In the second group are text which incite to proselytising, whether on the national territory as in Blake's poem "Jerusalem", often used as a hymn, or abroad. We cannot help noting how the missionary activities of the Anglican Church are wedded to the events of active colonialism, and how the hymns are also in fact a form of subtle political pressure.

I think it may be useful to provide some precise examples, accompanied by a brief commentary:

The Battle Song: Julia Ward Howe (1819–1910)

1. Mine eyes have seen the glory of the coming of the Lord;
   He is trampling out the vintage where the grapes of wrath are stored;
   He hath loosed the fateful lightning of His terrible swift sword:
   His truth is marching on.
2. I have seen Him in the watch-fires of a hundred circling camps,
   They have builded Him an altar in the evening dews and damps;
   I can read His righteous sentence by the dim and flaring lamps:
   His day is marching on.
3. I have read a fiery gospel writ in burnished rows of steel:
   "As ye deal with my contemners, so with you my grace shall deal";
   Let the Hero, born of woman, crush the serpent with his heel,
   Since God is marching on.
4. He has sounded forth the trumpet that shall never call retreat;

> He is sifting out the hearts of men before His judgement-seat:
> Oh, be swift, my soul, to answer Him! be jubilant, my feet!
> Our God is marching on.
> 5. In the beauty of the lilies Christ was born across the sea,
> With a glory in His bosom that transfigures you and me.
> As He died to make men holy, let us die to make men free,
> While God is marching on.
> 6. He is coming like the glory of the morning on the wave,
> He is Wisdom to the mighty, He is Succour to the brave,
> So the world shall be His footstool, and the soul of Time His slave,
> Our God is marching on.

Perhaps the success of this hymn is partly due to the possibility of singing it to the tune better known as "John Brown's Body", whose refrain "Glory, glory, Halleluiah" can also be inserted into the hymn itself. (In fact all the most bellicose hymns have tunes that can be easily sung, with rhythms adapted to marching, and this is certainly one of the elements that make them easier to remember). By singing these words, the group is manipulated into expressing bellicose sentiments; the description of the soldiers' night camp is a match for any good action novel, while Christ is implicitly compared, through the use of the phrase "Hero born of woman" to other heroes born of goddesses; it is explicitly asserted that the soldier of this army can die for the cause, and the image of God which emerges from it seems to have a great deal in common with that of some epic commander, but the vessel containing these sentiments, the church, is always kept present.

Onward, Christian soldiers! S. Baring-Gould (1834–1924)

> Onward Christian soldiers!
> Marching as to war,
> With the cross of Jesus
> Going on before.
> Christ the royal Master
> Leads against the foe;
> Forward into battle,
> See, his banners go:
> Onward, Christian soldiers,
> Marching as to war,

> With the cross of Jesus
> Going on before.
> Like a mighty army
> Moves the Church of God
> Brothers, we are treading
> Where the Saints have trod;
> We are not divided,
> All one body we,
> One in hope and doctrine,
> One in charity.

These words, which have a very martial tune, and of which I have quoted only two verses, also makes great use of military terminology, whose function seems to be to gather all warlike functions under the church's banner.

The second verse of "Jerusalem", however, which Blake certainly did not write as a hymn, but which has enjoyed huge popularity in this form, seems to express a state of personal exaltation in which aggressiveness is used for constructive purposes, always under the aegis and control of the church.

Jerusalem: William Blake (1757–1827)

> And did those feet in ancient time
> Walk upon England's mountains green?
> And was the holy Lamb of God
> On England's pleasant pastures seen?
>
> And did the Countenance Divine,
> Shine forth upon our clouded hills?
> And was Jerusalem builded here,
> Among these dark Satanic Mills?
>
> Bring me my bow of burning gold!
> Bring me my arrows of desire!
> Bring me my spear! O clouds unfold!
> Bring me my chariot of fire!
>
> I will not cease from mental fight,
> Nor shall my sword sleep in my hand:
> Till we have built Jerusalem,
> In England's green and pleasant land.

The text of "Jerusalem", with its emphasis on the building of the church, naturally brings our argument towards those hymns which incite us to undertake the missionary life beyond the sea. The collection has a separate section for these, around ten in all, but there are others of similar tenor, in the part dedicated to hymns for children, although containing the caption "Also for adults", as are also found in the section dedicated to Advent, and the one dedicated to social service (general, national and international), which also includes Kipling's "Recessional", which expresses a colonial version of the divine right of the monarchy.

(Also for adults)

P. Dearmer

Remember all the people
Who live in far off lands
In strange and lovely cities
Or roam the desert sands,
Or farm the mountain pastures
Or till the endless plains
Where children wade through rice fields
And watch the camel trains.

Some work in sultry forests
Where apes swing to and fro,
Some fish in mighty rivers,
Some hunt across the snow.
Remember all God's children,
Who yet have never heard
The truth that comes from Jesus,
The glory of His Word.

God bless the men and women
Who serve Him overseas;
God raise up more to help them
To set the nations free,
Till all the distant people
In every foreign place
Shall understand His kingdom,
And come into His grace.

Recessional: Rudyard Kipling

God of our fathers, known of old,
Lord of our far-flung battle-line,
Beneath whose awful Hand we hold
Dominion over palm and pine—
Lord God of Hosts, be with us yet,
Lest we forget—lest we forget!

With this first verse of Kipling's poem we can bring to an end our remarks about one of the ways in which the church assumes the task of managing group violence: it implicitly acknowledges the fact that human beings are violent, and indicates two conduits along which violence can be channelled in such a way as to make it socially acceptable: through the construction of a living church, and through the militant and colonialising exportation of personal aggressiveness merged with the bellicosity of the group and controlled by it.

But the in the past the state has also used means of pressure to contain bellicosity which did not pass so directly through specific organisations such as the army and the church: one might think that the Roman policy of "bread and circuses" is a kind of precursor to this, even though in this case the intention to keep the Roman people "quiet" was not in fact unconscious.

Similarly, the intentions of many writers for children, whose rather didactic books—I am thinking of *Cuore* by Edmondo de Amicis, for example, or *Kim*—were directly intended to forge a certain mentality, in which the calls to arms and the acts of heroism (in the former) and the subterfuges and lies (in the other) could all be accepted and held to be morally irreproachable because subject to the state and the empire, and at their service. The fantasy underling this kind of book seems to be connected with the idea that the good of the group has almost a redemptive effect on the misdeeds of the individual, who can lie and kill in its name with impunity. This renunciation of personal responsibility, certainly very remote from the conscious intentions of De Amicis or Kipling, in fact has quite pernicious consequences, as we can tell by reading the accounts of war crimes trials, not only those in Nuremberg, but more recently also those in which French soldiers were accused of atrocities in Algeria, the British for acts of cruelty in Ireland and in the United States for the My Lai massacre.

In this context of underground messages, what a state chooses to censure or praise is highly significant: a glance at school books, particularly in history, which in more or less all European states fall under some kind of control (albeit indirectly, through state exams) clearly shows a certain difficulty in confronting the problem of the belligerence of the state itself. Past heroes are praised, and this implicitly sanctions war, all the more if it is a war that can be considered defensive or a war of liberation. At the same time, colonialism is implicitly condemned, with British school books discussing at length the *end* of colonialism and the liberation of the colonised, but dealing very little with the previous offensive wars against those same peoples.

Conscious manipulations of group bellicosity

Any individual and any group of people may sometimes feel that their own emotions are being manipulated. A very common example of his is the emotion, often leading to tears, provoked by certain films, intentionally constructed as "tear-jerkers". In every single case, the film appeals to, speaks with, *only part* of the personality of the viewers (which is why one may also feel very irritated for having been "forced" to cry), and something similar happens when a leader tries to lead a group towards belligerent action. The fact that the orator is speaking only to a part of the personality of the individuals listening reveals the dishomogeneity in the group's response. The same individual may feel driven towards violent action, probably to the basic assumption of fight/flight prevailing in the group at that moment, followed shortly afterwards by dismay and horror, and a complete lack of desire to wage war.

The text by Isenghi quoted above clearly outlines the manipulations of the crowd by a D'Annunzio or a Mussolini, but also explains how it is that in popular culture one encounters expressions of the individual's hatred and fear of war, as in songs like the one from the First World War called "Gorizia, tu sei maledetta" [Gorizia, you are damned]. What emerges most strongly is the way in which the individual loses his individuality as soon as he becomes part of a basic assumption group, and how he reacquires it, along with his capacity for thought, when he manages to estrange himself from the group, when he becomes part of his own family once again, for example, or also when the same physical people who composed the basic assumption group find themselves in a different mental state. This change can follow on from a physical change (the patrol comes back to base and finds a different mental atmosphere from the one at the front) but it may also happen as a spontaneous shift.

We know too little about these spontaneous shifts in basic assumptions to be able to use them, which is why we must limit our discussion to deliberate manipulations, designed to touch those profoundly unconscious levels. The ones that we have seen so far are manipulations designed to touch the bellicosity of the group until it can be made to spill over into action—an enraged group committing a lynching. We have also seen how in various ways society, through the formation of specialised groups with the task of dealing with bellicosity, of sporting "symbolic wars", and an international policy of peace, attempts to avoid these disastrous outbreaks of violence. But a politics of peace, while it may be of fundamental importance, may not be enough to put a country in refuge from its *own* violence.

One of the reasons why we cannot simply trust goodness and the desire for peace of any political class is that, apart from the problems of unconscious bellicosity that these groups certainly have to confront,[3] there are also other unconscious elements which can lead a nation to war. Of these, perhaps the first insidious is intra-psychic envy. Returning to the Leviathan, and considering the government of the country as the ego, we can observe how in certain historical and documentable circumstances—and for many people, still part of their own memory—some governments have behaved as if they had great problems with intra-psychic envy. In the cold light of day it does not seem logical to send to the slaughter the group that is of the age that is potentially the most productive and enriching for the country, the young men of recruiting age. If we take into account, for example, the fact that D'Annunzio's speech in Quarto on 5 May 1915 was delivered "at the invitation" of the authorities, we may not think that the desire to inflame minds and lead Italy to intervene was not also concealed within the ego of the country.

The presence of envy on the part of the older generation (which will not have to go to war) is confirmed by the furious and quite

---

[3] Also, while individuals are trying to work together in the work group *par excellence*, which is parliament. It seems that when Verdi was Senator of the Kingdom he wrote a score using as libretto an argument among members of parliament, which ended blows. Unfortunately, it would appear that the score no longer exists, perhaps destroyed by the composer himself, and perhaps out of love of his country.

hostile reactions at the front during the First World War towards the "draft-dodgers" who stayed at home (Isnenghi, 1989), a shared rage common to all soldiers on all fronts, just as the desire to fraternise among themselves was common to them all. Unfortunately, as can be seen in the psychoanalysis of certain patients, intra-psychic envy is potentially boundless, and the individual risks destroying himself. It seems to me that there is a similar situation when anyone in a position of responsibility and power, such as the head of a government or a state, military advisers or politicians etc. seriously considers the possibility of using nuclear weapons, removing from his own consciousness the perception and awareness that it might be fatal for his own country, and perhaps for the entire planet.

Another, possibly cleaner, theoretical approach to confronting the same problem of self-destruction on a national scale is to consider that the country is managed by a power group which functions chiefly on the level of the "double" of the basic assumption of dependence. Within this mental ambit, the respective functions of leader and followers were reversed: it is no longer the leader who leads, cares for and protects the herd, it is the herd that must attend to the physical and psychical needs of the leader. The example that Bion gives of this is that of the pharaohs who bled Egypt dry and destroyed the lives of countless slaves to silence their own fear of death. The "personality cult" that Saddam Hussein plainly encouraged (we need only think of the ineffable television advertisement) may be an indication of the active (and fomented) presence in Iraqi society of the basic assumption of dependence, with the possibility that there may soon be a mirror reversal until it becomes a "double".

The problem encountered in confronting this point is the analysis of the intersection between the psychology of the individuals composing a ruling group and the behaviour of the same group when it is given ascendancy over one of the basic assumptions, but that would be an extremely lengthy process and would require knowledge of the protocols of decisions taken and the shorthand minutes of the discussions leading to the decision if it were to be done in an appropriate manner.

An education for peace

In my opinion, any education for peace, in order to be really efficient, would also have to take into account unconscious realities, not only conscious ones. It must be constructive, creative and not terroristic. It seems to me that these characteristics are also those of an education towards the freedom of the individual, a freedom that some authors, Galtung in particular, consider to be a fundamental element of the concept of positive peace.

But will there never be a way of helping the individual who lives in a group to guard against intentional manipulations (not least unconscious ones) which lead towards hatred and war? This is a major problem, because the fact of fearing group violence is not enough to control it, using unconscious means, and nor are there any guarantees about the absolutely good intentions of the political classes (of any country).

In recent years, educational theorists of many European countries have been active in the development of courses at many school levels, designed to create an education for peace within more traditional school courses. In fact, during a child's time at school which, although it may be effective from the point of view of putting students face to face with a certain reality—and the obvious manipulations (or ruses)—they leave the whole unconscious part of the problem in the realm of the unknown.[4] It also seems to me that there is a risk of alarming young people without giving them adequate protection or psychological reinforcement to confront reality without being upset by it and without falling into despair. It will be said that school is not a place of psychotherapy, and that teachers are not trained in this direction: but it is the place where children grow up, and which seeks to make them mature, which is why it does not seem out of place to me to use some techniques aimed at increasing their level of self-knowledge, in the context of a general education for freedom.

It would be enough to broaden, even only slightly, an activity that is already pursued in some Italian primary schools, namely the study of advertising. Basically, television, radio and print advertising is a form of propaganda full of hidden messages designed to manipulate consumers, in a way not very different in terms of the techniques used from wartime propaganda speeches. This is to say, a situation is presented as

---

[4] Popp (1988) writes (a) of the use made in photography classes of a peace demonstration as a topic of discussion with pupils and parents; (b) of having accompanied students to visit a military zone in their area, inviting them to check what the possibility of survival of the population would be if the NATO base, supplied with atomic missiles, were attacked; (c) and on a visit to bunkers reactivated as anti-atomic refuges, but in fact useless.

optimal, to which very good member of the group will try to conform as quickly as possible, at risk of feeling excluded.

Advertising admits no doubts, nor does it leave space for the individual to be able to think and act with autonomy or assess advantages and disadvantages. It is axiomatic when it identifies enemies ("Flies/mosquitoes must all die") and it has a great influence on young people in their choices of models (drinks, clothes, behaviour) which become determining for membership of a particular group. The study of these techniques of persuasion can also be started quite early in primary school, I would say with the second cycle, with the advantage of introducing children to the following ideas:

a. There are messages beneath the surface of what we think we see or hear and which influence us without our being aware of it.
b. If we blindly obey these messages, civic life becomes regimented and impoverished (we all become alike, we all have furniture at home by S or by Y, the same clothes, cars and food, while we do not all have the same character: if the actual way of living is also an expression of one's own mind, a flattening-out of this kind would be deleterious to our own individuality).
c. Hidden messages, designed to sell a product, do not invite to a wise or just way of living. (It is true that flies of mosquitoes are irritating, but their elimination changes the ecosphere in a very serious way, impoverishing it (we need only think of the rarity of water birds in rice fields) and the whole problem of the poisoning of the water table owing to an insane use of pesticides).

Confronting children, even quite young children, with these ideas does not strike me as scandalous, nor are psychologists necessarily required to do it, but it might lay the foundations for a certain habit of awareness, and in future of criticism, of our own way of being uncritical within a group, supinely accepting what the group presents as good and positive.

An awareness of the child's own individuality may be encouraged by a school encouraging an attitude of curiosity about reality. It is also true that that same awareness can be severely damaged by a school which tries to limit the exuberance of the pupils only through their premature regimentation—and this may be the imposition of a school uniform, school sport (in the sense of organised support for the school teams), the training of the school army unit—without, to contrast with all this, any attempt to look into the culture of freedom of thought.

A school that respects the individuality of the single pupil, inviting and encouraging them to think for themselves and to guard against propaganda influences of all kinds, is a school which is performing the task of preparing men and women in such a way as to choose and not to move from personal aggressiveness to its fusion and confusion in group bellicosity, and from group bellicosity to belligerence.

But another problem arises concerning the problem of education for peace at a school level; will it not be a system to place on the shoulders of young people the problems that adults do not feel capable of facing? It is not a disguised way of saying "you sort it out"? This kind of unconscious attitude, which is sometimes revealed as rampant in the most unexpected places (no one has ever heard a political or ecclesiastical appeal along the lines of "Old people for peace in the world!") shows how difficult it is to take on board the responsibility for a change in our way of thinking first of all. To confront this kind of task we would therefore need a permanent education for peace, which would touch every age group without exception, and this is certainly more difficult to organise.

The difficulties are of various kinds: the dispersal of the population, the fact that, once students no longer have to go to school there is no longer any kind of similar obligation in our own lives as free citizens (apart from military service, but it strikes me as a little too paradoxical to ask the state to educate its own soldiers to live in peace—or perhaps not?). And besides, even if we want to see things principally from the point of view of the education of young people, the example of adults is very important for them, so we cannot reasonably think of shrugging off the problem as if it did not concern us.

One thing that might be useful would be a research and study commission into the prospects of permanent education for peace, which strikes me as being of vital importance for our survival. In particular we need a serious collection of data on the national territory—and it would be even better if it also happened in other countries—to identify which are the negative teachings, the subtly bellicose ones, which we absorb every day almost without noticing. Among these I think there are certain television programmes, such as war films, scheduled uncritically without being compared, for examples, with films made by the enemies of the time.

Other areas worthy of study might be sports newspapers, with their well-known ability to incite supporters, and the ways in which "opinion-makers" in every field exert their influence. If we managed to explain how the hidden, and also the open, persuaders work in times of peace, we might be able to go on to think of systems of "defence" against the threat of manipulations.

My wish is that, as in an individual psychoanalysis, in the course of which the rigid and entirely unconscious defences of the individual have to be dismantled to leave us space for more flexible, articulate and efficient defences, the same path may be pursued by the social body, either as a Leviathan or as a set of intersecting groups. For this to come about, first of all we need a profound investigation to understand which defences are used against which real dangers. This is a task which requires a considerable interdisciplinary effort, involving cultural anthropologists, sociologists and psychologists, historians, philosophers and communications experts. It is only once we have realised the unsatisfactory nature of the defences used by society, sometimes ambiguously, to channel the aggressiveness of the individual into the group and then keep the group's bellicosity under control, that we will be able to start coming up with new defence systems that are conscious, or at least much more aware than before, with which to manage that fundamental human characteristic which, in the nuclear age, has become too dangerous to ignore.

CHAPTER EIGHT

The creation of mental models (1992): basic and ephemeral models

Psychoanalytic theory uses quite a high number of models of the mind, principally concerning three classes of theoretical problems: the *structure* of the mind, its *functioning* (the dynamics of mental events) and the *psychological development of the individual.*

Among these models are, for example Freud's two tripartite divisions (id, ego, super-ego, unconscious, pre-conscious, conscious), and also the Oedipal theory, which can be seen as a model when it is thought of "visibly" as a triangle.

The class of models of mental functioning rightly includes all the theories which deal with the dynamics of interpersonal relations, from the pair transference/counter-transference to introjections, to projection, to projective identification through to the theory of the proto-mental system that underlies group behaviours.

All of these models have in common at least two characteristics: they can be considered "basic" because they form the theoretical substratum of all of our work, whether with patients in psychoanalysis or with those in psychoanalytic psychotherapy, or with groups with different purposes. They are also "invisible" or at least "not said" within the analytic relationship. That is, we can have in mind the fact that something just said by a patient may be understood against a background of

Oedipal theory, but we do not say that to the patient in these terms, we use the words appropriate to the here and now, and keep our theories and technical terms out of the consulting room as far as possible. But there are also two other classes of models that we use all the time. These models are not so easily codifiable because they refer to passing, ephemeral events, in the session or the functioning of the internal world of the patient (or the analyst). A group consists of models that the analyst uses to mentalise and then to verbalise the analytic events, and the patient when he tries to communicate something that falls within a particular class of mental events for whose communication metaphors no longer seem adequate. The second group, on the other hand, is usually of more use to the analyst than to the patient, to describe the patient's mental structure at a given moment. While the models of the first group, which describe mental movements, are so ephemeral as to be able to describe them almost as "throw-away", those of the second tend to come back into our discussions with the patients, and I am inclined to see them as models of daily use, more natural than the basic models and also more verbalisable (and verbalised) in work with patients.

It is these two kinds of models that I want to talk about today, in the hope of being able to talk about them together, because they constitute a fundamental part of our daily work of which we speak very seldom. It also seems to me that there is at least the possibility that we are introducing into our work with patients a mental typology (or a modelisation of it) which is different from the classic one, and which it might be useful to explain.

The concept of mental movement

When I speak of analytic events under this heading, what I really want to do is refer to a very limited group of them—not, for example, the set, the acting, the performances as such, but something invisible, inaudible and intangible, which goes on below the surface, so to speak, phenomena perceptible through the senses. In the absence of a more elegant term, I will call the object of my remarks "mental movement". I could say, for example, that I think that the "form" of the movement of what I want to say today is more or less circular, because at the end I will return to a fundamental aspect of the Freudian division of the mind, but I would like to provide a better illustration of this concept of mental movement, referring to something known before moving on, to the two Bion's models of mental movement. Of these, one at least belongs, strictly speaking, the class of basic models, the model Ps ⇄ D. In this context, on the other hand, I am speaking about them because of their strong element of the *visualisation of movement* which is used to explain the phenomenon of the shift that the individual undertakes in his own mind from feeling submerged and persecuted in a universe composed of meaningless fragments to feeling that instead a new element has conferred meaning on the universe and put the fragments "in place".

The model of Bion's Grid, on the other hand, is what so far comes closest to a modelisation of the movements of analytic events, understood in broad terms, because it allows us to "map" the journey taken by the patient during the session, and this journey may also include acting, for example. From this point of view it is worth remembering that the precursor of the Grid was the "visualisation" in Bion's mind in the department of the military psychiatric hospital as a matrix in respect to which patients moved physically.

In any case, the desire to find some system to understand what happens between patient and analyst, and to communicate these passages and movements not only within the session but also of the scientific community is a very concise element of post-Kleinian analytic theory and in my view underlies a style of theoretical writing, and an ambit of apparently extra-analytic interest, which is worth exploring because it acts as a background to "ephemeral models".

"Vision" in analysis

In fact, the whole of psychoanalytic literature, since its beginnings, is scattered with terms to do with "seeing" and with metaphors taken from the visual sphere. One of the most concise terms is the English "insight", and Freud's letter to Lou Salomé, in which he speaks of blinding himself in order to see better has rightly become famous for his ability to "clarify" or "illuminate" a movement in Freud's mind, one of its ways of functioning.[1]

Besides, it seems almost impossible to describe a structural theory or a theory of functioning without referring to a drawing—we need

---

[1] Freud, S. (1916). Letter from Freud to Lou Andreas-Salomé, May 25, 1916. The International Psycho-Analytical Library, 89: 45.

only think of all the drawings by Freud himself, of Bion's reversed cube, used to illustrate the reversibility of perspective, to the journeys of reading indicated by Semi, or even from drawings by patients to the drawings by Melanie Klein's child patient, Richard, because certainly it is not only the analysts but also patients who privilege vision as a field in which to harvest fertile metaphors for understanding. A patient, E., who has recently thought of terminating the analysis, speaks, as an association with a dream, of the basket of games used for observation in the diagnosis of children which has been given to him by a psychotherapist who was losing his sight and who had decided to stop working with young children because he could no longer follow the games and decipher the drawings so well. The discussion of this association, which the patient had remembered after the session in which he had mentioned the dream, interpreted initially with the help of another group of associations, led to the unravelling of the patient's idea that his terminating the analysis made my blind to him, I wouldn't see him physically any more, only mentally. This interpretation allowed him to start exploring his compassion for the mother who "loses" her children when they grow up, and to make reparatory gestures towards his own mother, perceived as empty and unspeakably alone.

In contrast, metaphors that come from the auditory sphere are almost entirely absent, as if they were not perceived as useful for a clarification of internal or public communication, perhaps because they are felt to be particularly irreconcilable with verbalisation (or perhaps, as we will see below, because they come from a mental area of proto-verbalisation). One of Bion's patients said to him, "If I had a piano here, I would be able to make you understand what I want to say." But the application behind this is that the form of musical communication cannot be translated into the verbal form.

The wife of Masud Khan, a star in the Royal Ballet, when she was asked to talk about her own interpretation of a certain ballet, replied, "If I could put it into words, I wouldn't need to dance it."

The problem for us, as analysts, is that we have to put into words material which sometimes seems to be extraordinary refractory to this kind of transformation. I think that very often we find ourselves having to pass from a level of visualisation to one of verbalisation: it is true that patients tell us dreams—usually—in a verbal form, but with the request to "visualise" the dream. Meltzer suggests that dreams should be listened to with the eyes closed, so that they can then be verbalised for the patients, "enriched" by the interpretative dimension (Astor, 2005, p. 74).

But what is perhaps most difficult is passing from an obscure vision of mental movements on the part of the patient to their verbalisation in terms that are as clear as possible. When Bion speaks of the "language of achievement", in my opinion he is referring to a concise and clear verbalisation which carries meaning but is not saturated with it, the characteristics of the optimal formulation of an interpretation.

This, it seems to me, is a problem that goes beyond aesthetics, and I have wondered if what seems to be a tendency on the part of analysts to write about figurative arts, whether as an exemplification within their work or as an "applied analysis" might not have to do with a quite widely felt need to understand what are the relevant aesthetic elements in our work with patients.

The "beautiful" in analysis

There is no definitive answer to the question "What is beauty?", partly because the philosophical answers, however illuminating or detailed (I am thinking of Kant or Hegel or Cassirer) do not take into account unconscious thought or the interaction between subject and subject, at least not as we understand them today. On the other hand the psychoanalytical response to these comparisons, which can be encountered in the various texts which discuss individual works of art or individual artists, are partial precisely because they deal with specific problems. One might think for example of Klein, for example on *L'Enfant et les sortilèges*, and also of others.

But perhaps we can take from these works—and there are many others that I have not mentioned—certain fixed points: *the work of art must satisfy a need not only of the artist, but also of the viewer*; the need is emotional (an empty space to fill) but the satisfaction of the need also provides an intellectual pleasure. In the enjoyment of the work of art the experiences evoked in the viewer also have an important part to play, particularly the unconscious ones: that is to say that the viewer puts something of himself into the "dialogue" with the work of another. So we can see that the criteria for the formulation of an interpretation in the "language of achievement" correspond to the criteria for the enjoyment of a work of art: there must be a fertile marriage in the mind of the viewer or the analyst between the outward form, the content of this, the experience of the subject, without these three elements saturating the discussion to the extent that it cannot be taken further. That is, he who listens to the formulation, or enjoys the work of art, must be able still to be free to be able to add something to the experience. For the patient R., his previous experiences of mental contact with adults were such that they immediately and excessively saturated my interpretations, as I will explain below.

But perhaps interpretations also resemble works of art on a deeper level. In his study of Michelangelo's Moses, Freud stresses one vaguely unsettling element: he is not content to contemplate the statue as it is, static, but wonders what gesture Moses has just performed. This is not the question of an art historian or an aesthete, but specifically of a psychoanalyst, and it is the pivot on which all interpretation turns. *What is the mental movement that the patient has just performed?*

When Bion says that Leonardo's drawings of water or hair are formulations of mental turbulence, he is indicating the effort made by the artist to give a definite (and hence communicable, thinkable) form to one of his inner experiences, an experience of a period in a healthy psychotic part of the mind. Bion quotes, as an analogous verbal formulation, because it belongs to the same discursive universe, Milton's phrase: "Won from the void and formless infinite." Poincaré suggests that geometry is an attempt to give form to the perception of inner space even before external space. Freud suggests that external space is a projection of psychical space. From this point of view, joking but only slightly, we might say that fractal geometry is the geometry of psychoanalysis, and geometry of the healthy psychotic mind.

So we may say that a "beautiful" interpretation is an interpretation that catches not only the meaning of the here and now and of the internal objects active in transference, but that also, in order to reach its formulation, it must also have fished in profoundly unconscious places and brought up something of the mental movements in that realm. An implication of this on the aesthetic plane is that a "beautiful" interpretation will very easily become so only for the patient and the analyst who share the analytic experience, and seem a very poor and squalid thing to anyone else. In fact, it is quite difficult to write a clinical work that can seem even slightly convincing, because not even a faithful word-for-word account of the session gives ideas of the mental dimensions touched, seen and experienced which have informed these words. From the point of view of the frustration implicit in verbal communication, we are still in good company, when Verga can write to Capuana: "... the effect that any work makes in all of us, which leaves us discontent and unsatisfied, is the natural result of the miniaturisation, I would say, which the work of the imagination undergoes, losing everything it had that was vague and luminous in its concept to assume precision of colour and form."

Fishing tackle

I am deliberately using a rather thoughtless term, albeit one rich in Christian evocations, and which also recalls the depths of the unconscious, to try to find not too weighty an approach to the theme of ephemeral models, which are needed to seek to grasp and formulate an effective, "beautiful" interpretation. I probably feel this need for greater lightness because it is part of analytic work, which is in fact very burdensome, requires very deep concentration, and patients are usually very opposed to it, for most of the analysis, which is why trying to do it as part of daily discipline means swimming against the current. This last phrase itself a piece of fishing equipment: sometimes with some patients I feel not only as if I was swimming against the current, but more as if I were swimming in a sea of molasses, dense, with the traces of my strokes still apparent for a long time. This happens, for example, with a patient who is reduced to silent weeping after each of my interpretations.

In this particular instance, the tool assumes the form of a metaphor, and is easily verbalisable and communicable between me and me and between us—but not with the patient! It is a metaphor that includes various different elements—the sense of weight and effort, effort that I acknowledge I am making with this particular individual, who speaks very little and weeps almost as if "she were being wept" by the tears, which fall down her face without her making the slight attempt to wipe them away, she doesn't sob, as if the weeping did not belong to her, as if it were not hers. The metaphor of the swimmer in molasses allows me to make an assessment of how I feel with this patient, and then comforted by the material of the same patient, also allows me to interpret how she feels weighed down by everything, not only the tears, but even by the very air through which she walks.

Another type of ephemeral mental model is represented by the images which sometimes come to mind when we are in a very relaxed state of calm listening, close, I hope to the state of being without memory or desire, intensely concentrated and at the same time almost absent with regard to the external world. It is a state that might be considered one of "inner alertness", and the reason which I think it is burdensome is that the analyst becomes particularly vulnerable to the destructive attacks from patients, and I am probably also thinking about attacks that come from an actual hostility to psychoanalysis. To some extent this mental attitude must involve a lowering of one's own defences against one's own psychotic parts and those of the patient. The images that come to mind in these circumstances must be very carefully winnowed before being used as an element from which an interpretation should emerge—they must be able to be visible as part of an ensemble of elements, and one of the "rules" that I personally use to assess them, a kind of litmus test, it is to assess whether there is a reiterative element, a kind of recognisable configuration that reappears several times with different materials.

In late analyses of borderline patients, on the watershed of the terminal phase, with patients who are predominantly neurotic and not very disturbed on the level of thought, it may be the patient himself who supplies the elements of the repeated configuration. This is why the elaboration carried out by the analyst usually happens consciously, and clearly less disturbing than finding oneself doing elaborations that struggle to emerge from the unconscious. On the other hand, when this occurs, one also has to make a kind of internal investigation to follow the elements that constitute this elaboration. A fairly typical situation which illustrates this conscious work may be that of patient E., in the eighth year of analysis, who begins the session by giving me a cheque for a rounded-up sum and then starts talking about a cheque for a million lire that he had been given by his mother for his new-born daughter, describing it as "full of zeros, so empty"; towards the end of the session he begins to describe the way in which his older daughter wants the Emmenthal to be cut, the way she plays at making "bridges" with pieces of cheese, using the holes in the cheese itself, like the arches of the bridge as basic elements, then, of the construction. At this point it becomes possible to do an appropriate interpretation linking the zeros, the voids, the holes, the costs of the analysis, to me, on the coming week, to the bridge that the patient feels he must, and now can, build to the next session. But this is a light piece of work, because the patient himself is very close to conscious understanding of his own material.

In contrast with this level of mental elaboration, the situation in the session is much more disturbing for the analyst when a configuration that is really significant for the patient in fact appears as an actual emotional reaction that he cannot connect immediately with the facts of the session. A patient in the first phase of analysis seemed neither stiff nor particularly defensive, but in fact K. did not consciously feel any profound emotions.

This became definitively clear when she told me about the death of her beloved grandmother, when K. was ten years old and her sister six. His grandmother lived at home with them, she had been ill for some time, lovingly followed by her daughter (who had never been able to separate herself from her own mother). K. described a very gentle death scene, communicating an intense pathos to me, but while I had tears in my eyes, she was perfectly calm and did not seem even slightly touched or moved. I didn't know what to do with the rather intense emotions that I was feeling, and nor could I find a hook that would have allowed me to refer them to the patient except in a rather mechanical fashion. After quite a long pause, and one that was painful to me, K. told me that her sister had been sent away from home, to relatives on her father's side, on the day of the death-throes, and then after her grandmother's death she was allowed to find a soft toy on her bed, as a present from her grandmother, "who had gone away". This was all because otherwise her sister would have cried. It was only at this point that I was able to talk to K. about her unconscious need for me as a substantial container of the emotions that she couldn't feel. In this situation the significant emotional configuration became conscious for me, after what the patient had added to the discussion, but it was not yet conscious to her; however, in this first instance, it was "imprisoned" within me, I could not express it, in a similar way, but on a more attainable mental level, in the way in which K. could not feel the emotions, they were imprisoned inside her and out of reach.

The ephemeral model to which I refer in a situation of this kind is the idea of a similarity in mental structure between me and K., but with the events that occur inside the patient on deeper levels, and in me on levels that are a little more verbalisable. One might also speak of a kind of isomorphism, in the sense that the feelings of both crystallise, so to speak, in such a way as to create two similar mental configurations. But this kind of bi-univocal correspondence of mental events—which is once again something that allows us to work without a perception of great effort, even if it can be painful—does not always occur. There are moments when images come to mind that seem absolutely absurd, inane, inappropriate, and unconnected in any way with what the patient is saying (in the case of K., she was at least able to think or guess that the tears in my eyes were not entirely out of place or senseless, even if I couldn't think of their precise meaning with regard to the transference until K had given me other information).

One example of another type of image, which is disturbing because at first sight it seems like a simple incursion of images coming from an actually psychotic or simply frivolous place, may be the following, which comes from the second month of work with a patient, L. The patient told me, very calmly, about his family relationships, which turned out to be good—apparently he was a genuinely solicitous husband and father, attentive to other people's states of mind, anxious not to hurt, with good relations with his own parents, and I was able to listen in a relaxed manner. There were no "alarm signals"—a problem in paying attention to what the analysand is saying, for instance, or an awareness of tension—nor was there any kind of pressure on the part of the patient for me to intervene; something, however kept coming to my mind, something quite absurd in the context, an image of my fridge as if the salad drawer were dirty, the vegetables in it slightly stale, particularly all the lower parts of some celery stalks, as if they were beginning to rot. This image caused me considerable irritation because it seemed so irrelevant to me, were it not for the fact that I had thought that morning that the celery was no longer very fresh. Because the fact of having linked this thought to a previous thought of my own was not enough to silence it, I went on to wonder if it might be a key to reading, an unconscious interpretation on my part, and hence one with what L. was saying, and the image formed in my mind of a person whose emotional roots are rather cold, whose relationship with his parents seems to be spoiled at bottom by a fundamental defect.

Then, as if the information did not carry great weight for him, L. informed me that he had been brought up to a very great extent by his paternal grandmother, who lived in the front apartment on the same floor, and who had a very poor relationship with the parents of L., and I suspect that this was to the detriment of a warm relationship with his mother—or perhaps a substitution for a relationship that was not warm. I still do not know, however, how L. communicated to me that sense of coldness and of "not all right" in the course of the session, even though the image of the celery in the fridge, however domestic, was not in the end very much out of place. I have not yet succeeded in using this kind of perception of the patient in work with L. but it remains there in the background, it is part of the general picture and perhaps one day it will be possible to verbalise with him something that derives from it and is more visible, and graspable, in the here and now.

But the tools which allow us to fish in our unconscious are not always such clear images, and nor do they present themselves as metaphors, but sometimes I have a sense of having to allow things unknown to me to rise from deep strata, as sometimes the dreams of patients seem to come from areas that are not verbalisable, even if they may be very close to this level. The dream of a patient, R., who shares with another two patients a thought disturbance which makes the analytic work very difficult on a practical level, is a very good illustration of these two aspects of the depths of dream and the closeness of the interpretative work to a non-conscious level; I should also say that my more conscious interest in the problem of mental models is partly down to my work with these patients. The problem that they present (albeit in different modalities) is that of not being able to use my mind, not being able to approach me, enter me, bear mental contact. I could say in other words, words that come from a more sophisticated sphere of my thought, that this patient in particular cannot bear making use of the maternal reverie. The analytic work seems to advance, but on a mental level that is not the one on which I normally expect to work—but I will return to this point later on.

The story of the dream, which is a good illustration of the idea of mental movement—whether in the mind of the patient, or in mine in the course of the interpretation—occurs after an interpretation in which I had spoken to him about how he felt on the brink of a fundamental decision, namely whether or not to trust me and my mind and the possibility of using me as an analyst, as a counterpart to the analysis. The patient said: "I dreamed something that seemed almost like rounding a mark: it had this shape which he drew in the air—certainly a much faster and more immediate form of communication than verbalisation could be on its own; I think it's a palaeo-Christian sign. The first arm was accompanied by *la vinci* [you win it] and the second by *evincila* [deduce it], but the first *la* [it] was more like the musical note."

My immediate thought, that no yachtsmen would have appreciated rounding the mark in this way, because it would have made them collide, I took the liberty of acknowledging how difficult this dream was for me to interpret. But the patient gave a sense of waiting confidently, as if he thought I already had all the data I needed, and that he did not need to add anything.

At this point I felt the need above all to locate he dream in some mental space that could be grasped with a term: perhaps an indication of its provenance. That was a demand on my part, and I think the mental place of the dream is one of the elements that I am always trying to identify in the course of the interpretation—usually it is not so clear or so unique.

I began by saying that the idea of a palaeo-Christian sign indicated a "palaeo" mental zone with regard to the possibility of formulating verbal thought, and that he felt confidence in my ability to tolerate both the work on this level and the fact that he was *dando il la*—'setting the tone'". (This was a quite compressed reference both to material from the first months of analysis, and to a dream from around a year previously. I tend to make very brief interpretations to this patient, precisely because he saturates them too quickly with his own experience, which is why I try to ensure that they have a "wide mesh"). I replied with a little nod of the head, and he went on to say that as far as he was concerned his ability to trust the good working of my mind was really "a win"—meaning winning over years of extreme fear with regard to adults. Once he had rounded that mark, he was able to start using my mind in relation with his own to "deduce" (evincere) verbal thoughts: in fact, the "la" had become a word, no longer just a sound.

When I began the interpretation of this dream, I did not have the slightest conscious idea how it was going to end, but as I was speaking—and the tiniest gestures of the patient told me that I was on the right road—a long series of elements of R.'s analysis came to mind, for which I had a sense that the interpretation was taking shape "all by itself".

This sense of "growth" of an interpretation is something ephemeral in the session, I use it as a temporary mental structure of mine in which to classify the "auxiliary pieces" on which I am basing my interpretation—and in this case the pieces were very consistent. A non-ephemeral model of primitive mental functioning also presented itself to me in the background, namely the idea of my mother's mind, which contains the idea of the father, suffused with contrasting emotions.

This last concept, which belongs to the set of concepts relating to the sphere of the maternal reverie, acted as a "decoding device" or a "structuring element" for the different memories that this dream of the patient's brought to the surface: in the first few months of analysis he had spoken to me about his instrument for playing music and for listening to it, counterpointing it furiously and with a sense of rivalry with my instruments—and mine include a husband who is a musician, a fact known to the patient. But at the start of the analysis he wanted to play his music, he didn't want to hear mine or contemplate the possibility that I might have a musician-husband of my own in my head. In this dream, the same area of concepts has changed its emotional colour, and is acquiring meaning, suffused by greater tolerance: I can tolerate him giving the "la", he can tolerate using a musical note that is known as an element of common culture; it has been appropriated from a convention that allows harmonious communication (of all the members of the orchestra, of son and mother when he also has the father in mind). So the patient agreed to take something into his mind and use it serenely to communicate, even though the memory of what had gone before allows him to know that there is also potentially a hostile dimension, a possibility of ambivalence, or of emotional multivalence, which is very enriching.

The "palaeo" in this dream is a very sophisticated reference to a dream that he had about a year before. The associations with this dream were that the previous day he had had a very tedious day, having been obliged to go and have dinner with a family with a pair of twins less than a month old. Then he told me his dream: he had dreamed of dying: he felt that his body was disintegrating, his mind was disintegrating and his only remaining functions were his ability to hear sounds and feel emotions. Then someone from the same family fired a bullet at his head, but it didn't kill him immediately, it just speeded up the disintegration process.

At the time I was struck by the fact that, even though it was apparently a dream about his own death, the patient did not seem at all disturbed, displeased or anxious. I told him that rather than being a dream about his death, it was in fact a dream in which he was trying to come to terms with how he had felt as a very small child, who could hear words even if they did not yet have a meaning, and that he was starting to feel his own emotions.

The "la" the musical note of his recent dream, is also a very sophisticated form of "la-la-ing", lulling babies, and the refined adult version, stripped of disturbing elements, of the "sound of the surrounding universe", which in the dream of a year ago did not yet have a meaning and could not confer meaning, because it could not be an acknowledged basis of interpersonal communication.

It seems to me that these two dreams of R.'s, like many others, come from, or refer to, a mental area that is effectively preverbal and also pre-thought: in the course of the interpretation of the dream I have in the background an image of my mental activity which consists in grasping, in drawing out, collecting—almost mentally embracing—a nucleus which will then, when it is dressed up in words, become a verbal thought.

It is only at this point that it will be available for use—by me, with R., and, eventually, by R. to himself, and this only on the rare occasions when he does not have an attack of terror at the perception of our mental encounter, the kind of terror that fills him up and flings him out of his relationship to me.

Models of use, halfway between the ephemeral and the fundamental, visualisation of the analytic work

In the course of working with these and other patients, and also in the course of a kind of continuous monitoring of my own mental activity, which it is perhaps not entirely improper to call "self-analysis", I think I can acknowledge that I have constructed for my own professional use a model of mental functioning which, although based on classical models, does not precisely coincide with them. Or rather, I think it is necessary to have as instruments of analytic work some types of visualisation of the mental structure and mental events, and that these visualisations lead to the use of a specific and personal vocabulary. At this point I find myself face to face with Bion's advice that every analyst finds his own personal linguistic baggage: but now I know what lies behind that advice, what type of mental journey I have had to take to begin to understand it.

Above all, I find myself adding another dimension to the structure Conscious/Preconscious/Unconscious, that it is that of the degree of sophistication of thought, which can go from the naïve (the celery stalks) to a moderately sophisticated level, the one on which we begin to formulate interpretations concerning the stimulus of the here and now, to the very sophisticated plane of metapsychology, which we use to give a clear internal structure to our interpretations, even if it is not always explained either to the patients or to ourselves. R.'s dream about rounding the mark is a good example of these different levels of sophistication, because on the less sophisticated level he had to trace a gesture in the air: on the moderately sophisticated level he described his own mental movement as "rounding the mark", using a verbal metaphor, and on the very sophisticated level (which very often, and not only for him, acts as a kind of shorthand) has introduced the term "palaeo-Christian sign". This idea of dimension of sophistication is not in fact a fundamental model: it is a model of use, and a form of inner mapping of mine which signals to me the direction of the discourse of the patient (or mine), I use it to identify the degree of mental sophistication prevalent at that moment. Here I am referring to what I have said about patient R., with whom I sometimes find myself in contact with a very unsophisticated level of thought, more than happens with most patients. I think it has to do with the use of higher mental functions to collect and verbalise a very rough level of functioning in the here and now.

In fact the idea of mental levels is a basic level to which we continuously refer in our work to be able to formulate the interpretation in as detailed a way as possible, because it speaks at the appropriate level.

I have, for example, sometimes found myself submerged by a patient who almost always spoke about a level of psychotic fragmentation, largely disguised by the more fully functioning level of her personality, but which were not the significant levels, or the ones with which I should have addressed if I was to respond to her in a significant and meaningful way.

Another patient, Y., has invaded me, and attacked my integrated levels of thought to such an extent that I had to take a long, visual, roundabout route to understand her. The first year of analytic work with Y. was dominated by decay, not only hers, because this patient fell under the category of those who bombard the analyst with words. I found it very difficult to extract any interpretations that seemed convincing to me, or which breached the wall of words with which Y. seemed to surround herself. She complained that she could not communicate with her family, she could not tell she wanted to get married, and did not receive any adequate responses to what she said: and all of this was clearly visible, because it was reproduced in detail in the analytic situation. I could not see the person I was talking to, and she felt that I could not hear her. Sometimes the rivers of words induced a forced state of drowsiness in me, making me think that the theory that should have helped me was that of the projection inside me of something, but I couldn't work out what. She was unable to use analysis of the transference, and my attempts to think with her about her inability to use my interpretations were similarly unsuccessful.

In the first session after the summer holidays, Y. began the usual bombardment, and I couldn't stay awake: I felt I was drowning and coming back up spluttering, with a strong sense of anxiety. I started to feel desperate; that sleep could have no other easy explanations (tiredness, over-exertion, a cold, etc.) because I was well and rested; it must have been something that was happening between Y. and me, but I didn't know what. The session came to an end, leaving me without the slightest idea of what Y. had told me—and in fact she gave me a quizzical, disconcerted look as she left. I deduced that she had told me something very important and that having been unable to listen to her, I hadn't replied adequately to her communication. In reality I was so crushed by the experience of the session that I didn't even know if she had given me good or bad news.

At the end of this session I had my lunch break, and found myself turning round in my hands a postcard I had bought during the summer, partially written and never sent. It was a very particular photograph of a beach—there was no context (bay, coast, sea or sky), but only the random multicoloured stones that make up the coarse shingle on the beach. Many of the stones looked broken. All of a sudden I understood what Y. was projecting into me: I remembered her way of articulating phrases, or rather disarticulating phrases: "Yes, of course, because you know, errr, I was going to say. The other day—no, because ..." contextually I was able to understand why it was so painful for me to listen to her that I closed myself away in turn in a defence of sleep. In practice she was crushing my mind with the bombardment of fragments of verbalisation.

What I find curious about this experience is that, even though somewhere in my mind I had not only the concept of the Ps $\leftrightarrows$ D oscillation, but also the drawing of the coloured balls that illustrates it, I needed to see physically a similar drawing—but really chaotic, before I could start to think in a truly operational way. This seems to me to be an indication of the fact that I at least am much more inclined to think in terms of visible configuration, probably to the detriment of auditory configurations: I do not know to what extent this might be a common experience in our work, even though I suspect it is. The reason why

I have spoken at some length about this patient is that my experience with her leads to two ramifications in the discussion of mental models, which are rather important, and which concern both our way of conceiving what Meltzer has termed the psychoanalytic process and a fundamental aspect of the whole of psychoanalytic conceptualisation. This term which Meltzer uses is one of his models of analysis; it is a model which strikes me as too linear to be able to map my experiences of analysis, which is why I am more comfortable with the idea of analysis as a mosaic.

In certain ways, it is a static mosaic because the pieces, the tiles, are placed by the interaction between patient and analyst in a chronological order: but the analyst has to be able to use those same pieces as if they were part of a personal kaleidoscope, reorganising them in one's own mind with the aid of one's own "chosen facts"—the basic models. The elements of dreams often recur in different configurations as they unravel in the course of the session, different levels of interpretation made possible by new contributions from the patient, stimulated in turn by the previous interpretation.

The other intermediate model, with which I would like to conclude this discussion, has to do with boundaries: the mental boundaries between people, and the inner mental boundaries in each individual which separate the various mental zones. One of the first tasks of psychoanalytic theory has been to trace the boundaries between the various parts of the mind (again, the systems of Conscious, Preconscious and Unconscious are the example of choice). But Freud found himself in difficulties when he had to admit that the term "unconscious" also indicates a mental quality of something that belong to another system (ego, super-ego, id, for example). Sometimes in work with patients we effectively have a sense that something has crossed a boundary, an unconscious state has become conscious—we recognise it in ourselves, not least in my "understanding" of patient Y. In these circumstances, I find myself using the term "crystallise", because for me it is a good description of the visible emergence of something that was present but only potential (or unconscious).

But we are not always dealing with objects that move across boundaries: sometimes they stay in their area, but as if they were changing their (mathematical) sign. I think this was the difficulty that Freud found himself confronting. When I want to indicate this type of change I often find myself using the term "suffuse": in the case of R., I think I can say that the area of proto-verbalisation and proto-thought gradually comes to be less suffused with terror and therefore more usable. This is not why the area will never become a more sophisticated area of thought: it will always have the same functions and the same status as a "palaeo" area, a smithy of thoughts, it will always be something that is behind thought: but it gradually starts to be informed by many different emotional colours.

It would also be useful to make more than a nod to the way in which the concept of the internal boundary and interpersonal boundaries, particularly in work with groups, is connected with the basic model of the container-contained, and with all the conceptualisation of projection, introjections and projective identification, but I do not want this discourse on the three levels of mental models, the basic, ephemeral and intermediate models to go on so long that it leaves no space for debate, so I think it is better if I stop here.

CHAPTER NINE

Experiences in Groups revisited (1992)

What I would like to present for your attention today is a twofold journey of reading—or rather rereading—Bion's *Experiences in Groups* (1961). I have wondered if, and in what way, this text might be considered seminal for Bion's thinking in the works that followed, and secondly, to what extent Bion "kept the promises" expressed in *Experiences*. We might probably discuss this second point quite quickly, in the sense that at least superficially the promises were not kept.

Before venturing into this tangled wood, I would like to remind you of two things that it seems to me to be useful to keep in mind against the background of all the rest of the discussion: the first and more technical is the chronological position of different texts of Bion which speak plainly about groups, texts most of which were published between 1930, with "The war of nerves: the reaction of civilians, the social spirit and prophylaxis" in *The Neuroses in War*, via *Psychiatry at a Time of Crisis* in 1948 through to the final chapter (Re-View) of *Experiences in Groups*, in 1952. The last text that should be part of this list is *Attention and Interpretation* from 1970. The second aspect, which is quite substantial, is the importance of groups in Bion's practical life, because practice and theory are certainly not separable.

Personally, I consider that the awareness of the importance of the group in the life of the individual is something that entered the mind of the child very early on, and remained there as a "given" of existence that life itself never denied. Even before encountering a rough, but clearly expressed, codification of groups ("Are you A or B?") at his first school in England at the age of eight, Bion had lived in an extremely complex society, subdivided according to membership groups, meaning that of the British Empire in India at the turn of the century. His experience of this society, formally divided into rigid castes on the Indian side, and informally into equally rigid groupings on the side of the English, was probably anomalous with regard to most of the English children, above all because his father had married an "Anglo-Indian" woman, of mixed blood, and did a job (civil engineering) that led to his living in very close contact with the Indians and far from the cities or garrisons frequented by the English.

Then the child moved among the various social groups quite naturally, not paying much heed, consciously at least, to their boundaries. It may be supposed that he underwent a kind of "culture shock" when he arrived at a school in England, a school in which life was subdivided into school classes, "houses", dormitories, "studies" (the privilege of the older boys) and sports teams.

It would seem that in the course of his years at school the boy had learned to adapt more or less to these boundaries and to the functions of the various groups, although without ever identifying totally with any of them in a way that he found convincing. Emblematic from this point of view are the attempts of the adolescent boy, and later the young officer, to join a group that had crystallised around the basic assumption of dependence (the prayer group at school)—attempts which couldn't help revealing a fundamental sense of ill-disguised foreignness. This impression of belonging without identification emerges even more strongly when we read the accounts of the First World War and of Bion's experience as a very young tank troop officer. The terrible muddy bloodbath that was Bion's First World War, made even worse by the stupidity and almost complete lack of contact with reality of the superior officers, planted the emotional foundations of an understanding "from within" of cohesive power in a small group—the tank crew, in good and bad ways, in the adversity of external circumstances and the capacity for solidarity and love between the boys in the tank. It is certainly no coincidence that the codification of the idea of a group as a specific entity was born out of the experiences of yet another war, the Second World War, in which Bion was enlisted as a military psychiatrist.

Bion's career in the years from the end of the war to his death in 1979 always kept faith with regard to this need to be part of society, and to be at its service: apart from the institutional roles within the Tavistock Clinic and the British Psychoanalytical Society, he was part of the consultation committee into the law on the decriminalisation of homosexuality in Great Britain, he worked as an advisor to the Justice Department of the United Sates, and he followed as a supervisor the work done with a group of boys held in a Californian prison for resisting the draft (this was at the time of the Vietnam War).

Let us now turn our attention to the issue of the *Experiences* in Bion's work, and start with a brief nod to the regrets that Bion mentions in his Introduction to *Experiences in Groups*. Bion developed his best-known theories on groups over a period of about ten years, the first published work being in 1943 (*Intra-group tensions in therapy*) and the last (*Group dynamics—a review*) in 1952. These two works, the first discussing experiences in a military hospital in war-time, and the latter a more definitive theoretical reformulation, along with seven central chapters, form the book known under the title *Experiences in Groups*. We may deduce from the publication date of the collection that Bion wrote the Introduction to *Experiences* at some time during 1959 or 1960, when he was already working in the direction of *Learning from Experience* (1962b) and *A Theory of Thinking* (1962a). In his introduction Bion mentions two aspects of group dynamics that he had not explored satisfactorily in his previous works (the chapters that compose the book), namely sovereignty and power: all he says on the subject is that in such small groups sovereignty and power cannot develop to maturity: "The mature form is extrinsic and impinges on the group only as an invasion by another group."

He adds that he intends to discuss these matters in another volume if he has time, and that contextually he will speak about the extra-economic sources of the value of money, "which not only are important in themselves but also contribute significantly through their influence on economics to the dynamics of sovereignty and power".

In fact that volume never saw the light of day, which is a shame not least because it would appear that Bion was of the opinion that group dynamics, we might perhaps say, the classes of group dynamics change according to the size of the group, which is why it would seem logical to deduce that he maintains that the theories set out in

Experiences had value only for groups of limited size. My idea on this is that the limit in terms of size is the visible and auditory limit: the individuals in the group have to be able to speak to and see one another. This implies that an important part of communication within the group is conveyed via means that are not exclusively verbal, and that will probably turn out to be Bion's idea, if we note the assertion at the end of his introduction about the central importance of Kleinian theories of projective identification and the interaction between the paranoid-schizoid and depressive positions, and appears even more clearly in a close examination of the last page of *A Theory of Thinking* (1962a), a text to which I will return. For the time being I wish only to mention the fact that the criticisms Bion makes in *Psychiatry in a Time of Crisis* (1948) about the vicarious nature of participation in the life of the group that following events (athletic, political or other) through television are presumably intended to link to the perception, not fully clarified at the time, of the fundamental importance of direct encounters between people to a fullness of meaningful communication. That is to say, if individuals cannot perceive each other directly, communication is so impoverished that it becomes a falsification of itself, and ceases to be a real communication.

In *Cogitations* (1994) Bion briefly mentions "extra-economic sources" of the meaning of money, but in too telegraphic a manner for it to be considered a satisfactory development of his thought. He adds:

> There are certain "uses" of things in themselves that could be analogous to "uses" of modes of expression; they might form the basis of, or one axis of, a new Grid. Thus: money may be used to measure the status of a man or a woman, as in *wergild*, bride-purchase, religion. It can then be transferred to measure exchange values (commerce). It can then be debased in the sense of both change of base and change of value, i.e. to give substance to a fiction. For example:
>
> A) Analyst fee: low ←→ high; to correspond to psychoanalytic value of the psychoanalyst, i.e. a measure of value.
>
> B) Analyst fee: low ←→ high; to cloak and hide the value of the man or woman "psychoanalyst". The monetary value is debased as the communicative value of speech, the "currency of words", becomes debased.
>
> In A the money derives its value from the person to whom it is assigned, accredited, paid. In B, the person derives his "value"

from the possession of money that, already having value from its origin, is used to cloak his worth.

This brief passage grants us a glimpse of the type of turning that Bion's thought was taking, or would have taken had he continued along that path.

I think that the reason why Bion did not develop beyond this kind of intuition, and that his thoughts on Groups took a different turn which would then "keep him busy", so to speak, for the rest of his life, following, at least in part, the line of development suggested by the use of Kleinian theories on projective identification and the oscillation Ps ⇌ D for the understanding of an aspect of group life. From the beginning of *Experiences*, Bion explains that he wants to study the behaviour of the group and not that of single individuals: that is, the group in the military hospital is treated like a unit, not like a collection of individuals to be treated singly. In spite of this clear statement of his position, paradoxically Bion's goal, as a military psychiatrist, was to "turn out men who are respected, socially in harmony with the community and thus available to accept responsibility for the life of the community, both in peacetime and in war." From this we can see that for Bion the fact of being part of a group, a community, was of prime importance for the individual and his mental wellbeing. He resolved the paradox, implicit in devoting himself to the wellbeing of the individual while looking exclusively at that of the group, by bringing neurosis to the centre of everyone's attention, as a problem of the group and not an isolated problem of the individual.

But later on, and we can see this clearly in *A Theory of Thinking*, Bion began to examine the relationship between the individual and the group, in terms of physical individuals, and the relationships between the individual and the internal group, in terms of fantasies or conceptualisations of the mind. This second line of thought can immediately be seen as very rich—we need only think of the fact that it leads to *A Memoir of the Future* (1975–1979).

In fact Bion was vaguely aware of the overarching importance of the individual-group opposition from his schooldays, in which he so plainly felt himself always to be in difficulties with regard to his own less than total membership of school groups, and that awareness of the clash between individuality and group behaviour is something that has grown and clarified over the course of the last twenty years of his life.

Certainly, the clash between these two aspects of the individual is not only problematic for Bion, but also fundamental for the very possibility of his being able to think about it. In this context it is worth mentioning a brief note in *Cogitations* for 16 May 1959:

> The individual analyst has two main contacts: his patients and society. In the first certainly, and in the second probably, he will have it brought home to him how little he knows and how poor his work is. In this respect his position is not unlike that of the soldier in war who is aware of his own troubles but not of his enemy's. It must therefore be borne in mind that the fundamental importance of our work demands that kind of fortitude and high morale which places the welfare of the analytic group and its work before the welfare of the individual analyst, and sometimes before the welfare even of a particular patient. This, taken in conjunction with the isolation in which analyst and patient work, means that the analyst must, in addition to the commonly recognised equipment, possess a social consciousness of a very high degree—common sense must never be allowed to become dimmed, even when work is concentrated on the more arcane and narcissistic attributes of the analyst's patients. In other words, when concentration is focused predominantly on psychotic mechanisms, the non-psychotic aspects of the work must be as present to the analyst's mind as his awareness of the nonpsychotic aspects of the psychotic patient's personality are in the analysis he is conducting. Or, to put it another way, the analyst must ever cease, even in the midst of his analytic work, to be a member of one or more social groups.

Elsewhere in the same note he also says: "Publication is an essential of the scientific method, and this means that common sense plays a vital part. If it is inoperative for any reason, the individual in whom it is inoperative cannot publish, and unpublished work is unscientific work." By "publish", Bion certainly means "make public", an act that involves making one's own thought available to the community, but also subjecting one's own thought to the criticisms of others, as well as arranging one's own thoughts so that they can receive the contributions of others. Here we are really at the heart of the problem of the relationship between individual and group.

In the last chapter of *Experiences* Bion says:

> I hope to show that in his contact with the complexities of life in a group the adult resorts, in what may be a massive regression, to mechanisms described by Melanie Klein as typical of the earliest phases of mental life. The adult must establish contact with the emotional life of the group in which he lives; this task would appear to be as formidable to the adult as the relationship with the breast appears to be to the infant.

Later in this chapter, Bion does not develop his interactions between the basic assumptions and projective identification in any great detail: he speaks of the latter as something which concerns both the analyst and the leader of the group: they are both seen as "receivers" of the projective identifications of the group. The analyst should be capable of acknowledging this phenomenon when it happens—even though Bion himself notes that it is far from easy to do it—and make use of them to interpret, while the leader remains wrapped up in the web of projective identifications and acts accordingly.

At this point it may be interesting to follow the vicissitudes of some of the concepts contained in the quotation preceding this paragraph.

Let us start with the development of the concept of projective identification. On the penultimate and last pages of *A Theory of Thinking*, Bion discusses, very briefly, in fact, *realistic* projective identification as the means by which communication is effected:

> ... it does also develop as a part of the social capacity of the individual. This development, of great importance in group dynamics, has received virtually no attention; its absence would make even scientific communication impossible. Yet its presence may arouse feelings of persecution in the receptors of the communication. The need to diminish feelings of persecution contributes to the drive to abstraction in the formulation of scientific communications.

This is without a doubt a later step further, not least because here Bion introduces the idea that projective identification (which exists in a good relationship between infant and breast, in which the mother effectively uses the child's own perceptions to set the process of thought in motion) is in reality something that is continuously present as a mental activity throughout the whole of one's life. This is connected with what he is saying, more or less at the same time, in *Cogitations*, about regression:

> I consider that the behaviour of the patient is a palimpsest in which I can detect a number of layers of conduct. Since all those I detect must, by that very fact, be operating, conflicts are bound to occur through the conflicting views obtaining contemporaneous expression. In this way, the conflict that is so important to the patient's sufferings and to theories of dynamic psychology is, according to me, accidental and secondary to two different views of the same situation (...) Winnicott says that patients *need* to regress: Melanie Klein says they *must not*: I say they *are* regressed, and the regression should be observed and interpreted by the analyst without any need to compel the patient to become totally regressed before he can make the analyst observe and interpret the regression.

So, perhaps at this point we might try to make a synthesis which Bion himself did not make, but which would let us see something in the relationship between the concept of the basic assumption and the presence in the group of projective identifications.

The Italian term *assunto di base*, now commonly used, is not in fact a very faithful translation of the idea that Bion was trying to express: in English, "basic assumption" includes the idea of a mental state which is at the same time common to all and also *taken for granted*, and it is from this last characteristic that it derives its irrevocable force.

I think that the innate preconceptions of the individual, the preconceptions which are at the root of the realistic projective identifications of the infant, are called into play by the presence of the group, and which share with basic assumptions the level of "taking something for granted", something that must not be questioned. In my view, what must not be questioned is the goodness of the group, its availability to accept the individual and the projective identifications of these like a good mother, who is able to elaborate the projections of the infant and return them to it in a form that it is able to bear (*A Theory of Thinking*, 1967c).

I think a correlation may be assumed between the basic assumptions and innate preconceptions, whose form of communication is projective identification. This correlation—as if basic assumptions were a kind of summation of the innate preconceptions via a network of projective identifications—would justify the numerical limits of a "Bion's" group—that is, a group in which phenomena may be rendered explicit partly by use of the heuristic instrument of the concept of basic assumption. That is, communication via projective identification requires the contemporary presence of individuals and their reciprocal reactivity on a larger basis than the solely verbal. (It might be conjectured that projective identifications travel on very primitive sounds, on the sense of smell, as well as on vision.)

In this mental context, of very primitive and tough unconscious expectations, if we try to imagine how the members of the groups described by Bion in the second and third chapters of *Experiences* feel, we might think that it was something rather disagreeable for them, precisely because the things that are taken for granted, and taken for granted, what is more, were called into question on quite regressive but still active levels.

I do not know if this attempt at conflation of the theory of realistic projective identification and basic assumptions can really hold up—perhaps it is something that would be worth talking about later on.

For the time being I would like to turn my attention, quite briefly, to the fact that the continuation of this discussion about groups in *Attention* (1970) is organised in a completely different way, even if he is also discussing modalities of the relationship between the single individual and the group. In this text the theoretical climate and the interests of the author are completely different; there is no longer any sign of the basic assumptions, or more generally of the internal dynamics of the groups, but also seems that these aspects of theorisation have not been developed further. In reality one would have to have a long discussion just to begin to understand the sudden transformations of Bion's theory over the almost twenty years between *Experiences* and *Attention*, so I think it would be more useful to conclude the discussion of the development of group theory as it is expressed in *Experiences* here, and instead look at the text from another point of you in order to identify, if possible, precursors of ideas that will be developed later, even much later, and which can be considered seminal for other areas of Bion's thought.

One of the elements that I consider important is that kind of precursor of the Grid set out in the description that Bion gives of his "visualisation" of the training department. He says:

> The organisation should if possible provide a means by which the progress of the patients could be indicated, so that the psychiatrist

could tell if a man were fit for discharge. It would also be useful to have an indication of the patient's direction, of his effective motivation, so that an opinion could be formed about the sort of work to which he should be discharged.

I found it helpful to visualise the projected organisation of the training wing as if it were a framework enclosed within transparent walls. Into this space the patient would be admitted at one point, and the activities within that space would be so organised that he could move freely in any direction according to the resultant of his conflicting impulses ...

Various forms of the grid return in Bion's work—we have already seen an example above—and the importance that he placed on visualisation was always notable, whether images used to clarify his own thoughts, or images created by other people to communicate, from works of art to ideograms.

Apart from this, we can also find a characteristic of his personality in the phrase "... my determination not to attempt solution of any problem until its borders had become so clearly defined ..." and sense in this characteristic the mentality that would develop the idea of "free and fluctuating" attention until it became that mental attitude that uses Keats' negative capability as an instrument of knowledge, the theorisation of analytic practice that appears both in "Notes on memory and desire" (1967) and in *Attention*. Certainly, this is a theory that does not concern groups, because it is something that exclusively concerns the dual psychoanalytic ambit.

As I have already suggested, however, there is a very specific and very Bionian way in which work with groups has contributed to theorisation about the mental structure that emerges so clearly in *A Memoir of the Future*. In the quote from *Cogitations* about regression we may glimpse the foundations for a conceptualisation both of the mental structure and of some mental dynamics, which has little in common with the Freudian version. The key word here is *palimpsest*, but in later years that idea seems to make way for the idea of an internal group consisting partly of the personality—this idea is clearly expressed in one of the Brazilian lectures. I think we may deduce from *A Memoir of the Future* a later evolved idea of mental structure in which the mind is much more like an enormous kaleidoscope constantly in motion within, which is why the aspects that appear "in the window", so to speak (that is, they are conscious for the individual or appear to others) can be very different.

This is to say that Bion seems to have adopted a model of the mind in which all the aspects of the personality in their chronological personifications are simultaneously present. When I use the term "personification" I am thinking of the characters of *Memoir*, but also of the "Miracle" and "Mystery" plays of medieval England. These latter plays included above all representations of the vices and virtues, as if they were at war for the salvation or damnation of the soul, which is very like a representation of what we are more used to thinking of as the moral (or immoral) agencies of the personality.

This idea of a simultaneous presence of archaic and evolved aspects seems to give a much more dynamic and lively picture than is given by Freud's tripartite divisions, which appear much more static. But it is also different from Bion's assertion "I say that the patients *have regressed*": they have at the same time regressed and not regressed; it just depends which part of the personality is in the foreground on the stage at any given moment.

I have the impression, although I do not think it would be right to engage in an exploration of this territory now, that this type of conceptualisation of the internal world- as populated by a congregation of parts of the personality—has significant implications, both concerning Freudian theories of mental structure and repression, and for Kleinian theories of internal objects. Certainly, in the general economy of Bion's work, it has the characteristic of drawing together many different threads of discussion, and many of the sources of his thought contribute to the massive canvas of *A Memoir of the Future*.

I think that in conclusion we may say that the concept of the group has undergone a notable evolution in the course of Bion's work, from social group to internal group, but a constant remaining preoccupation is the idea of dynamics within the group as the element that is fundamental to the group's qualities, its characteristics, and also as an indicator of mental health.

CHAPTER TEN

Some notes on the theories of structure and mental functioning underlying *A Memoir of the Future* by W. R. Bion (1993): festschrift for Francesco Corrao

The following annotations on the theories underlying W. R. Bion's book *A Memoir of the Future* (1975–1979) are largely the fruit of the translation work, along with Gianni Nebbiosi, of the first volume of the trilogy, *The Dream*. At this occasion I should like to dedicate them to Francesco Corrao as a form of thanks for his great intellectual courage and his generosity in giving space in his own internal world to the ideas of Bion, from the outset, when they were very little known, but feared and attacked out of all proportion as "strange, abstruse and unorthodox". Not only did Francesco Corrao give space within himself to these ideas, he also introduced them to others, by popularising and studying them, and implicit within this activity is a very important teaching concerning the transmission of psychoanalytic culture. Bion's ideas in Corrao's mind were not left as foreign bodies, as relatively non-interactive guests, but were later developed and used as a basis and as stimuli for the thought of Corrao himself (1977). It is true that with regard to the history of science it is important to be able to attribute correctly to their authors the paternity of the concepts used, but it is also true that thinking dies if it is not refertilised and subsequently developed in the generation and the mind of each thinker.

From the point of view of translation technique, *A Memoir of the Future* posed a number of problems, some of which are certainly also common to other "difficult" translations, as for example the use by the author of a very large vocabulary and the difficulty of understanding the more audacious passages. But *The Dream* presented other problems that one does not normally encounter when preparing for a tradition, problems which sometimes become so acute and pressing that they slip into "nightmare". These problems may be classified into two groups: the ones which most specifically concern those who address the text as a translator, and those which emerge even when one is only trying to read the text. If we deal with the latter first, (given that before becoming translators we were readers, a state to which we then return once the translation is complete), we see that they are present on different levels: some derive from the emotional impact, an impact which affects different areas of the reader according whether it is a first, a second or a tenth reading. Other problems emerge for the reader on the intellectual level—not only concerning the swift understanding of the text, which is already arduous enough for reasons to which I will return—but because in reality writing is woven in with a theorisation about the structure and the working of the mind which is revealed and rendered explicit only gradually, through the discussions of the characters. It might be said that this treading technique, which expresses a precise intention of Bion's, that of presenting first the reality of an emotion or a mental state (paranoid-schizoid, for example), and then discuss it "using reason", corresponds to a form of *Nachträglichkeit*. So it presents the reader with a difficult challenge, both on the emotional and the intellectual level, because a participation and an interaction with the book is required on every plane.

The specific difficulties facing a translator are also relevant to all readers, because, like few other books, this text needs to be retranslated into the emotional terms of the reader himself, which is why each new reading is almost a new translation—even within a single linguistic range, the universe of the discourse of the single individual who cannot necessarily call upon more than one *linguae*, even though he might use several *linguaggi* (languages of the body, of childhood, of the emotions, etc.). These characteristics, which I will go on to describe in greater detail, have required from the translator a specific and unusual attention not only to the meaning the words used, but also to what we have defined as the "specific emotional weight" of terms, which we have tried to carry faithfully from one language to the other. One example of the difficulties that we have found is given by the use of expletives on the part of the characters: we have discovered that in terms of "emotional weight", where an English speaker will curse, an Italian will swear. If it were only a matter of translating a direct discourse, there would not be many problems, but very often the same curse is then used by Bion as if it were an "idée Mère", generating an associative verbal chain, which might in turn descend from the Italian swearword used by us in the translation because it is emotionally (but not linguistically) more appropriate than the curse.

Our choice has been to try to stay as faithful as possible to the emotional impact of English, even if that faithfulness sometimes seemingly obliged us to distance ourselves from the terminology of the original.

All of this effort and attention to every single word—why? To what end must a book be translated so scrupulously, why must we experience so intensely every passage and every change of mood? The reason is very simple, and it is the fact that the writing of the text is self-referential, in the sense that it is that which is being discussed. Perhaps this concept will become clearer if we take a closer look at the *Dream*.

The theories of structure and the mental functioning—which I would be more inclined to call the "mental movement"—cannot be defined exclusively in terms of Kleinian theory, even as expanded by Bion in his theory of the thinking of the individual and the group. I think we can still object that perhaps the term "structure" is not so appropriate to indicate the type of thing that I think Bion wants to talk about, in the sense that it *ipso facto* gives the impression of something rather solid and constructed which does not perhaps correspond very well to the image of mental functioning that he is trying to delineate. But the reason I tried to maintain the term structure is partly historical, given that my discussion cannot help descending from Freudian topics, and also plays in part on the ambiguities of the term, because our mind is always in search of certainties and life-rafts to cling on to, not least to be able to talk about a rather difficult text. Fundamentally, the theories of mental structure are used as points of reference and touchstones when we work with mentally disturbed people, to be able to "get an idea" of the degree and type of disturbance they suffer from, of the evolution of this, of its history. They are also useful on a more personal level of introspection with regard to our own mental health. So it is important to have a clear sense in your own mind of what kind of theory of mental structure is being referred to at any given moment, and perhaps that also applies when we set about reading *The Dream*, a book that fundamentally calls into question Freudian theories about mental structures, while at the same time taking its lead from them.

In terms of a close examination of the new model of the mind that Bion outlines in *A Memoir of the Future*, this text can be considered precisely as an example of this area of which the author speaks, in which he allowed the as yet untamed wild asses of his own thoughts to roam freely, before guiding them back to a beautiful domesticated theorisation. It is as if the book were a sort of testing ground on which Bion carried out a study of a modality of thought which emerged more and more clearly to him in the course of his evolution as a psychoanalyst. To start with, I would like to give a rough description of the mental structure that emerges from the text, before refining it later on. The model is approximately that of a huge multidimensional stage (one would like to add "directed by Ronconi"). In my view, the genesis of this model has a long story, traceable through hints in Bion's work beginning with *Experience in Groups*, in which he gradually lays the foundations for what will go on to become the Grid. The model, as it develops, is also enriched by multiple contributions from other cultural fields—first of all English literature, very rich, from its earliest days, in theatrical works, in the broad sense, but to be performed by a group and in public. The medieval works called "Morality Plays", for example, put on the stage characters who are personifications of vices and virtues, and this is a cultural furrow that Bion pursued by introducing some aspects of the mind as characters in *A Memoir of the Future*.

But these are aspects which are relatively easy to trace, elements of the composition of *A Memoir of the Future* which do not give an idea of its specificity as the fruit of the work of a psychoanalyst. On the other hand, in the construction of the text there is something specifically analytic in the text, which is not just part of the technique of writing the text, but also an element which reveals a certain type of the theory of the mind; not a structure, precisely, but rather a mental functioning, a mental movement. It is precisely the exaggeration of this element, to highlight it to a greater degree, that has made the translation work so difficult. We need to take a few steps back to illustrate the subject more clearly, and try to retrace this theory in the course of its development, from its genesis in Bion's work. The correct name of the theory is "dream-work-α".

Bion does not refer to the theory in this name, until the notes published posthumously in *Cogitations*, but the notes concerning this topic contained in this volume were probably written in 1960. In the works published when he was still alive, however, we find traces and hints of this concept. For example, all discussion of the need to work without memory and desire, without yearning for comprehension, are part of this broader conceptualisations about how the mind of the psychoanalyst at work really functions, and about what happens in "practical" terms during a session. One of the chief published indications of the direction in which Bion's thought was taken is found on pp. 123–124 of the English edition of *Second Thoughts*, in the "commentary"— presumably written in 1965 or 1966; it discusses the problem of whether or not to take notes concerning analytic work. After saying that he had carried out various experiments on the subject, he goes on:

> ... the most evocative notes were those in which I came nearest to a representation of the sensory image; say an event visually recalled. The evocation however was not of the past but of interpretations wise after the event. In short the value of the notes lay not in their supposed formulation of a record of the past but in their formulation of a sensory image evocative of the future.

Here I think we have the seeds for the very title of the trilogy, but apart from this consideration, which is far from trivial, I would like to place the emphasis on a different element contained in this discussion, which I consider to be extremely important: the formulation of a sensory image, as a constitutive factor of thought. It is at this point that it might be a very great help to consult a draft of a work contained in *Cogitations* (1994), entitled "Communication". In a section of this book (pp. 179–180), a section entitled, "dream-work-α", having briefly described what the dream-work means for Freud, with the compression, distortion, displacement and disguise of the dream-thoughts, Bion continues with the description of a process that has analogies with the mental processes described by Freud—hence, to some extent, the name—and that refers to a varied series of phenomena, connected, however, with Freudian ideas:

> In the state of mind of relaxed attention necessary in making observations, the individual is able through his senses to establish

contact with his environment. He is aware of his sensations and could, if required, describe what they are—as I, for example, can describe the colour of the paper on which I write, my hand holding the pen, and so on. Similarly you, the reader, can make observations of your experience as you read the word printed on the page.

Bion continues with a description, using an example, of the way in which dream-work-α functions as part of a process of mental assimilation. He says:

> … suppose I am talking to a friend who asks me where I propose to spend my holiday; as he does so, I visualise the church of a small town not far from the village in which I propose to stay. The small town is important because it possesses the railway station nearest to my village. Before he has finished speaking, a new image has formed, and so on.
>
> The image of the church has been established on a previous occasion—I cannot now tell when. Its evocation in the situation I am describing would surprise no one, but what I now wish to add may be more controversial. *I suggest that the experience of this particular conversation with my friend, and this particular moment of the conversation—not simply his words but the totality of that moment of experience—is being perceived sensorially by me and converted into an image of that particular village church.*[1]
>
> I do not know what else may be going on, though I am sure that much more takes place than I am aware of. But the transformation of my sense impressions into this visual image is part of a process of mental assimilation. The impressions of the event are being re-shaped as a visual image of that particular church, and so are being made into a form suitable for storage in my mind.

Then Bion explains that the visual image, in this instance, that of the church, is the one that he calls "element-α", briefly discusses the characteristics of the β-elements, and goes on to say:

> If my contention is correct, the production of α-elements is of the first importance: on an adequate supply of these elements depends

---

[1] Author's emphasis.

the capacity for what Freud calls "unconscious waking thinking", the ability to entertain and use dream-thoughts, the capacity for memory, and all the functions of the apparatus that Freud tentatively suggests come into existence with the dominance of the reality principle. ("Two Principles of Mental Functioning" [1911b]). (Bion, 1994, pp. 179–180)

In later notes (for example p. 277), Bion stresses the fact that the dream-work α, which here already becomes "α-function" serves to store emotional experiences in a communicable form. It seems to me that the type of literary technique that Bion used to write *A Memoir of the Future* is strongly indebted to the idea of compressing very powerful emotional experiences into a series of visual images, sometimes quite disconnected from each other, called to the mind's eye by the strong evocative power of the words that Bion uses.

In giving the first volume of the trilogy the title *The Dream*, I think he wanted to indicate to readers a kind of mental attitude that could ease reading, not only as if something that goes under the title of "dream" had a more valid passport to be accepted by us, but also a useful signal to predispose the mind to read. But this is a constructed waking dream, of which the author was aware and responsible (often we do not feel responsible for our dreams, but only of our fantasies, which in general we guard against relating, except, laboriously, in analysis—and it is much easier, even in those circumstances, to relate a dream).

Then Bion related a dream, conscious and constructed, a chain—if only it were only a chain, it is a real tangle of α-elements. These are often single words, with a very strong evocative power, taken from poetical texts, from songs, from the author's experiences in war and peace, love and hate. The important thing, when reading, is not the minute reconstruction of the sensory terrain from which the α-elements emerged, a kind of reversal of what the author did, but to allow the text to become evocative for us. This obviously did not apply to the translators, who repeatedly found themselves getting to grips with the need to try to go back to the origins, in so far as that was possible, of the α-elements intentionally constructed by Bion, to be able to formulate in Italian others which would have an analogous evocative power. Luckily the author often used compressions of terms taken from two, three or even more literary works, and it has been possible to make a faithful reconstruction of them using Italian translations. But of course the knowledge, for example, of the Bible, or of hymns, differs greatly from one country to another, and from non-conformist Protestant, as was the missionary environment of Bion's childhood and his school, and a Catholic, Jewish or lay environment. In some passages of the Dream we looked for analogous elements in Italian culture that might have the power to recall to the mind a complex and specific state of mind like the one evoked by the English text.

The second volume of the book is called *The Past Presented*, and this wordplay also indicates concept of mental structure, which is illustrated by the unravelling of the text. Where Bion brings on-stage different characters or voices, these often come from "past" parts of the personality, like somites, but are made "present". In my opinion, this way of seeing the mind as a big stage on which is performed not the drama of six characters in search of an author, but of the author grappling with a crowd of mental parts, each of which rises to become a character in its own right, in fact allows a glimpse of a conceptualisation of the mental structure that is much more chaotic than the Freudian one. The mental elements, at least when they have the status of α-elements, seem to enjoy a notable mobility, moving between conscious and unconscious—Bion had, however, eliminated the preconscious from his own theoretical baggage, considering it superfluous—and the ego or super-ego functions seem to be subdivided among different agencies of the personality—Myself, Bion, Psychoanalyst and Priest, to indicate only a few. Perhaps it might be argued that the dinosaurs Albert Stegosaurus and Adolf Tyrannosaurus also express aspects of the id.

This kind of conceptualisation of the mind raises problems concerning two pillars of Freudian theorisation, repression and regression. If Bion's repression is not so very different, because it may be considered as the outcome of a struggle for a position at the front of the stage, if not exactly on the gangway, a struggle in which some characters lose and are banished to the wings, only to reappear somewhere at the least opportune moment, regression, as seen by Bion, notably shifts the emphasis with regard to the previous theory. Hitherto, the analyst who maintained that he was dealing with the regression of a patient concentrated his own attention on "past" characteristics of the present situation. Bion's concept, on the other hand, suggests thinking of the regressed patient as a person who is using only some archaic, infantile, adolescent etc. aspects of his own personality, aspects which are always there—but in the wings—and at the same time bearing in mind the fact that we are dealing with an adult, who contains elements that come from his entire lifespan. Seeing regression in these terms sometimes allows us to pick up signals of the active but rather disguised presence of other parts of the personality: we may have the sense that a patient is "capitalising" a little, and not only, of course, in terms of regression.

Another type of theoretical problem is posed by the theatrical image of the mind. If the elements populating the mind are the ones we have seen, what is it that constitutes relations between the elements? Freudian theory indicated in the term "investment" ("cathexis") that which must explain the emergence of one feeling or thought more than another, but Bion makes no use of this concept. Instead it seems to me that apart from the oscillatory motion between major and minor integration (Ps $\rightleftarrows$ D) and projective identification, the latter presented to the reader in an unmistakable manner through dialogue between the two dinosaurs, Bion in fact brings into play all the mechanisms of dream-thought to "glue" together the various elements, and also to unglue them: so we find pages of associative chains, the compression of two or more words to create a significant neologism, fleeting allusions to the names of people who represent a whole theory—Lobachevsky, for example, and so on. So we may say that Bion brings together the α-elements with mechanisms of the dream-work-α. But the author also counts on the fact that the reader will have emotional reactions towards the work, reactions that become the contribution of the individual reader to the fabric that is being woven. However it is true that we may expect this kind of collaboration which, every now and again, and the start and the end of every book, speaks directly to the reader in a short dialogue, in which the author usually denigrates himself as he expects the reader to do, but every now and again darting an arrow in the direction of the unfortunate victim—the penultimate dialogue beings with: "I see you turn to the last page as you always used to do." This expectation of collaboration with the reader's emotions is analogous, and pursues the same kind of role, as expectations on the part of the patient (however unconsciously) that the analyst's emotions will be called into play. The analyst must expect this consciously, and be available in this sense, and this aspect of the reading of *A Memoir of the Future* beings me to another dimension of his book.

During our reading we find ourselves wondering if there is any point continuing—the book is so difficult, sometimes unpleasant or at least disturbing—and this is question that the author expected the reader would ask himself. Bion gives no reassurances in this regard, even when clearly behaving as an analyst in this respect, but leaves it up to the reader to discover whether it is worth, or whether it has been worth, the trouble of going on. In the course of the translation it gradually emerged that a deep reading of the text is so evocative of one's own emotions that it is disturbing, certainly, but also unleashes a mass of thoughts about our own way of working with patients and about the patients themselves.

This happens above all because the structural and functional theory hidden in *A Memoir of the Future* confronts us with the necessity, and the possibility, of making a rigorous revision of the concept of the counter-transference. Bion did not use this term very often in his theoretical texts, but by using it he restricted its meaning until it coincided with the idea of "that part of the relationship between analyst and patient that remains unconscious to the analyst". For this reason was also unable to speak of "using his own counter-transference" in analytic work, the counter-transference was a mirror image of the transference in the patient and therefore unconscious by definition. So this was a terminological contradiction that had no meaning, and in this, in the end, negative meaning of the idea of counter-transference, Bion was very close to Freud's opinion.

If we also restrict the use of the term in this way, we must perhaps find another term for something that happens within the analytic session, which is beginning to be much more accepted as a worthy object of investigation, in fact shamefully admitted as a "problem", in whispers and only with colleagues who are also friends: I am referring to the events connected with the operation of the analyst's dream-work-α (because obviously it is much easier to follow and untangle that of the patients). We find ourselves becoming distracted, thinking of other things—images come to mind which seem random to us, irrelevant, nonsensical, or freighted with significance and emotion for us but not pertinent to the patient or the work that is progressing with him. I think that giving dignity to the dream-work-α, as Bion implicitly did in *A Memoir of the Future*, gives us the possibility of exploring with greater calm and with less of a sense of guilt, our own dream-work-α. I think that a minimum of introspection allows us to distinguish between genuine distractions, due to tiredness or also to the emotional pressure of some personal event, and this other phenomenon, which deserves to be studied in much greater depth and by many people so that we may start to understand it a little better.

One note that is very illuminating about the technical aspects of this problem can be found in *Cogitations* under the title "How to Stay Awake":

> Since it is essential that the creative worker should keep his α-function unimpaired, it is clear that the analyst must be able to dream the session. But if he is to do this without sleeping, he must have plenty of sleep. The need for this now becomes apparent as a way by which α-function can be preserved for the sake of analysis, i.e. neither for waking up nor for going to sleep, but for a special and entirely new function, and not—as has hitherto been supposed—because the capacity for judgement is peculiar in being easily and rapidly fatigued. It is because α-function is by intended to make sense impressions or an emotional experience available either to the unconscious or to the conscious, *or* to make wakefulness or consciousness available to the emotional experience—as, for example, in learning a skill, from walking to fighting. Making oblivion available is not the same as repressing, but if the analyst has not had enough sleep, the α-function may produce oblivion.

In this quotation, Bion locates the α-function on a kind of frontier, unlike the "dead" frontier of the Tartar Steppe which "gives no thought" (but causes obsessions); this, on the contrary, is the frontier which seems to be the place in which thought forms, like a mountain range which looks like the cradle where clouds are formed. The α-function is almost like a policeman directing the traffic of the elements that constitute thoughts, on either side of the watershed, a policeman who makes it possible, for example, to "forget" of all the movements needed to walk—a short time after having acquired this skill, we no longer think about how to do with it, we just walk and that's it.

In the short passage quoted above, Bion refers to the relation between oblivion/sleep and α-function. The sleepiness of the analyst in the session is a problem to which he returns every now and again. As a general rule it is seen as a shortcoming, certainly as something about which the analyst almost always feels guilty, at best, as the fruit of a more or less pathological interaction between patient and analyst. While all of these aspects remain important, what Bion says suggests that it may be an occupational hazard. When the analyst is trying to be as much in contact as possible with the part of his own mind in which the α-elements are more fluidly available for the construction of thoughts, he is, precisely because of this availability, also in as defenceless a state as possible with regard to the reception of the patient's emotions—but also, perhaps, of projective identifications, which are not always benevolent. Apart from the possibility that the patient might launch an attack on the analyst's ability to think, and manages to make him go to sleep with, for example, the use of hypnotic tones of voice, there is also a possibility that the analyst, receiving from the patient emotional and conceptual "information" that is extremely painful in nature, finds himself curling up in a ball to protect himself and, rather than going to sleep, goes into a kind of mental "armour" which makes him feel out of contact with what the patient is communicating and, at the same time, suffocated by the armour, from which he tends to emerge with the sensation of having been in a state of apnoea.

It seems to me that with the help of the conceptualisation of the α-function and the storage zone of the α-elements to construct thoughts, we may understand something about the efficient functioning of our minds while we are working. I would like to give a practical example of this: the preamble to the story, so to speak, what would be the day's residues if one were oneself relating a dream, is that it rained very heavily in Turin, immoderately, and many of the streets had enormous, deep puddles. The events of the story contain a patient who, at a late point in the session, falls unusually into a rather long silence; I find myself having a very clear image of a long, broad, very dark puddle beneath a leaden sky, running along the right-hand side of the central carriageway of a wide Turin street. To the right of the water is a wide, grassy central reservation and then the service road. I seem to be at the wheel of some kind of vehicle, not defined, and to avoid passing through the puddle I head to the right, and steer towards the central reservation. This image had absolutely nothing to do with the previous material of the session, it is not a part of the road that I usually travel along, and it was not raining at that moment. Then the patient says:

> You know, there's something I think I should tell you, but I really don't feel like it, it's very hard for me, and I've avoided it until now, but the other day at the conference a psychoanalyst delivered a long dissertation on your father's work, I didn't understand it at all, and I didn't understand it even after two psychoanalysts began dismantling the dissertation.

At this point I had the sensation of having struck, in my visual imagination, something of the quality of the silence of the patient, of his desire to "avoid", but also something that was not so clearly verbalised by him, that is, his sensation that talking about father–child relations was something that led him to dark, grim thoughts.

In what way can I make use of an experience of this kind? Above all, realising that the α-function on its own does not have the status of a thought exactly, but needs other contributions, in this case what the patient has verbalised, at least to begin with. But even if I can formulate my thought about father–child relations, I am not yet in a position to use all of this to make an interpretation. So that this may occur, we need other data common to the patient and to me—something said, a sigh, to which I can also connect my emotional experience compressed into the visual image. These other data do not always appear quickly, in the same session, for example—sometimes one has to wait a long time before the data of the patient which "vindicates" the appearance of one's own α-element can be caught and communicated. It is for this reason, I believe, that Bion also describes the α-elements as "evocative of the future".

Having said this, it might be useful to return to the purely theoretical aspects of this discussion and try to see the relation between the α-elements and the α-function and Freudian ideas about mental structure and functioning. In short, the α-function and this kind of store of α-elements do not, I believe, have the status of structures in the Freudian sense of the term, because they seem to be too mobile to deserve it. An analogy that comes to my mind is that of the role of the gerund in English grammar, which can be either a verb or a noun, either static or indicative of movement—it is in fact referred to as a "verbal noun". The α-function is a "motor" of activity which will become thought, it is also a component of it, and the store of α-elements is in the frontier zone between conscious and unconscious—a little like Lago Maggiore, whose waters may be equally Italian or Swiss depending on the hidden currents.

Bion speaks of the α-function of the analyst as if it were a novelty, but perhaps this is not entirely true, because it seems to me that what Freud says about the hypnagogic experiments of Maury and Ladd refers to this kind of phenomenon. But it is true that it is only beginning with Bion that we begin to think of the α-function as a quality of mind that the analyst is able to use specifically in his own work, refining it as an instrument, learning to use it creatively. By learning to use it, I mean trying to acquire the discipline necessary to be relaxed, without memory or desire, without the urgency to "say something", to give a polished meaning to the events of the session. This discipline seems to ease the emergence from our own unconscious of the "ideograms" of the α-elements, which can never be forced to show themselves, but only invited to do so.

It would therefore seem that we must declare that the model of the mind and the theorisation of mental functioning that emerge from *A Memoir of the Future* are different enough from the Freudian conceptualisation, and yet the general effect of the reading is that it is a book much more rooted in Freud's thought that other Bion's texts. It is possible that this effect arises from the fact that Bion's thought, in the course of the whole book, is very firmly rooted in the sixth chapter of *The Interpretation of Dreams* (Freud, 1900a), extending the dream-thought and the dream-work still more specifically to the realm of α-elements by the analyst in the same way as the production of oneiric images on the part of the patients. This procedure, allied as it is to the emergence of thoughts about psychoanalysis at a remarkable level of abstraction and generalisation, means that the Bion's text is in turn a good example of the production of scientific thought. But these are characteristics specific to Freudian thought, and perhaps it is not least because Bion fully belongs to this great tradition that his thought cannot be heard as if denying Freud, even though he had developed a model of the mind that was much more agile and dynamic, and one which also acknowledges the fundamental status of Kleinian theory.

CHAPTER ELEVEN

From free-floating attention to dream-work-α (1993)

In *Recommendations to Physicians Practising Psychoanalysis* (1912e), Freud first introduces the term "evenly suspended attention", in the course of an open discussion of what we would now call the mental attitude of the analyst. For some time I have felt curious about the connections between Freud's ideas on this subject and those of Bion, not least because the idea is reinforced more and more in my mind that Bion was in fact very close to Freud's thought, much more than appears at first glance. The enterprise of translating the first volume of *A Memoir of the Future* had as its corollary a sort of "treasure hunt" in search of the roots not only of quotations or word-plays with which the text is scattered, but also about the origins of the psychoanalytic concepts used by Bion: and this search brought me closer and closer to Freudian sources.

Today I would like to try to take part of that journey towards the sources of Bion's thought because it seems important to me with a view to a greater understanding of the mental forces at play when it comes to making an interpretation: I think that Bion was very curious to know what happens to the mind of the analyst at work, because that tiny fragment of mental activity, apparently so specific and limited, is also pertinent to the considerably wider field of mental functioning in general and in all scientific fields; and perhaps artistic fields as well. Taking my cue from some of Freud's earliest works, then, I will attempt to identify and illustrate first of all Bion's theorisation and then the type of clinical phenomenon to which this theorisation corresponds.

In the Freudian text of 1912, various hints are made towards elements that will later be found in Bion's text "Notes on memory and desire", in which they caused a scandal and were felt to be abstruse, authoritarian, and above all "new". But in fact, Bion was raising some of the same problems that, in an apparently "soft" way, Freud had raised before.

According to Freud, the first problem that an analyst confronts when he starts having more than one patient per day, one of the things that seems quite difficult, almost impossible, is to remember all the data concerning all the patients. The technique for doing this successfully, according to Freud, is very simple: "It rejects the use of any special expedient (even that of taking notes). It consists simply in not directing one's notice to anything in particular, and in maintaining the same 'evenly suspended attention', as I have called it, in the face of all that one hears." In fact, the only previous occasion on which Freud has said anything similar is in Little Hans, where he asserts, very shortly after the beginning of the presentation of the material in the form of a letter from Hans" father "It is not in the least our business to 'understand' a case at once: this is only possible at a later stage, when we have received enough impressions of it. For the present we will suspend our judgement and give our impartial attention to everything that there is to observe."

In the "Recommendations", Freud goes on to say that not fixing the attention on a particular point implies that the analyst is not making a selection from the patient's material, a selection that might be invalidated by his own inclinations or expectations:

> ... if he follows his expectations he is in danger of never finding anything but what he already knows; and if he follows his inclinations he will certainly falsify what he may perceive. It must not be forgotten that the things one hears are for the most part things whose meaning is recognised only later on.

He adds that this rule is the necessary counterpoint to the fundamental rule of analysis that the patient should follow, of communicating everything to the analyst without making a selection.

This rule is not followed by patients just as the rule of free-floating attention is not followed by analysts, and we shall see that both have, in their own way, good reasons for disobeying.

Let us continue with Freud, who formulates the rule for the analyst in these terms:

> He should withhold all conscious influences from his capacity to attend, and give himself over completely to his "unconscious memory". Or to put it purely in terms of technique, "he should simply listen, and not bother about whether he is keeping anything in mind.
>
> What is achieved in this manner will be sufficient for all requirements during the treatment. Those elements of the material which already form a connected context will be at the doctor's conscious disposal; the rest, as yet unconnected and in chaotic disorder, seems at first to be submerged, but rises readily into recollection as soon as the patient brings up something new to which it can be related and by which it can be determined. (...) ... a conscious determination to recollect the point would probably have resulted in failure.

The Freudian work that we have followed thus far takes rather different paths, also returning to the theme of his own unconscious by the analyst, with a recommendation (we are only in 1912) that any aspiring analyst should have himself analysed before beginning to work with patients, to "purify himself" of his own resistances. I would, however, like to point out one last point that Freud makes *en passant*, that "the doctor's unconscious is able, from the derivatives of the unconscious which are communicated to him, to reconstruct that unconscious, which has determined the patient's free associations" (Freud, 1912e).

In this last sentence there appears a fine oxymoron concerning the *determination* of the *free* associations of the patient, which are of course consciously felt as free by the patient, while they are determined by unconscious associative chains.

We can draw from this very short Freudian text, of which I have only cited a few elements, practically all the theory of the technique that seems specifically Bion's: it is rather as if the latter had picked up a magnifying glass and observed each individual Freudian sentence, turning it into a kind of expanding universe.

"It is not in the least our business to 'understand' a case at once," Freud says to the father of Little Hans, and from this we may derive the whole of Bion's discussion of the progression from K to become O—this is a complex discussion which would take us a long way towards considerations of Bion's mysticism, which I shall leave aside for the time being.

"... suspend our judgement and give our impartial attention to everything that there is to observe." It is here that the connection occurs between the suspension of memory and desire, elements to which Freud alludes in his warning not to follow one's own inclinations or expectations, but as I have said above, this rule is not rigorously observed by analysts, and this, in my view, is connected with quite disagreeable experiences that the observation of the rule may sometimes encourage. Freud goes on to talk very briefly about the fact that the analyst must make use of his own "unconscious memory", and underlines the fact that it, for the moment, seems to be disconnected and in chaotic disorder, that it seems at first to be submerged.

Bion's expansion of these brief allusions is truly remarkable: from those few words comes all theorisation of the dream-work-α, and some of the intuitions about the oscillation $Ps \rightleftharpoons D$.

According to Bion, the mental discipline required to work without memory and desire has a very precise purpose, which is that of easing the unconscious thought of the analyst, which is not only what Freud calls "unconscious memory", but something more active. Freud speaks of unconscious wakeful thinking as being similar in its formation to the dream and what Bion calls dream-work-α is the name that he gives to the results of a later inquiry into this field: how the unconscious thoughts of the analyst at work arise, in what form they appear, and how the analyst can make use of them.

Bion does not refer to the theory by this name until the notes published posthumously in *Cogitations*, but the notes on this subject contained in this volume were probably written in 1960. In the works published during his lifetime, however, there are traces and hints about this concept. One of the first indications published of the direction that Bion's thought was taken are found on pages 123–124 of the English edition of *Second Thoughts*, in the "commentary", presumably written in 1965–66.

Here he discusses the issue of whether or not to take notes about analytic work. After saying he had performed a number of experiments, he goes on like this:

the most evocative notes were those in which I came closest to a representation of a sensory image; say, an event visually recalled. (...) The evocation however was not of the past but of interpretations wise after the event. In short the value of the notes lay not in their supposed formulation of a record of the past but in their formulation of a sensory image of the future.

It is at this point that it may be a very great help to consult a draft of a work contained in *Cogitations*, entitled "Communications"[1]. In one section of this work (pp. 179–180), the section entitled "dream-work-α", having briefly described what the dream work means for Freud, with the compression, distortion displacement and disguise of the dream-thoughts, Bion continues with the description of a process which has analogies with the mental processes described by Freud—hence, in part, the name—and which refers to a different series of phenomena, albeit related with the Freudian ones.

In the state of mind of relaxed attention necessary in making observations, the individual is able through his senses to establish contact with his environment. He is aware of his sensations and could, if required, describe what they are—as I, for example, can describe the colour of the paper on which I write, my hand holding the pen, and so on. Similarly you, the reader, can make observations of your experience as you read the word printed on the page.

Bion goes on with a discussion, using an example, of the way in which the dream-work-α functions as part of a process of mental assimilation. He says:

... suppose I am talking to a friend who asks me where I propose to spend my holiday; as he does so, I visualise the church of a small town in the village in which I propose to stay. The small town is important because it possesses the railway station nearest to my village.

The image of the church has been established on a previous occasion—I cannot now tell when. Its evocation in the situation I

---

[1] Also discussed in Chapter 10, in relation to A Memoir of the Future [Ed.].

am describing would surprise no one, but what I now wish to add may be more controversial. *I suggest that the experience of this particular conversation with my friend, and this particular moment of the conversation—not simply his words but the totality of that moment of experience—is being perceived sensorially by me and converted into an image of that particular village church.*[2]

I do not know what else may be going on, though I am sure that much more takes place than I am aware of. But the transformations of my sense impressions into this visual image is part of a process of mental assimilation. The impressions of the event are being re-shaped as a visual form of that particular church, and so are being made into a form suitable for storage in my mind.

Bion then explains that the visual image, in this instance that of the church, is what he calls "α-element", briefly discusses the characteristics of the "β-element", and goes on to say:

the production of α-elements is of the first importance: on an adequate supply of these elements depends the capacity for what Freud calls "unconscious wakeful thinking", the ability to entertain and use dream-thoughts, the capacity for memory, and all the functions of the apparatus that Freud tentatively suggests come into existence with the dominance of the reality principle.

In later notes in *Cogitations* (for example, p. 277) Bion stresses the fact that the dream-work-α, which is already becoming the α-function, is used to store emotional experiences in a communicable form. One very illuminating note on the technical aspects of this problem appears in *Cogitations* on page 120, under the title "How to keep awake":[3]

Since it is essential that the creative worker should keep his α-function unimpaired, it is clear that the analyst must be able to dream the session. But if he is to do this without sleeping, he must have plenty of sleep. The need for this now becomes apparent as a way by which the α-function can be preserved for the sake

---

[2] Author's emphasis.
[3] Discussed in identical terms in a different context in Chapter Ten. [Ed.]

of analysis, i.e. neither for waking up nor for going to sleep, but for a special and entirely new function, and not—as has hitherto been supposed—because the capacity for judgement is peculiar in being easily and rapidly fatigued. It is because α-function is by nature intended to make sense impressions or an emotional experience available either to the unconscious or the conscious, *or* to make wakefulness or consciousness available to the emotional experience—as, for example, in learning a skill, from walking to fighting. Making oblivion available is not the same as repressing, but if the analyst has not had enough sleep, α-function may produce oblivion.

In this quotation, Bion locates the α-function on a sort of frontier, different from the "dead" frontier of the Tartar Steppe, which "does not give thought" (but obsesses); this on the contrary is the frontier which seems to be the place in which thought forms, like a mountain range which looks like the cradle for the formation of clouds. The α-function is almost like a policeman directing the traffic of the elements that constitute thoughts, on either side of the watershed, a policeman who makes possible, for example, the "forgetting" of all the movements needed to walk—a short time after having acquired this skill, we no longer think about how to do with it, we just walk and that's it.

If we take into account the need to be able to dream the session—which is to say, use in a disciplined way within the session the level of one's own mind governed by the rules of the formation of oneiric images (or sounds)—we can understand the Bion's insistence on the need to keep out of range memories, recollections, desires (or inclinations or expectations as Freud would say) because they clearly impede the free functioning of the dream-work-α, being the product of operations taking place a very different level. This is an aspect of the problem of the mental attitude of the analyst which opens up the whole discussion of the way in which some mental functions—perfectly healthy and appropriate at other times—may become membranes acting as a caesura to interrupt the relationship between the analyst and a certain part of his own mind. Perhaps Freud would have numbered them among the "resistances" of the analyst, but the impression that the discussion is too complex to be liquidated in this way, even though in this case we should not pursue it beyond, however fascinating it might be.

In the short passage just quoted, Bion hints at the relationship between oblivion/sleep and α-function. The analyst's drowsiness during the session is a problem to which he returns from time to time. Generally it is seen as a defect, certainly, as something about which the analyst almost always feels guilty, come what may, as the product of a more or less pathological interaction between patient and analyst. While all these aspects still have their importance, what Bion says is an opening onto the possibility that it might be an occupational hazard. When the analyst is trying to be as much as possible in contact with the part of his mind in which they can most easily form the α-elements, and these in turn are more fluidly available for the construction of thoughts, he is himself the cause of this availability, even in a state of maximum defencelessness with regard to the reception of the patient's emotions, but also perhaps projective identifications, which are not always very benevolent. Aside from the possibility of the analysand launching attack on the analyst's capacity for thought, and succeeding in putting him to sleep, for example, through the use of hypnotic tones of voice, there is also a possibility that the analyst, receiving from the analyst emotional and conceptual "information" that is very painful in nature, finds himself curling up in a ball to protect himself: and rather than falling asleep, he goes into a kind of "mental armour", which makes him feel out of contact with what the analysand is communicating and, at the same time, suffocated by the armour, from which he tends to emerge with the sensation of having been in a state of apnoea. In situations of this kind, we may understand why, as I have mentioned before, it is not always possible for the analyst to allow himself the luxury of having been in the relaxed state of mind appropriate for the formation of α-elements; he can not always observe the Freudian rule of "... suspend(ing) our judgement and giv(ing) our impartial attention to everything there is to observe".

On the other hand, there is also the other side of this coin of forced drowsiness. We have all, I think, experience of analysands, or phases of the analysis of a given analysand, in which it seems that our attention is kept painfully alert, and the degree of weariness at the end of a session of this kin, is similar to the weariness that we feel when we have been prevented, by external factors, from sleeping during the night. The observation of Freud's recommendations leads to the production of α-elements on the analyst's part in collaboration with the analysand: the analysand's hostility towards this enterprise can succeed in damaging the analyst's capacity for work in quite a serious manner. Somewhere Bion says rather sadly that each patient has the analysis he deserves, and this comment is certainly a reference to the fact that not all analysands allow the analyst to make the best use of his own capacity for making pertinent and usable α-elements. The ideal state in which to work may be considered as a state of "inner wakefulness" in which we are intensely concentrated and at the same time as if absent from the external world, and it is burdensome because it makes the analyst vulnerable, not only in terms of the hostile attacks of the analysands, but also in terms of the attacks that may come from an actual unconscious hostility towards psychoanalysis. To some degree, this mental attitude must involve a weakening of one's own defences against one's own psychotic parts and those of the analysands. The images that come to the analyst's mind in these circumstances must be very carefully sifted before being used as elements of an interpretation: it must be possible to recognise them as parts of a set of elements and in some way coherent with the analysand's own experiences. One of the rules that I use personally in evaluating them, a kind of "litmus test",[4] is to check whether there is a reiterative element which indicates the presence of a recognisable configuration. I would like to give two brief examples of clinical work which in my opinion illustrate first a minor use of the dream-work-α and then, in the second example, a major use of it. The difference of mental level on which I find myself functioning is on a par with the different mental levels on which the two analysands habitually work in the session.

In the first example, my mental work was not on very deep levels, even though both my conscious and my unconscious mind worked in harmony, and this is a situation that arises when it is the analysand himself who provides, almost consciously, the elements on which to base an interpretation, in such a way that their concatenation (or, if we prefer, the emergence of the "selected fact" which makes visible the design of the mosaic on which all the pieces previously seemed to be scattered; as Freud says, "as yet unconnected and in chaotic disorder").

At the start of the session, the analysand pays me with a cheque for a rounded sum; in the course of the session he talks about the cheque for a million given to him by his mother for his newborn daughter, describing it as "full of zeroes, so empty" and then, towards the end, he describes the way his older daughter wants the slices of Emmenthal cheese so as to make "bridges", using the holes in the cheese as a base element of the construction. At this point it becomes possible to make

---

[4]The same description is used tin a similar context in Chapter 8. [Ed.].

an appropriate interpretation that connects the zeroes, the voids, the holes, the costs—including the emotional coasts—of the analysis, with me, with the coming weekend, with the bridge that the analysand feels he must, and now also feels he can, make with the next session. This is certainly a "light" work, not least because the analysand himself is very close to the understanding of his own material (he was already in the pre-termination phase).

The second example that I would like to introduce is in stark contrast from the point of view of the mental level on which the analysand—and also the analyst—functions. An analysand who suffers from a disturbance of thought which has made the analytic work very slow for many years (he used to fall asleep all of a sudden, unable to bear mental contact with me) tends at first to function in the session in an area that is not yet verbalisable, and then draws out words from this mental zone. Mostly this takes the form of relating a dream on the spot, so to speak, even if recently he has stopped going to sleep and speaks to me about images that have come into his waking mind.

In this session,[5] which I should like to relate, the analysand gets off to a reasonably good start, in the sense that he manages to remain awake enough to tell me, with a good crop of details, that he isn't in fact sure whether or not he wants to have a serious relationship with a certain girl that he met some time before. I interpret that he feels on the brink of a fundamental decision, which is to trust me and my mind, and the possibility of using me as an analyst, as his counterpart in analysis, or not. He falls suddenly falls asleep almost instantly when faced with the verbalisation of this idea, but when he wakes up, perhaps ten minutes later, he tells me:

> I dreamed something that looked like rounding a mark: it had this shape (which he drew in the air—certainly a much faster and more immediate form of communication than verbalisation could be on its own). I think it's a palaeo-Christian sign. The first arm was accompanied by "la vinci" [you win it] and the second by "evincila" [deduce it], but the first "la" [it] was more like the musical note.

My immediate thought is that no other yachtsmen would have appreciated rounding the mark in this way because it would have led to a

---

[5]This material was discussed also in Chapter 8. [Ed.].

collision, and I took the liberty of acknowledging how difficult this dream was for me to interpret; because I have a sense that the analysand is trustingly waiting for the interpretation, as if he thinks he has told me enough, and doesn't need to add anything else.

The only association I can work on is "the palaeo-Christian sign": it is useful to me because it allows me to begin to situate the dream in a mental place, "palaeo", with regard to the possibility of formulating verbal thoughts. I begin, then, by saying precisely this to the analysand, and add that he is feeling a sense of trust in my capacity to tolerate both working on this level and allowing him to be the person who "sets the tone"—*dà il la*. (This is a fairly compressed reference both to material from the first few months of analysis and to a dream from about a year before, which the analysand showed that he understood by nodding his head.) I go on to say that for him to be able to trust the sound functioning of my mind is really a victory (vincere). A victory over years of fear and profound mistrust. When he rounds this particular mark, he may start to use my mind in relation with his own to "evincere" (deduce) verbal thoughts: in fact, the "la" has become a word, no longer a pure sound.

When I began the interpretation of this dream, I did not have the slightest conscious idea how it would finish, but as I was speaking, and the tiny gestures of agreement on the part of the analysand told me that I was on the right path—I never felt "out of contact" with him during the development of the interpretation—a long series of elements from this person's analysis presented themselves to my mind, spontaneously and without my having to make any effort, which gave me a sense that this interpretation took shape all by itself, delving deep within me.

These elements included a dream of his own birth from about a year before, in which the analysand had felt a state in which he could hear sounds and have sensations but did not understand words and wasn't able to verbalise anything, a reference to an apparatus "for making music" (a mega-galactic hi-fi) in opposition to my own apparatus which includes my ears and a musician husband in reality and in my mind, and last of all, the idea of the harmony of the orchestra which "prende il la"—"takes the tone"—at the beginning of a rehearsal, and is able to work together by virtue of submission to a discipline, originally a convention, a convention that has acquired significance until it has become a "meaning".

While the first elements were part of the story shared by me and the analysand, the last one, a fleeting image of the RAI orchestra from Turin, was a real α-element, a précis of complex thoughts and emotions which moved from considerations about the analysand's ability to tolerate human commonality, to feelings of affection for my husband, and I think also for the analysand, which seemed in the end to tolerate my existence as a person, without being a source of unspeakable terror. This last fact, along with later associations on the part of the analysand, allowed the analytic work to continue on a level which contemplated the fact that the mother had an image of the father in her own mind … and so on.

In my opinion this kind of development of an interpretation can occur only in optimal working conditions, with a relaxed mind and without a feeling of stress, of tension, of yearning for an answer. This does not happen very often in the course of an analysis, and when it happens it is a happy moment, and often such moments coincide with the formulation of a mutative interpretation. I think there are also examples of what Bion meant when he spoke of "at-one-ment" with the analysand.

But there are also moments when we find ourselves dealing with unexpected thoughts of our own, thoughts that seem alien or formless, the product of a distraction, but which in my view are really α-elements whose meaning will be guessed sooner or later. I am referring to those visual objects which do not at the moment strike us as pertinent or appropriate, and which to have nothing to do with the patient's material. Of course, we may also find ourselves being seriously distracted—although this too is a phenomenon to be taken into account, and from which we can learn something either about ourselves or about our relationship with the analysand—and the genesis of these images of which I am speaking is not always easily comprehensible, whether it is something that emerges from the analytic relationship or simply internal to the mind of the analyst.

I would like to give one practical example of this—the preamble to the story, so to speak, what would be the day's residue of oneself relating a dream, is that it had rained a great deal in Turin, immoderately, and there were huge and quite deep puddles in many of the streets. The events of the story contain an analysand who, at a late stage in the session, falls (unusually) into quite a long silence; I find myself having a very clear image of a long, wide and very dark puddle beneath a leaden sky, which runs along the right-hand side of the central carriageway of a wide Turin street. To the right of the water is a wide, grassy central reservation and then the service road. I seem to be at the wheel of some kind of vehicle, not defined, and to avoid passing through the puddle I head to the right, and steer towards the central reservation. This image had absolutely nothing to do with the previous material of the session, it is not a part of the road that I usually travel along, and it was not raining at that moment. Then the analysand says:

> You know, there's something I think I should tell you, but I really don't feel like it, it's very hard for me, and I've avoided it until now, but the other day at the conference a psychoanalyst delivered a long dissertation on your father's work, I didn't understand it at all, and I didn't understand it even after two psychoanalysts began dismantling the dissertation". At this point I had the sensation of having struck, in my visual imagination, something of the quality of the silence of the patient, of his desire to "avoid", but also something that was not so clearly verbalised by him, that is, his sensation that talking about father–child relations was something that led him to dark, grim thoughts.

In what way can I make use of an experience of this kind? Above all, realising that the α-function on its own does not have the status of a thought exactly, but needs other contributions, in this case what the patient has verbalised, at least to begin with.

But even if I can formulate my thought about father–child relations, I am not yet in a position to use all of this to make an interpretation. So that this may occur, we need other data common to the patient and to me—something said, a sigh, to which I can also connect my emotional experience compressed into the visual image. These other data do not always appear quickly, in the same session, for example—sometimes one has to wait a long time before the data of the patient which "vindicates" the appearance of one's own α-element can be caught and communicated. It is for this reason, I believe, that Bion also describes the α-elements as "evocative of the future".

Having said this, it might be useful to return to the purely theoretical aspects of this discussion and try to see the relation between the α-elements and the α-function and Freudian ideas about mental structure and functioning. In short, the α-function and this kind of store of α-elements do not, I believe, have the status of structures in the Freudian sense of the term, because they seem to be too mobile to deserve it. An analogy that comes to my mind is that of the role of the gerund in

English grammar, which can be either a verb or a noun, either static or indicative of movement—it is in fact referred to as a "verbal noun". The α-function is a "motor" of activity which will become thought, it is also a component of it, and the store of α-elements is in the frontier zone between conscious and unconscious—a little like Lago Maggiore, whose waters may be equally Italian or Swiss depending on the hidden currents.

Bion speaks of the α-function of the analyst as if it were a novelty, but perhaps this is not entirely true, because it seems to me that what Freud says about the hypnagogic experiments of Maury and Ladd refers to this kind of phenomenon. But it is true that it is only beginning with Bion that we begin to think of the α-function as a quality of mind that the analyst is able to use specifically in his own work, refining it as an instrument, learning to use it creatively. By learning to use it, I mean trying to acquire the discipline necessary to be relaxed, without memory or desire, without the urgency to "say something", to give a polished meaning to the events of the session.

This discipline seems to ease the emergence from our own unconscious of the "ideograms" of the α-elements, which can never be forced to show themselves, but only invited to do so.

Bion's thought about clinical technique is very firmly rooted in Freudian thought, even if it extends dream-thought and dream-work even more explicitly into the realm of unconscious wakeful thinking, and deals with the production of α-elements on the part of the analyst to the same mode of producing images on the part his patients, bearing firmly in mind the fact that we are also dealing with products from the unconscious of each.

In a sense we may truly say that the analyst must perform continuous self-analysis, because he must unravel his own α-elements, just as he must interpret the ones underlying the dreams of his patients, always remembering to try to identify the way in which the dream-work has operated on the individual elements.

It may seem a very long road, the one that leads from equally suspended attention to the α-elements of the analyst's thought, passing through the paranoid-schizoid position, the $Ps \leftrightarrows D$ oscillation, the dream-work, but in reality, at the end of the journey, when we return to the Freudian text, we find we have travelled a very short distance: we have not even left the house, we have only used a magnifying glass that has given us infinite space in a nutshell.

CHAPTER TWELVE

Inside and outside the transference: more versions of the same story (1995)—or: history *versus* geography?

Geography
Is about Maps.
Biography
Is about Chaps.

—G. Clerihew Benson

*Delimitation of the field of application of the term
"patient's history"*

According to the statute of the IPA in 1994, the term "psychoanalysis" refers to a theory of the structure and function of the personality, to the application of this theory to other branches of knowledge, and finally to a specific psychotherapeutic technique. I think that this mixture of the three elements, theory, applied, psychoanalysis and therapy, is present in the mind and the practice of every analyst, but that the proportion of the "ingredients", so to speak, can vary greatly from individual to individual, just as it can vary in the course of the evolution of the individual analyst—the position of Freud himself moved away over the years from the initial concept of the "patient's history" has a particular connection with the idea of therapy, perhaps originally having been borrowed from the concept of anamnesis, which is a typically medical concept.

But it may be that this opinion of mine is particularly influenced by my English linguistic background, because in English "anamnesis" (in Italian "anamnesis") is commonly termed "history", and the Italian phrase *raccogliere l'anamnesi* becomes "taking the patient's history". From this reflection, however, while it might reflect a purely linguistic influence, we may derive two main series of thoughts: first of all, the possibility that the "patient's history" has a specific and limited field of correct and appropriate application within psychoanalysis. It does not add much, for example, to the application of psychoanalysis to other branches of knowledge, in the sense that I do not think it can have reasonable applications. The second series of thoughts, or perhaps a corollary of the first, concerns the possibility that, in my opinion, its usefulness in the course of a psychoanalysis is limited, and that sometimes its use may even be harmful if the analyst wants to concentrate on the functioning and psychical structure of the patient, and in fact aim (deliberately) at its cure. When Bion speaks of working without memory and desire, one of the desires which must in his view be eliminated is that of cure: and perhaps Freud was not very far from something of the kind when he warned of the necessity of renouncing the *furor sanandi*. But I will discuss this below at greater length.

I have wondered in the past how the phrase "patient's history" [*storia del paziente*], in its various meanings, has always provoked in me, for a long time now, a sense of irritation and unease which has grown over the years. While I was trying to jot down some preliminary thoughts for the writing of this work, a kind of answer to this question began to appear: and it is substantially this attempt at an answer that I should like to share with you this evening. To start with, the universe of discourse indicated by this phrase "patient's history"—even if we wish it to limit it to the area of psychoanalysis as therapy—is not entirely clear: does it refer to the events of the patient's life, in that the patient relates a kind of chronicle of himself in the very first sessions, or perhaps in that the patient relates a story of himself throughout the course of the analysis; or even to what the patient thinks is true concerning his own past? When Freud, in "Constructions in analysis", speaks of "historical truth" as a nucleus of delusions, he is only touching upon a topic which seems to me to be a kind of minefield, full of traps and snares, and the source of a certain confusion. The reason for my rather unfortunate state of mind is that, while it is clear that the analysis of each individual patient may be aimed at allowing the patient know as deeply as possible the truth about himself, I am not in fact convinced that the most appropriate formulation about this truth necessarily occurs in "historical" or "narrative" terms. I do not think it is only an idiosyncrasy of mine, but I do believe that there is some more serious motive underlying this sensation; it is true that in the course of my analytic work with patients it has been very rare for me to find myself thinking in terms of "history" or of "temporal and/or concatenation". So I think it might be worth talking more openly about this difference that I notice between "history" and what I effectively do while working, and I hope you will want to debate with me something that I experience as a methodological and theoretical problem touching the very essence of what we do while we are with our patients. The concept of the "patient's history", then, falls within psychoanalysis as therapy: but it also concerns the theory of the structure or function of the personality.

The tiles of the mosaic

At first, years ago, when I became a little more consciously aware of the faint unease I felt about the growing tendency to "narrativise" psychoanalysis, I thought there was something "wrong" with my way of feeling, and I tried to set it aside, but this technique of vague and more or less conscious denial was not in fact very efficient. When I started thinking about my this evening's paper, after an initial and quite enthusiastic support for the general idea, and after an unstable trace (of a "double" story) flashed into my mind, it was joined by a series of doubts, stronger and stronger, so strong at a certain point that they advised me to apologise to you, to withdraw the work that I had already done, and completely avoid the problem of having to write a paper on a topic that leaves me so perplexed. It did not seem polite to cancel the paper: but equally it may not be very polite to "demolish", or at least resize, the central topic of a series of scientific papers. You will forgive me, I hope, if in the end I decided to try to share with you my unease and even irritability with regard to the concept of "history", hoping that doing so will be more acceptable than a total silence would have been, or insufficiently convinced support of a thesis.

It seems to me that the problem consists of different "pieces", as if they were the tiles of a mosaic scattered around the place and still waiting to find an underlying theme (a "selected fact"). These tiles include:

1. A strong contemporary tendency to "narrativise" a psychoanalysis, and even a single session, or part of a session, which seems to me to go far beyond the Freudian conceptualisation of the "constructions in analysis", and which I find grating.
2. In contrast with this tendency there is my sense—which has grown over the years and been reinforced by experience—that any attempt made in the course of the analysis to create a historical narrative of the life or development of the patient soon comes to sound strained, even though I could not at first have said whether this was due to the patient's material or something else.
3. The repeated experience of a mental attitude of mine—*post hoc, propter hoc*—regularly left me time that it found (in the sense that it did not seem to bring it from anywhere) and that, from the patient's point of view, if (or when) the patient said to me "this and that happened because first ..." I found myself, also regularly, calling into question the completeness of the temporal and causal sequence, which was instead presented to me as if it were adequate in itself. More briefly, what happened was a premature and precocious saturation of curiosity, both mine and the patient's, which is why we were left with something like a sense of emptiness, a path leading nowhere.
4. A growing interest on my part to try to work as harmoniously as possible with the primary process of the patient—and thus also my own—with a view to try to collect thoughts "as they were born", and see which operations they undergo as they emerge from the inner chaos. (My patient Guglielmo, whom I shall discuss below, has stimulated me a great deal to work in this direction, probably because the analytic work was for many years so rarefied that I had to deal with mental levels that often did not reveal themselves sufficiently to be able to be picked up in a reasonable manner. To be able to work with him, on the other hand, it was actually necessary to work in and on fleeting moments in which he was awake, and try to understand what he was doing with the experience of himself in the session).

Working like this to try to collect the nascent thoughts means paying a great deal of attention to phenomena of condensation and displacement, to considerations of representability and secondary revision. I suspect that considerations both of representability and secondary revision are connected with "narrativisation" or the production of "stories" of various types, and that it is an mistake to suppose that they have a stronger" or in some way "more concise" meaning than other organised structures of the material.

Finally, I should like to add another tile, from a different source, so to speak: I have also found myself approaching the problems of the patient's "history" from a direction which in fact has nothing to do with this kind of topic, while I was trying, that is, to understand something about the substantial difference, from the point of view of the therapist and her inner setting, between psychoanalysis and psychotherapy.

The "double history": about "historical truth"

I think it may be useful to try to start with the "double history"—precisely, inside and outside the transference—that I intended to use as a "clinical vignette" for this evening (when the plan for this paper was very different) because, however, it allows me to illustrate one of the reasons why the "real history" of the patient always leaves me with a sense of suspicion, if not actually of "uselessness", of the narrow point of view of analytic work. This is the "double history" that I wanted to relate. It clearly brings out the question of the truth that analysts are seeking: it does not appear that it is historical truth properly speaking, because the knowledge acquired, the explorations pursued within the internal world, indicate that the internal truth does not correspond—for many years during the course of an analysis—with that external truth to which the "common sense" of the group or the individual would lend its support and approval. It also seems to me that the patient's internal truth is something that should evolve in the course of the analysis; the analytic par should be able constantly to come closer to the truth, but the truth itself lies in becoming, it is not timeless and immutable (if it were, there would be no reason to have oneself analysed—what for?). The historical truth of which Freud speaks, on the other hand, seems to be intended to have a quality of "now and for ever", and therefore to be intended as an immutable truth.

Topology

Now I would like to turn my attention to the other tiles of the mosaic that I mentioned at the start. It is not in fact a matter of chance, but perhaps it does not place sufficient weight on the fact, that Freud spoke very often, and at length, about mental topology. And he spoke about it much earlier and at much greater length than he spoke about the patient's "history", in the form of "constructions". In reality, there are several "topologies" discussed theoretically—we need only think of Matte Blanco, of Corrao—as proof of the fact that analysts have "always" dealt with the visualisation of the mental in terms more spatial than historical or narrative.

Bion, in *Cogitations* (and also elsewhere), presents a topological approach that is very different from the Freudian to the problem of the conceptualisation of mental activity, particularly as regards the theory of thinking. In fact, the Grid is itself a form of "map" of the movements of the analytic session, both those of the patient and the analyst. It may appear on first examination that his approach, like that of Klein, is exquisitely and solely dynamic, but in the course of the years the theorisation of paranoid-schizoid and depressive positions was gradually formulated in terms that increasingly call to mind a rather topological image. This is not to say, however, that the Ps ⇌ D oscillation does not remain an essentially dynamic fact: but the description of the moment of the choice of the "selected fact" is a description that lends itself well to a visualisation that is precisely topological. You will perhaps remember the little game done with a piece of cardboard pierced with holes at regular intervals, in each of which was inserted a coloured peg, apparently at random. Someone need only say the word "triangle", and we "see" that each peg, with others of the same colour, is in fact part of a triangle, at first "invisible". This is a visualisation of the theory according to which the scattered "facts" of the paranoid-schizoid position, following the selection of one of them, acquire significance and coherence, because the selected fact supplies a key to reading that was not previously there.

In my opinion, this theory about mental functioning gives the idea of the existence of a mental place. But it is not so easy to see what the points of contact between this kind of theorisation of mental space and Freudian topology might be, because we would have to consider that we are dealing with a dynamic fact that lies in the ford between the system of the Unconscious and the system of the Conscious, but not in the Preconscious. The fact that the word "ford" comes spontaneously to my mind stresses my tendency to think of the mind in geographical terms;

this is probably an almost inevitable development, given the Kleinian habit of thinking in terms of an "inner world". I should perhaps make an elision between the two terms of the clerihew quoted at the beginning, and acknowledge that my way of thinking of psychoanalytic work, as well as my way of thinking during the work, requires a sort of "geography of biography" along most of the course of the analysis, and not so much a "history" of the biography.

The selected fact: time/cause/others

In the various passages of the *Cogitations* in which he speaks of the "selected fact", Bion stresses one fundamental element, which is that if the selected fact is time, the key to reading, or the arrangement conferred on the scattered elements, is a "causal" key, according to the rule of *post hoc, propter hoc*. In modern terms, it is also a narrative key. The problem, or the difficulty, from the point of view of analytic work with the patient, is that the most appropriate selected fact might very well not in fact be time, which is why, if we wish to pursue the "history" of what has happened, we risk losing sight of other important elements. For example, in the course of a patient's account, there may gradually—and also sometimes suddenly—arise in the analyst's mind a very clear perception concerning a reiterated "element" of the discourse, such as jealousy (clinical material).

The relations between mental objects: temporal or a-temporal?

If we look at Freud's work "Constructions in analysis", we find the famous analogy of the archaeological dig, in which Freud says that the advantage that the analyst has over the archaeologist is that the finds are still alive. This seems to militate in favour of the idea that we are really dealing much more with a map of the mind than with its history, in spite of the "construction" that Freud immediately goes on to supply, a construction, amongst other things, which seems curiously flat and uninteresting, as if it fell within the category of "causal" or "historical" interpretations that lead nowhere. Too often the introduction of the narrative key or the construction makes us lose sight of the possibility that relationships between the mental objects are of another kind: Bion suggests in fact that other kinds of relationality to be taken into consideration can be expressed in terms of the four mathematical operations, but also remaining only within the Freudian theorisation of the primary process we may identify a series of relationships (superimposition, juxtaposition, reversal, displacement) which cannot be described adequately in narrative terms. This, of the non-linear relationships between the mental objects, strikes me as a promising line of research, in the sense that it alerts the analyst to the possibility of assessing the patient's material for non-temporal selected facts. In this same type of ambit of thought, Bezoari and Ferro's concept (Ferro, 1992, p. 401) of "functional aggregates" may be very fruitful, and it seems to me that their "aggregates" are very appropriate to a conception of the mind in terms of a multi-dimensional, even stratified, topology. I do, however, find rather contradictory the coupling immediately suggested on the following page between the theorisation of "functional aggregates" and narrativisation. It places a strain on both the patient's material and the way of working of the analyst, who, in my view, needs to leave himself more time to see possible non-causal links between the elements of the material, and forces a kind of premature closure of the state of doubt and uncertainty that may risk his making explanation-interpretations which notoriously fail to explain or interpret anything. This necessity is what Bion is talking about when he describes the way in which the analyst has to "have patience"—even for a long time—before he is able to reach, if only in a transient way, "safety".

If Freud is right to say that the unconscious is ignorant of time, it does not seem to me that we should necessarily seek to introduce it into conscious verbalisation. The following assertion of Ferro leaves me very perplexed: "If the micro histories developed in the session reach, no matter where they come from, the communication of the patient and the reverie of the analyst, in the here and now of the session, they organise themselves into a story that they must be able to share and construct together." Above all, we need to see how the micro histories that develop are connected with the communications of the patient and the reverie of the analyst, since it is possible, in my view, that the seductiveness of the idea of history is such that neither patient nor analyst realise sufficiently that there is something ahistorical and atemporal in play. And then the shared construction of a history, given by Ferro almost as obligatory, is something which, in my view, happens, if it happens, in the last months of an analysis, and as part of the work of discovery of what the analysis is, and of why this particular patient decided to do an analysis with this particular analyst (and perhaps also, reciprocally, the analyst will be able to discovery why he has taken this particular patient into analysis). In my experience, the only time of historical construction with which I feel at ease occurs when the patient begins to check his own evolution in the course of the analysis, when he really begins to be on the home straight, so to speak, and the risk of acceptance of a construction not to do (or not to see) something else effectively diminishes.

Psychoanalysis or psychotherapy?

In the introductory section of this paper, I said that I have encountered the problem of inner relations within the opposition of history/ geography, also arriving from an apparently totally different direction, from considerations on the relations between psychoanalysis and psychotherapy and on the distinction between them. Thinking along the lines that I have now tried to indicate, I have convinced myself more and more that my way of working with patients might be more usefully compared with the revelation of the topology (or geography, if we prefer) of the patient's mind, because it certainly does not follow a linear trajectory and I do not seem to find many indications of trajectories of this kind in patients' material.

The fact of trusting oneself very much to "free-floating attention" in the concentrated form of reverie favours the emergence of "self-selecting facts", and these quite rarely have connotations of any temporal (and hence causal) considerations. The reason for this is that the reverie is an instrument that is refined to pick up the movements of the primary process: this is the thought that must be picked up *in statu nascendi* and interpreted, not that of the secondary process, in which time and cause have their appropriate role.

In reality, the idea of a map (perhaps with "hic sunt leones" and question marks along the lines of "inland sea?" in many of its parts) is not enough to give an image of the wealth and dynamic complexity of the mind while it is being studied during an analysis, and I have found a metaphor which strikes me as a little more appropriate in an unexpected place, namely in a novel by Asimov (1982). This novel describes a computer installed aboard a spaceship, which can produce a holographic image of the galaxy, an image that changes according to the position of the ship, giving the impression to the person "looking" at the image that he is in fact "inside" the galaxy. (Anyone who has only sailed among terrestrial islands is well aware that what is seen—the reciprocal positions and shapes of the islands—changes by the minute as one approaches or moves away from them).

But if for the analyst the understanding of the personality and mental functioning of an individual patient passes through something that can be compared to the creation of a galactic map in continual evolution, while, that is, the analyst is also evolving, how many maps at a time can we reasonably expect to be able to keep in our minds?

The distinction between what I think we may define as the vitality of the "galactic map" and the member that we might have of a patient once the analysis is concluded is a very important one; the memory does not seem to require any more effort than remembering anything else, while the maintenance of the "mapping" is a real task which I think requires a notable expenditure of mental energy. It also calls for the regular practice of at least four or, even better, five weekly sessions, and requires a great availability on the part of the analyst to make his own mind and his own mental functioning available to the patient. I am of the opinion that more than a dozen—at most—patients is in fact impossible to "keep in mind" in this dynamic way. My experience also leads me to think that trying to work in this way with only one or two sessions a week is destined not to work very well: the patient has no time to become accustomed to the analyst's strange way of working—and neither does the analyst to the patient. (It takes a certain familiarity born of long and regular practice before the analyst can allow himself to enter the state of relaxed concentration necessary to favour the emergence of his own α-elements, and patients also have to learn to be patient with regard to this kind of procedure.) Seeing patients less frequently, then, implies not being fully able to use the technical instruments that we have at our disposal, not least because it is at least likely that if patients are seen for fewer sessions, they are seen for longer, not least for simple economic reasons, and the question arises of the unsustainability of the effort. As a consequence of this effort there is a tendency, automatically, I would say, to make use of the best known and most familiar mental categories, and, above all, the most conscious: Kant (1781) himself maintained that the categories of time and cause were categories *a priori*, categories, that is, which are part of our mind and not of the world of things-in-themselves. This means that they are categories which we impose upon the world—which could be entirely different, and we will never know—and which we impose them almost automatically, above all if we are tired and overloaded with patients. What psychoanalytic theorisation has been able to add to Kantian theory is that there are also other inhabitants of the mind, the unconscious modalities of thought—the primary process first of all—which require our attention as analysts, more, I would add, than the categories of thought of the secondary process require it. These considerations, then, constitute the connection between the patient's history and the problem of the differentiation between psychoanalysis and psychotherapy. In my view, the work of psychotherapy with a few weekly sessions must be based largely on the use of secondary thought on the part of the analyst, with a consequent "historiography" rather than a "geography" of the patient. A psychoanalyst, on the other hand, attends to the mapping of the inner world.

Conclusions

I would not like to be considered someone who wants to demonise or demolish the concept of the patient's "history". I want only to try to stress something that strikes me as an important fact: an excessive attention to the idea of "narrative" blinds us to the possibility that things might be different. The narrative seems to be something that patients (and also analysts) take as if it had a special, protected, status—and hence, for this reason, allows them to feel "in place". One often hears a patient complaining/apologising (as if they had done something wrong and wanted to be commiserated with and forgiven) when they bring a dream "in pieces", "just a few images", "just a flash". This means that, every now and again, the dream has escaped into a secondary revision that has imposed on a group of scattered images the semblance of a narrative. Some of these dreams may be interpreted in such a way as to reveal a superimposition and a multi-determinism that are absolutely fascinating.

My patient, G. is a specialist in the production of these flashes, and has a high tolerance for the fact that they are not narratives, while other patients remain upset, as if it were dangerous to dream things that cannot be linked together. I think they experience this as something that reveals their madness, and I maintain that in fact it reveals the functioning of the primary process. From this point of view, Kekulé's dream of the snake biting its tail is a truly extraordinary example: it is also an example of the wealth that can be drawn from an examination of our mind aside from a premature narrativisation.

It is precisely this need always to leave ourselves the possibility of making discoveries about mental functioning, this obligation, in a sense, to keep faith with the explorative aspects of psychoanalysis, which makes me doubtful and a little disturbed about the "historicisation" of patients and their (and our) analytic experience. I think that the "history" of the patient has an important role—for the patient, as a starting point for their analysis, at least, and then, within the analysis, in the final phase, as a reconstruction of analytic stages. But I also think that the correct role of history is situated outside the transference, not within it, where instead we must try to arrive at the most recondite processes of the mind, allowing ourselves to think that perhaps the tendency to make a history of the analysis or the session is a defence against the transference and against the violence and urgency of emotions and unconscious thoughts. Ferro himself acknowledges this, somewhat between the lines, when he acknowledges that in fact the analyst flees from the transference when he makes interpretations such as "she had this kind of relationship with her mother". While one is in the midst of work with patients, then, the analyst, in my view, would do well to keep out of range his own tendency to "historicise", to "make constructions", because it is an activity that distracts attention from the here and now, from the transference, then, and in consequence, from our most precious and most specific heuristic instrument. I could close, a little polemically, perhaps, by saying that while many people can write history, discovering geography is a privilege reserved for the few.

CHAPTER THIRTEEN

The concept of the individual in the work of W. R. Bion, with particular reference to *Cogitations* (1996)

Every now and again in the works published during his lifetime, above all in clinical and non-clinical seminars, Bion refers to the idea that a person's somatic confines do not correspond to the confines of their personality.[1] I think this is quite a curious concept—albeit an intuitively attractive one—but if we stop to think for a moment, it becomes incomprehensible. But there are some passages in *Cogitations* which shed a little light on what Bion himself meant by this idea, and I think they may be useful as a basis on which to launch a discussion on the subject, on its possible relevance and its usefulness above all with regard to his psychotherapeutic work with groups—but not only with groups.

What I would like to do today is to present some pertinent Bion's texts, refer to a clinical passage and then, with you, to see whether this kind of conceptualisation of the individual confers greater significance to the clinical data and can be used as a heuristic instrument in the various clinical situations. Bion's discussion of what constitutes an

---

[1] Bion was influenced on this point by the writings of Alan Watts (1966), who wrote of the "myth of the skin-encapsulated ego" [Ed.].

individual is articulated around certain nodal concepts that should be examined one by one before we attempt to clarify the links between them. The concepts are: Common sense; Narcissism; Socialism; Myth as group dream.

But all of these concept hinge on that of the α-function or α-elements seen as fundamental mental activity, the basis of thought: that is, the mind's capacity to experience an emotion and enclose that experience within a visual image or a sound so that it can be stored and used later for unconscious wakeful thinking and for dream-thought.

In the discussion of a passage by the British philosopher Braithwaite, Bion observes:

> This at once raises the question, what is common sense?—a problem that has received inadequate attention because without modern psychoanalytic technique and theory, it is impossible to make any useful approach to the question, or perhaps even to realise that a most significant phenomenon lies embedded in the term, which is itself a striking emanation of common sense.
>
> Let us approach it clinically: a patient enters the consulting room, notices that the couch is in some disorder but, making only a minor adjustment, lies on it and proceeds with his associations. In due course evidence from his associations indicates that at this particular juncture, and taken with sundry other facts not germane to this discussion, he is experiencing an increase in anxiety and, furthermore, that the anxiety has as its ideational content the disordered couch as part of the furniture of a scene of parental intercourse. This conclusion, and the interpretation that is the psycho-analytic act by which it is expressed, is arrived at on the basis of observed facts seen in the light of a psycho-analytic hypothesis. But common sense tells this patient that he is lying on an ordinary couch and that ordinary people, as he himself might say, would know that that is what it is and that its disorder was due to the movements of the previous patient upon it.
>
> To prevent too minute a discussion, I propose that we may now say that common sense is a term commonly employed to cover experiences in which the speaker feels that his contemporaries, individuals whom he knows, would without hesitation hold the view he has put forward in common with each other. Common sense, the highest common factor of sense, so to speak, would support his

view of what the senses convey. Furthermore, he has a feeling of certitude, of confidence, associated with a belief that all his senses are in harmony and support each on the evidence of the rest. In this sense also, private to the individual himself, the term, "common sense", is felt to be an adequate description covering an experience felt to be supported by all the senses without disharmony. As contrast, I may cite the experience in which a tactile impression of, say, fur—sudden and unpredicted—gives rise to the idea of an animal, which then has to be confirmed or refuted visually; and so, it is hoped, the common-sense view is achieved.

But there is a difficulty. So far one might say that the patient's view is essentially at one with the strictly scientific view that Braithwaite investigates after limiting the scope of his survey in the way I have shown above. The analyst, however, is also able to claim that his interpretation is based on common sense; but it is common only to some psycho-analysts who may be presumed to witness the same events and make the same deductions.

(...) The serious problem can be emphasised if I maintain that the hypothesis on which I base my interpretation is itself an embodiment of common sense in the sense in which I have already described the term. The hypothesis purports to be a generalisation from "common sensations" applicable on an occasion when there arise again "common sensations" that appear to lend themselves to generalisation in the same hypothesis.

(...) Clearly I am attributing a very important position to whatever it is in the psyche that is ordinarily called common sense whose function it is to determine the "common sense" of the sensory experiences. Furthermore, it may seem that a certain minimum of sense experiences is necessary before it can be reasonably said that common sense can determine what is the sense that is common to all of them. This is a folklore version of the sophisticated scientist's need to establish adequate correlations.

It is appropriate at this point to stress how, in this short passage, Bion links the common sense of the individual with that of the group, in the sense that a) there is a formal resemblance (the senses of the individual are seen as analogous to the contributions of individual members of the group); and b) the individual refers to the group to discover "what may legitimately be thought".

But Bion also asserts, with regard to common sense, that it can be an object of attacks:

> (18 July 1959)
> (An inability to dream and hatred of common sense)
> implies
> (destructive attacks on all linking and anti-social acting out)
> The anti-social acting out is an attempt to destroy the common sense which the patient cannot get rid of. In analysis it contributes to the danger of murderous attacks on the analyst. The analyst's common-sense interpretations are attacked by being seen and felt as sexual assaults. But does the patient actually feel them as sexual assaults, or is this an instance of anti-social, i.e. anti-common-sense, attacks on common sense, a sort of "You're another" retort to someone who is felt to frustrate?
> (…) Is this his conscience playing up both him and me by being delinquent, by being a delinquent super-ego which knows how to produce the maximum anxiety?
> How does this link up with the common sense? The most obvious would be Freud's early super-ego which he equated or associated with social guilt. If this is so, Freud's denial of guilt before the Oedipal situation, except for social guilt, is a more fruitful theory than Melanie Klein's. But splitting attacks on the super-ego, common sense, would lead to a mass of super-egos—the bizarre objects I spoke of in "Differentiation of the Psychotic from the Non-psychotic Part of the Personality". It is a murderous super-ego. He rebels against it but it is itself delinquent.
> What is the relationship between common sense, super-ego, and narcissism?
> The super-ego is certainly opposed to his existence: it is opposed, *a fortiori*, to his living. It is opposed to morals, e.g. his dream: his father makes a sexual approach to his wife while he (the patient) looks out of the window helplessly.

Here Bion has introduced the term "narcissism": in the next passage we will also see the introduction of the term "socialism", which for Bion has nothing to do with politics, but concerns the social values of the individual, in contrast with his values towards himself, which Bion defines as narcissism:

> I am reminded of the Millais Culpin case: the patient committed suicide after an interview when Culpin told him that analysis was not suitable for him. Culpin was blamed by the coroner and attacked in *The Times*, which suggested that an end should be put to psycho-analysis.

With this patient (of Bion's) it is essential never to forget that we are dealing with a schizophrenic. In other words, we must never forget that the patient is full of homicidal and also irresponsible feelings, and that common sense, that is, the common sense of society, imposes a particular diagnosis and a particular attitude of individual members of society towards the patient. A resistance with regard to these principles brings with it the sanctions that the group always threatens to apply to those who oppose resistance to its principles. The patient's "common sense", however invisible and difficult it might look, tells him precisely this, because the patient is blessed with common sense, even if he makes rather uncommon use of it.

Even if the analyst must never stop being a member of his own group and must consequently be sensitive to the principles of the group and the risks he runs if he ignores them, must not however allow the "socialism" of his orientation to obfuscate the vivid and immediate reality that he has in front of him in the consulting room. The patient knows this as well: he is willing to pursue his own role in imposing a weighty sanction should the analyst fail to behave with the perspicacity required not only by his work, but also by the absolute determination on the part of the patient that the analyst—with his behaviour of exclusive commitment of his attention to the patient (whatever the cost to the analyst)—sustains narcissism against his own "socialism". (And the patient is also determined that the analyst should be socially ostracised just as he is.)

The analyst is thus forced to experience the split that the patient himself suffers between his own narcissism and his own socialism. The existence of this split is made apparent by the patient's reactions to the cures offered by the analyst for his narcissism. We have seen that the patient experiences the consciousness present in the analyst with regard to pressures and social obligations, but also feels pressures which have their origin in the urgent demands of his narcissism, and that he does so while exploiting the interest that the analyst shows in his well-being as a sign of the analyst's inability to demonstrate that common sense that everyone, except the analyst, is expected to possess.

Bion says some other things about the socialism/narcissism divide, still connected to the concept of "common sense":

> There is something curious about this kind of defence which is analogous to an interpretation in which the elements are so ordered that the narcissism of the patient is spared. But I have already said that narcissism, apparently primary narcissism, is related to the fact that common sense is a function of the patient's relationship to his group, and in his relationship with the group the individual's welfare is secondary to the survival of the group. Darwin's theory of the survival of the fittest needs to be replaced by a theory of the survival of the fittest to survive in a group—as far as the survival of the individual is concerned. That is, he must be possessed with a high degree of common sense: (1) an ability to see what everyone else sees when subjected to the same stimulus, (2) an ability to believe in survival of the dead after death in a sort of Heaven or Valhalla or whatnot, (3) an ability to hallucinate or manipulate facts so as to produce material for a delusion that there exists an inexhaustible fund of love in the group for himself. If for some reason the patient lacks these, or some similar series of capacities for attaining a strong degree of subordination to the group, he has to defend himself against his fear of the group—which is known to be indifferent to his fate as an *individual*—by destroying his common sense or sense of group pressures on himself as an individual, as the only method by which he can preserve his narcissism. In the extreme form of defence in the psychotic the result of these destructive attacks appears as a superabundance of primary narcissism. But that is an *appearance*—the supposedly primary narcissism must be recognised as secondary to a fear of "social-ism".

This digression brings me back to the psychotic defence against interpretation, which I have said is analogous to the attempt on the analyst's part to avoid communicating, through interpretation, any element which constitutes, or which can be seen as representing an attack on the patient's narcissism. In practice this means avoiding the clarification of illusional, delirious and hallucinatory mechanisms, with a view to making the patient feel loved, for fear that such a clarification might show him that the love he desires to feel he is receiving does not in reality exist. In turn, this means that the analyst must communicate in various ways that he loves the patient and that, from this point of view, the analyst is a representative of the common sense of the patient's social group, a social group that loves him more than he loves himself. Of course this latter conviction may find support in the patient through a conviction on his part that the analysis itself is an expression of such a love of the group for him.

Or, in terms of the experience of early childhood, that the breast is a gift that he is given by the family group.

To the extent to which the patient manages to avoid attacks on his narcissism, he experiences a hallucinatory gratification of his yearning for love. Like any other hallucinatory gratification, this too leaves the patient unsatisfied. So he has greedy recourse to a reinforcement of his capacity to hallucinate, but, of course, this has no corresponding increment in his degree of satisfaction.

> Narcissism and social-ism.
>
> These two terms might be employed to describe tendencies, one ego-centric, the other socio-centric, which may at any moment be seen to inform groups of impulsive drives in the personality. They are equal in amount and opposite in sign. Thus, if the love impulses are narcissistic at any time, then the hate impulses are social-istic, i.e. directed towards the group, and vice versa, if the hate is directed against an individual as a part of narcissistic tendency, then the group will be loved social-istically. That is to say, if A hates B, as an expression of narcissism, then he will love the society. "I hate B because he is so harmful to the society that I love", might be an assertion symptomatic of what I would call a state of narcissistic hate of A for B. I maintain that in a narcissistic statement there is always implied a social-istic statement. The two must go together: if one is operating, so is the other.
>
> If follows that if narcissistic hate is felt for A, then social-istic love is felt for B. If A is one person, then B will become a group of people all possessing the admirable characteristics that distinguish B from A who lacks them. Put in still other terms, if one group of impulses is dominated by narcissistic trends, then the remaining impulses will be dominated by social-istic trends. Let X be a person: if his hate impulses are social-istic, his love impulses will be narcissistic. But suppose his impulses towards himself, say love impulses,

become narcissistic, then all his other impulses will become socialised, and he will split himself up into a "group". Love of self need not be narcissistic; love of the group need not be social-istic. At one pole is one object: at the other pole an infinitude of objects. At one pole there will be one object to which one group of emotions will be directed: at the other pole a number of emotions will be directed to the infinitude of objects that owe their numbers to a splitting of one object.

In Freud's work, the social field in which the individual works is taken as "given", but now it is essential that the environment must become the object of further theoretical studies. Only in this way can narcissism and the narcissistic psychoses be understood."

The schizophrenic's relationship is not with the analyst predominantly but with the analyst + himself. That is to say, it is predominantly a social transference—dualism to narcissism.

But in postulating socialism as the other pole of narcissism, I had in mind the idea that the patient's socialism menaces his primacy as an individual, and the group demands of him subordination to aims lying outside his personality. This is especially true with regard to aggression. Is it also true of morality? Is there a moral instinct which is also bi-polar, one in which the patient is impelled in conflicting directions because his individual moral view conflicts with the moral view he holds as a member of the group?

The conflict in the individual between socialism and narcissism

In his paper, "Instincts and their Vicissitudes", Freud makes the suggestion that the relation between the ego and sexuality may be regarded in two apparently equally well justified ways. In the one, the individual is regarded as of prime importance; in the other, as a transitory appendage to the germ plasm bequeathed to him by the race. He postulates, expressly disavowing any greater authority for his statement than that appertaining to a postulate, that the conflict is between sexuality and the ego instincts. He suggests that study, particularly of the schizophrenias, might require modification of the theory.

I agree that one side of the conflict is associated with the ego, but it seems to me that difficulties are caused by making a division between ego instincts on the one hand and the sexual instincts on the other. A more fruitful division is one between narcissism on the one hand, and what I shall call socialism on the other. By these two terms I wish to indicate the two poles of all instincts. This bi-polarity of the instincts refers to their operation as elements in the fulfilment of the individual's life as an individual, and as elements in his life as a social or, as Aristotle would describe it, as a "political" animal. The exclusive mention of sexuality ignores the striking fact that the individual has an even more dangerous problem to solve in the operation of his aggressive impulses, which, thanks to this bi-polarity, may impose on him the need to fight for his group with the essentially possibility of his death, while it also imposes on him the need for action in the interests of his survival. There need be no conflict, but experience shows that in fact there is such a conflict—not between sexuality and ego instincts, but rather between his narcissism and his socialism, and this conflict may manifest itself no matter what the instincts are that are dominant at the time.

The ego is involved, for the ego is that which establishes a connection with internal and external realities. It is therefore within the ego that the conflict between narcissism and socialism has to be fought out. This struggle contributes to the forces that lead, in certain circumstances, to the splitting, and in extreme cases the weakening and finally the destruction—of the ego. But the ego is also under attack because it is the part of the personality that leads to the awareness of the conflicting demands of the group and the individual and is therefore felt to be the cause of the pain the individual experiences on account of the ego's contact with both external or group realities, and internal or ego-centric realities—i.e. because of its contact with the demands of narcissism and socialism. There is, therefore, in extreme cases, a weakening or even destruction of the ego through splitting attacks that derive from the primitive instinctual drives which seeks satisfaction for both poles of their nature and turn against the psychic organ that appears to frustrate both alike. Hence the appearance, noted by Freud, of hatred of reality—now hatred of the ego which links with reality—characteristic of the severely disturbed patient seen in the psychoses.

It will be remarked that this view demands a revision of our ideas of the narcissistic neuroses and psychoses: they must be considered as cases in which primary narcissism is matched by an equally strong "socialism" or group membership."

To these fragments I should like to add a passage on myth as a group dream, because it strikes me as pertinent:

The Tower of Babel: the possibility of using a racial myth

Can we, at such a crisis as this, fall back on a racial myth on the off-chance that it is a tool that has not yet outlived its usefulness? Let us interpret, for *our* purposes, the story of the Tower of Babel. I propose to use this story in a manner analogous to the use to which a scientist might put an already existing formula of mathematics. The mathematical construction may have been invented without any intention that it should be used as the scientist proposes to use it, or indeed without any intention that it should be used at all. Yet the scientist, despite the mathematician's avowal that his formula has no meaning at all, may decide that he has found a realisation that is the counterpart of the mathematical formulation and will use the formulation accordingly. This I shall now do with the story of the Tower of Babel.

First, I decide that the story is formulated in *Genesis*, but I might as easily decide to write my own version. This story I do not interpret: I use it to interpret a problem of mine. When I say I might decide to write my own version, I do not mean that the basic elements of the story can be altered. Some transformation is necessary which is not an interpretation of the story, nor yet a sophistication. It is not an operation such as Freud proposes for the elucidation of a dream: it consists in a recognition first that the story is a social version of the phenomenon known to the individual as a dream—it even has some resemblance to the consciously sought selected fact; it is an emotional experience that has been subjected to α-function.

There must be many such myths that are not recognised at all, except in a pejorative sense in which some unlikely story, or one that the listener does not wish to believe, is dismissed as a "myth". We cannot now say how they started, nor are we able to observe the process of myth-formation, if any, at work in our midst. If an individual, some anonymous genius, invented it, then we may suppose that the process is one marked by the following steps: the individual has an emotional experience; it is transformed by α; it is published. In almost every instance nothing further happens, for the emotional experience is of too particular a nature to be at all widely significant. It might then be regarded, by analogy with scientific method, as a hypothesis, not false in itself, but applying to events of such extremely rare occurrence as to make it pass unnoticed, in the way that a mathematical formulation (Poincaré, *Science and Method*) might be perfectly sound yet never be employed because no realisation had yet been perceived to which it might be applied as the algebraic system corresponding to its representative scientific deductive system. This must be the case with virtually all so-called dreams; they express, thanks to α-function, the stored and communicable version of an emotional experience. To this extent the narrator of his dream has been able to render the experience communicable, and has even published it, but the emotional experience itself—and consequently its α-formulation—has small social value because of its extreme particularity. But there are others that might be grouped on an ascending scale of generalisation until we reach, through myths of national significance, those, such as the Oedipus myth or the story of the Tower of Babel, which are felt to be of so nearly universal significance that their publication spreads over wide areas of racial and national thought and is also repeated in time. The individual who is able to transform such an emotional experience, by virtue of his α-function, into material that be stored, communicated and finally published must belong to the category we loosely call "genius". But my point is that we must regard these stories (and later I shall consider actual historical events too) as being parallel with the algebraic calculus produced by the mathematician not simply to represent a specific already-existing Scientific Deductive System (SDS), but as a mathematical formulation that has not at the time, but may at some future date turn out to have a realisation to which it is applicable.

The dream of the individual must be taken to mean that certain α-elements are constantly conjoined. The α-elements in themselves, and their constant conjunction as shown by the dream, must be regarded as of equal significance. The α-function has then served the purpose of making storable, communicable, and publishable an emotional experience that is constantly conjoined and has made it possible to record the latter fact. How does this relate the ordinary, apparently non-recurrent dream to the recurrent dream? If myth and manifest content of a dream are to be regarded as the group and individual versions of the same thing—and that thing an assertion that certain α-elements are constantly conjoined—to what use are we to put this statement? If we are to regard it as analogous to $(a + b)^2 = a^2 + b^2 + 2ab$, then presumably we need to know how the statement has been constructed and what the rules are that have to be obeyed if we are to use the statement correctly. At first sight the mathematicians appear able to do this; we can say something about the way these letters, a and b, are being used, and we can explain the rules by which their manipulation is to be guided. We can also show that certain problems can be solved if recognise that the elements of the problem can be adequately represented by this algebraic formula. Furthermore, we can be taught how to recognise that a given problem would be aided by this particular formula rather than another, and we can pass on that information. There is, nevertheless, a gap: some individuals are more easily able to understand the explanations and to grasp when and how such a formula can be applied to advantage than others who are thought of as being mathematically ill-equipped. It is not only the mathematically ill-equipped who have difficulty in accepting the mathematical explanation of fundamentals of procedure, as mathematicians and philosophers show by their discussions of these problems, which are inseparably bound up with the nature of mathematical ability itself. But nevertheless there is no doubt that mathematicians have formed a method of recording and communicating their formulations which makes teaching of the formulations and their use assume an enviably uniform and stable discipline—at least to me who proposes that myth and dream should be regarded as corresponding to algebraic calculi and therefore as capable of yielding, after scrutiny, the tools that can interpret, through their suitability to represent a problem, the problem itself, and so open the way to its solution.

After a long passage that I consider appropriate to leave out today, Bion says some other things concerning the interpenetration of individual and group: "… Suppose an analyst did not include in his canon the Oedipus myth: it would be an indication for considering to what extent he was able to regard other psychoanalysts and himself as embracing the same discipline and therefore able to communicate with each other profitably." This is very significant in terms of the level of interpenetration of the individual analyst and the group of analysts: it means referring to a specific myth as if to a common legacy of α-elements, choosing, in a sense, to be a member of a culture and agreeing to be part of it. This means, in terms of the passages that I read before on the subject of common sense, agreeing to be a member of a group to rely on with regard to a kind of generally accepted structuring of reality. Obviously this is connected with the acceptance of the moral principles of the group, a discourse which leads straight to the problem of the articulation of the theory of basic assumptions with what Bion is saying in *Cogitation* (written shortly after the papers of *Experiences in Groups*).

I think the insertion point in the theory of common sense occurs with relation to the work groups, that is, the group that functions efficiently until it is disturbed by the appearance of a basic assumption. I would like to finish with a rather long passage, which follows directly on from the other and describes one of the ways in which Bion thought he might use myths. I find it not only illuminating, but also amusing.

> But this, though important, is relatively not so important as the part that association on chosen myth, and selection of the myths on which to associate, plays in the promotion of psychoanalytic intuition and, more precisely, in the repair and reinvigoration of the analyst's α-function. Perhaps for the first time my suggestion makes it possible to give a practising analyst precise advice, and even instruction, on how to keep in training. He should not bother so much with attempts to keep notes about patients but to take, say, the Oedipus myth, and write his free associations on it, nothing the date. This he can repeat as often as he likes—the free associations will never be the same for different dates. If, amongst his associations, a patient's name appears, that name can be indexed if he feels he needs notes on his patients. This procedure can be repeated five days a week, for the same myth or for such other myths as he feels disposed to include in his canon; and he can discard and return to any given myth as often as he chooses. It would be as well to use a version, or versions, of the myth for whose historicity there is scholarly evidence, as, other things being equal, it seems that a version that has withstood the passage of centuries is probably more likely to have powerful appeal to the human mind than one that may be an ephemeral aberration and therefore of too great particularity.
>
> This procedure promotes analytic intuition in the following way: suppose the Oedipus myth is the chosen exercise; it will not be chosen unless it has some immediate relevance for the analyst, and its relevance must be that the analyst has an emotional experience that

is either repeating, or threatening to repeat, itself. Even this will not explain the choice of myth, but the analyst can draw his own conclusions on that matter at his convenience. The point is that his free associations should show him what the features are, in his present situation, which are interpreted and given a meaning by the myth on which he has chosen to associate. It will again be observed that this course of action differs from the accepted view of analysis. It is not using conscious material to interpret the unconscious; it is using the unconscious to interpret a conscious state of mind associated with facts of which the analyst is aware. The interpretation of the dream will give meaning to the known facts and feelings of the analyst's life, just as scrutiny of an ordnance survey map can give meaning to natural features clearly visible to the traveller and bring him to a realisation of the point that he has reached on his journey. The myth embodies the constants and variables valid for any period of life: the free associations ascribe the immediately current values to the variables, and the scrutiny of the material reveals the problem, which is the step essential to its solution, if any.

Now let us apply the Babel myth to the destruction of the α-function. One point that immediately obtrudes is the hostility of the Deity to the aspirations of men who wish to build a city and a tower to reach to Heaven, and to make a name for themselves to prevent their being scattered. The people are making bricks and slime, which are then to be put together to make the tower to reach Heaven. It seems like an artificial breast-penis. And what of the name to prevent scattering? The word as a hypothesis which brings the scattered objects together and keeps them so? It is the God who is opposed to the hypothesis, the word (as hypothesis), and it seems as if the people who *have* come together are to be scattered; the hypothesis or selected fact is to be destroyed, the fragments scattered upon the face of all the earth. This is an attack on an attempt to reach Heaven: it is an attack on linking—the language that makes co-operation possible.

Provisional conclusions

One of the curious things that can be deduced from the reading of these scattered fragments—which I have cut from the substantial text of *Cogitations* and sewn together again to regroup a little better the comments on the same topic—is that Bion is at the same time *very* Freudian—when he re-adopts the theory of the premature super-ego as a mental entity which incorporates the moral sense of the group (rather than that of the father)—and he is also very Kleinian when he asserts the importance of the environment, and above all the assertion of narcissism as secondary and not primary, secondary as regards fear of the human environment. These facts in turn stress the extent to which Bion was a member of his group—awkwardly, it is true, both for himself and the others—but being fully a part of it. Above all, studying what it means to be part of a group for an individual.

In these texts, we see what is only glimpsed in *Experience in Groups*, which is the work group at its best, that group on which the individual can rely to give strength and substance to his own human relationships.

We also see something that allows us to give a little more substance Bion's idea that the individual and the group have quite impermeable confines, which is really about a continuum which leads from socialism at one end to narcissism at the other. But, as we can also see from the chapter in *Attention and Interpretation* on the mystic and the group, it is above all the individual that is permeable to the group, permeable and most of the time, defenceless. The group is able to defend itself against the intrusion of new and disturbing ideas, it does not like the individual and is always willing to sacrifice him to the service of its own survival—and perhaps also to the service of the survival of the status quo. The problem shifts from the terrain of Rousseau and the noble savage and from Hobbes and his *homo homini lupus* to the terrain of the bivalent interaction between the infant and the outside world. The group preserves the family, the family as a small group, interacts with the infant for better or for worse: the individual who grows up will be equipped with powerful instruments that come to him from the group, social common sense (always in evolution, thanks to the contribution of the individual members of the group) as a testing tool and the common legacy of α-elements enclosed in myths, but will also have to defend himself against the group and the excessive power of unconscious group communication.

CHAPTER FOURTEEN

The two sides of the caesura (1996)

The slamming of the door alone might be too abrupt a caesura
(At the end of a session it's better to have a patient who's irascible but full of thoughts)

The concept of "caesura", which Bion developed on the basis of a phrase of Freud's, is an appropriate topic to approach a broader consideration of "evolution and fracture".
This is a phenomenon that occurs in a minor or more consistent interruption in the general course of events. It is a fracture in itself, but it can have an evolutionary importance and become the stimulus of a future evolution, if sufficient care is taken to interpret it in depth. In Bion's works, the concept may be linked to two others that the author made truly his own, one coming from one of his very first publications *Experiences in Groups* (1961) and the other taken from Attacks on Linking (1959), composed shortly afterwards. The two criteria which, in my opinion, seem pertinent to the theorisation of the concept of caesura are "reversible perspective" and "links", which can obviously be criticised. Even though they are both among the first concepts of Bion's thinking, they pass through all his works and serve to elucidate one another.

My intention in these pages is to use these concepts, trying to merge them in a certain sense, without depriving them of their individuality, and to demonstrate how they can be used by the analyst who is listening to his patient.

Of course I do not wish to imply that the psychoanalyst must seek, among the patient's words, a detail implying the presence of the caesura. The therapist, in fact, should never seek something in particular, but adopt "polyphonic listening" in such a way as to record everything.[1] It may, however, happen that the concept of the caesura enters the analyst's mind as a "pre-selected fact" and, encountering an element of the session that attracted his attention, creates a valid starting point for his interpretation.

There are different types of caesura that can be extracted and classified during the psychoanalytic session, for example: the patient falls asleep, or turns round on the couch, coughs, sneezes, hesitates over saying a word, stammers, interrupts a sentence half-way through, etc. There are also other, deeper types of caesura, which are not so clearly marked, which is why their presence appears less obvious to the psychoanalyst.

These caesuras may underline the passage from one mental state to another—for example, when the patient completes part of his unconscious process—without an apparent presence of transference, or at least without the transference being predominant at that moment.

Then, obviously, there are a myriad of caesuras which are illustrated by the patients stories: fainting, falling asleep, waking up, being under the effect of anaesthetics, having "crises", like a kind of recurring event, and so on. But as these must be treated on an equal basis with any other topics as indicators of the course of the session and the transference until that point, I will not discuss these aspects any further.

In any case, in the concept of caesura there is the implicit idea of a change from one state—mental or physical—to another, and this often includes the idea that there is a perceptible difference in the quality of the two states: birth includes within itself the concept of "being inside", darkness, the regularity of sounds and physical pressure, which contrasts starkly with "being outside", light, the chaotic sounds of life and the absence of a container. Otherwise, another obvious physical

---

[1] In my writings, prepared on the occasion of *Encontro Bienal*, São Paulo, 16–17 November 1996, "Dall'informe alla forma" (in this volume).

manifestation of the caesura, such as fainting, for example, may be perceived as a passage in the opposite direction: from the light and sounds of the world to the sound of blood pulsing in the ears, silence and darkness.

Let us take a step back for a moment. What is the caesura? What did this term mean originally? What did Freud mean by it? Or at least, what degree of importance does this term have in its context? The definition in the Oxford English Dictionary, referring to Greek and Latin prose and poetry, describes it as a division in metric verses while, referring to English writings, it adds that the pause or the interval are connected to the *meaning* of the words. A more general definition indicates the caesura as a synonym for interruption, interval, leaving aside the idea that it should be, or could be, significant.

The Freudian quotation (1925) that mentions the caesura, and which inspired Bion, says the following: "There is much more continuity between intrauterine life and earliest infancy than the impressive caesura of the act of birth would have us believe." Bion plumbs this concept at the end of a brief essay entitled "Caesura":

> There is much more continuity between autonomically appropriate quanta and the waves of conscious thought and feeling than the impressive caesura of transference and counter-transference would have us believe. So …? Investigate the caesura; not the analyst; not the analysand; not the unconscious; not the conscious; not sanity; not insanity. But the caesura, the link, the synapse, the (counter) transference, the transitive-intransitive mood. (Bion, 1977)

So we may note that Bion has taken and broadened the idea, only implicit in the use that Freud has made of it, that the caesura is important in itself, and not only the idea that there is a continuity in both its sides. But there is another aspect of Freud's thought that Bion has taken into consideration, even though he has not made it explicit, which is that the "caesura of birth" is intimately connected with the most general theory of anxiety, and more specifically to signs of anxiety.

We are a long way from maintaining that caesuras, in what the patient presents, could always manifest themselves as signals. They do not necessarily prompt anxiety in the analyst, but they still alert him to the probability that the patient is expressing anxiety at an unconscious level; *exactly as* on certain occasions he can become aware of the affect that he is anxious.

The anxiety that the patient feels on a conscious level might not coincide at all, or correspond only partly, to what he feels at an unconscious level.

Meanwhile, we may say that for Freud a "caesura" was simply a rift, a gap—slight or more consistent—between two phases of a process; while Bion puts into relief another aspect of the problem, concentrating greater attention on the concept of the gap, suggesting that we probe it further.

The gap, the intervals, the interruptions, have acquired the value of "analytic objects" by themselves, without necessarily being macroscopic gaps like the phenomena of hysteria in the absence of awareness, but they can also manifest themselves in the form of tiny fractures or recesses that characterise the communication of some of our analysands.

So we might maintain that while Freud emphasises continuity (interrupted by external events), Bion stresses the interruptions of this continuity, and this is not a predictable event. Some of Bion's examples concerning events similar to caesuras (links, synapses) are events with an intrinsic character, which are part of the individual experience (like a tangle of silk thread), and cannot be understood if they are thought of as external interferences with regard to a situation which, on the contrary, should progress regularly.

Other concepts which Bion likens to the caesura are without a doubt interpersonal, just as they are internal to the person themselves (for example the transference and its counterpart in the analyst). Instead, the passage from transitive to intransitive has more to do with an interior change in the subject (such as the transfer of a thought from an unconscious to a conscious level), even though this is certainly linked to the concept of the "I-You" dialectic.

It must be possible to think of the implicit presence of continuity as a sort of fabric of experience, interrupted by a break: if a subject, during this interruption, "looks back", experience refers him to a specific emotion, which could be diametrically opposed to what he might perceive as "looking forward". This formulation of mine, which may be subdivided into terms of "time and direction", which are not universal characteristics of the caesura, is a simple attempt to describe some of the vents which occur in the complicated moment in which the caesura manifests itself. This description could be made clearer by quoting one of Bion's most important formulations concerning the idea of reversible perspective:

> The psychiatrist must see the reverse as well as the obverse of every situation, if he can. He must employ a kind of psychological shift best illustrated by the analogy of this well-known diagram. The observer can look at it so that he sees it as a box with the corner A B nearest to him; or he can view it as a box with the corner C D nearest to him. The total of lines observed remains the same, but a quite different view of the box is obtained. Similarly, in a group, the total of what is taking place remains the same, but a change of perspective can bring out quite different phenomena. (Bion, 1961)

In reference to this quotation I should like to say, first of all, that the reversible perspective is something that happens quite frequently in a classic (two-person) session of psychoanalysis, as in a group.

At the moment when the "box" suddenly changes position in front of your eyes, the caesura is happening. This transition between what happens before and what happens after the caesura can seem violent, as in the case of the patient who, shortly before having to leave the consulting room and hence the comfortable state of mind that they have during therapy, manifested signs of sadness.

Among the most difficult and painful things in dealing with caesuras is the need, encountered by the analyst, to keep in mind both sides of the phenomenon and remain alert to both positions of the "box".

This need is only noticed empathetically by the patient after a major completion of the analytic journey, precisely because the caesura has a relevant role in maintaining a state of anxiety and, I believe, in suppressing the awareness of this unease.

Bion believes that the *caesura* seems to indicate a connection between anxiety and a kind of "reversible perspective" (although he does not say as much outright), as happens for example with the blushing (accompanied by intense pallor) visible in the patient who does not have the ability to express this sensation in a much more explicit manner.

In the example that I have taken from *Experiences in Groups*, it seems difficult to understand on a practical level the structure of both sides of the caesura; while at a conceptually more abstract level it may become simpler. The following quotation, taken from *Cogitations*, constitutes a good example of what I mean by "both" sides of the caesura:

> One of the weaknesses of articulate speech is shown in the use of a term like "omnipotence" to describe a situation that in fact cannot

be described at all accurately with a language that is of one kind only. "Omnipotence" must also mean "helplessness"; there can be no single word that describes one thing without also describing its reciprocal. (Bion, 1992)

Reading this quotation, we should understand that the expression "omnipotence" refers to the concept of caesura and implies a kind of connection that invites us to look in "both directions".[2]

In synthesis

These three cases, in my view, show how in the practice of analytic work the fact of recognising the use of the caesura on the part of the patient often leads them towards an evolutionary leap in their analytic work—as we were shown by the story of the life of Miss H., who married after three years, and is happily expecting her first child. In this case, it might seem a posteriori that she uses caesuras to reach another caesura: she was so defeated by the caesura of marriage or the severity of the links with her family that her anxiety produced a profound series of caesuras which fragmented her ability to communicate with others and prevented her from proceeding with her matrimonial plans. The work with Miss H. and Miss D. shows how the identification of a caesura is often closely linked to the perception of "reversible perspective". I have had to think of certain comments by Miss D, and how they were interruptions of her extenuating silence, before making advances in the interpretations (even if the very fact of being beside her as she wept, which her mother had not done, just as she had not been able to weep as a child, even during the painful analyses in hospital, was without a doubt a therapeutic advance during this period of silence). I also had to "see" the interruptions in the stones (quoted by the patient) and link this signal sent from heaven with Miss H.'s way of speaking, rather than looking at the stones and trying to listen to the words. And again, in the case of Miss T., the verbal lacunae in the story of her dream in some way reflected the sensations relative to her crises and her shaking,

---

[2] Italian editor's note: I am omitting the detailed clinical material for reasons of privacy. I note that this is not strictly indispensable for the full use of the theoretical part.

and my highlighting of this fact made it easier for her to find the words to describe her unconscious thoughts concealed behind her behaviour.

Even though I have not dwelt for long on the aspect of connection of the caesura, I maintain that it is clear from the clinical material presented that these patients use the interruptions with the intention of creating a connection. But these are only pseudo-connections because each of them is a kind of shaky bridge over an abyss of anxiety, "Do not look down!"

But if the analyst is lucky enough to be able to feel that the bridge has a dull and unconvincing sound, and that the patient can do so as well, or is helped to do so, it becomes possible to "look down" and see something of this abyss and the monsters that live there. Sometimes to describe why a dream is interrupted or why someone sleeping wakes up, it is equally important to record the beginning of a dream and its apparent content. In this way, the caesura/interruption may sometimes be transformed, through the reversal of perspective, into a caesura/connection with a subsequent evolutionary passage.

CHAPTER FIFTEEN

Bion and the group: knowing, learning, teaching (1996)

Between epistemology and agnoiology

When Dr. Romano invited me to address this conference, first of all I had emotional reactions: of pleasure on the one hand, with the sense that with this kind offer I am truly being paid a great honour, and of unease on the other.

These reactions have been followed by the process of "thinking about it". The thought had to deal with two main threads: the first was what would be the content of my paper, and the second consisted of the slightly curious question of the fact that the simple proposition of delivering a paper, let alone its contents, prompted *in primis* emotions, and only subsequently reflections.

In reality the two threads are not so split, because talking about Bion and the group to a group which in all likelihood is already very familiar with Bion's work in this field inevitably prompts rather precise concerns; to mention one, the fear of being superfluous and boring. But there are also more internal links between the two threads of emotional relationships and more abstract thoughts, as I will try to show in the course of this paper.

The fear I felt probably played an important part in the decision not only to limit my intervention to a very specific attitude of the many applications of Bion's theories to intra-group relationships, or relationships between the individual and the group, but it also directed my attention in an even more specific way towards problems connected with the asymmetrical communication of the individual with the group.

But let us begin with a more detailed look at the emotions aroused in me. In the first instance Dr. Romano spoke to me about a section of the conference "about epistemology", and it was precisely with regard to this term that my dismay spread very quickly. This word regularly produces in me the sensation of not understanding a thing, of not even understanding what it is about; it sends me running for the nearest dictionary, as if I can't even believe that I know what it means ... and all of this spiced with a strong sense of unease, if not of actual guilt, given that I have a philosophy degree: I should at least remember what it is about, broadly speaking if not more than that.

But why am I telling you this boring story about a small and shameful panic attack? It isn't because I was seized by a sudden need to confess publicly my substantial ignorance, or just to bring them onto my side (as if I was expecting an audience so critical that it would spill over into hostility) but for a series of different reasons. Above all, I would like to explain that we all tend to react emotionally to a group, even though obviously the emotions may vary, and a great deal between one individual and the next. This beginning, perhaps a little too anchored in my reactions, also supplies a twofold possibility for the development of the speech that I wish to give, so I hope that you will forgive me for being excessively personal, and not dismiss it as an example of flight into narcissism dictated by fear of the group.

The twofold development begins on the one hand with a consideration of the problems of the individual with regard to the group and on the other in my sense that something is missing in the concept of epistemology, and that if I managed to identify what it is that is missing, perhaps I would have a better understanding of the concept (and also remember it, as a direct consequence of my understanding). At this point, you will perhaps be saying to yourself that all of this seems to have nothing to do either with Bion, or with groups, or with learning or teaching ... leaving only knowledge, if this can be compared and made equivalent to understanding. This criticism strikes even me as valid at the moment, but we will see whether all these things do not once again become part of my argumentation.

In *Experiences in Groups*, Bion says that the confrontation and management of the group for the adult individual is a task as difficult as the relationship with the breast for the infant. This assertion has various implications, as Bion himself argues in various passages, notably towards the end of *Theory of Thinking* (1962a) where, speaking about communication, he says that this is originally:

> ... effected by realistic projective identification. It may develop into a capacity for toleration by the self of its own psychic qualities and so pave the way for normal thought. But it also does develop as part of the social capacity of the individual. This is of great importance in group dynamics; its absence would make even scientific communication impossible. Yet, its presence may arouse feelings of persecution in the receptors of the communication. The need to diminish feelings of persecution contributes to the drive to abstraction in the formulation of scientific communications.

From this point of view, I have allowed myself a rash move, beginning to read a text that should be a scientific communication at a conference with something to be considered non-abstract, that is, a description of emotions, not even slightly distanced with the excuse that they are "a patient's", but acknowledged as "mine". Obviously, I could have begun differently, in a more solemn manner, and so risk less: but I wanted to keep you informed about an emotional reaction on my part, not because I think it is any way special or interesting, but because, on the contrary, I think it is almost universal, with the aim of producing a situation in which one might be able to imagine an important part, perhaps the fundamental nucleus, of the object of the discussion: the conscious and unconscious emotions that are part of our ability (and our inabilities) to communicate.

Communicate is a term at once clear and not very specific, while the title of this paper contains three terms, two of which, learning and teaching, constitute two possible aspects of communication. In my view, the three terms in the title are interconnected: in order to learn, and then to be able to teach what one has learned, one must first of all be able to know, but the acquisition of knowledge necessarily passes through a mental zone in which the emotions are sovereign, and are primitive.

By primitive, I do not mean unsophisticated, but rather "primary". As such, these emotions include love and hate, envy, gratitude towards the other—whether it be a partial object, a breast, a person or a group, and a group of emotions which arise as a consequence of the perception of the quality of one's own transient state of mind, that is, a sense of wellbeing or of being persecuted. As Bion says, this capacity for perceiving the quality or emotional colour of one's own state of mind constitutes one of the outcomes of a good development of realistic projective identification.

To return to the example given at the start of this paper, some of you may be amused, and this might be the summation of loving sentiments and gratitude towards me, and of harmony with me, which can produce a perception of one's own state of wellbeing, while others might have felt irritated and annoyed, as the summation of feelings of hatred and/or envy and something persecutory—perhaps the very fact that unpleasant emotions and feelings are provoked, or even at most emotions of any kind at all.

Then if it is true that even in apparently less emotional situations, or at least those in which there is a highly structured group, something that should in itself encourage the control of the emotions, with well-defined roles—speakers and listeners—we must instead confront a series of emotions that are rather naked and rough, how do we then place ourselves in non-structured group situations, such as those described by Turquet in *Threats to Identity in the Large Group* (1975)? One of the things that Turquet says is that the assumption of a role in a group is part of the primary survival strategies within the group, and this attempt to "survive" in the group, as Bion says in *Cogitations*, is something that characterises the individual during the whole span of his life. So perhaps one of the first things that we try to do when we find ourselves in a group is to adopt a role that can be recognised by the other members of the group.

One of the first social roles, of a large social group which includes a child, past the years in which he is "the child" *par excellence* (and often referred to in these terms) in the bosom of the family, is the role of scholar, of student. This is a role which can however, also quite naturally, last for twenty years—we get used to it, in fact we can get so used to it that we become a member of the legion of "eternal students" (degree after degree, specialisation after specialisation). Sometimes we actually have a sense that this kind of learning is not designed to accomplish the growth of the individual, but rather satisfies a defensive need, that of attaching oneself to a role that is already known and used as a cocoon.

It seems, however, that those who want to learn something have to come to terms with various factors, and that the situation of the child proudly facing her first day at school is more complex than the gymslip, the tie and the lunchbox would lead us to understand (not to mention problems of separation anxiety). In my title, I have separated two voices that might seem almost synonymous, knowing and learning, but I maintain that they are not. We may consider knowledge to be a private fact, internal to the individual, even if certainly calls into question the individual's capacity to relate first and foremost to a primary object, whether it be breast or womb, to set in motion the thought processes that will lead to knowledge, to the individual's ability to say "I know this". The knowledge of anything also implies having an "inner common sense", a convergence of a significant number of senses in the absence of sensory contributions which deny the resulting data: in *Cogitations*, Bion speaks of the sensation of fur which must be comforted by senses different from the tactile to be able to assert that an animal is present (perhaps the senses of smell and hearing—if we do not hear any sound and notice no animal smell, it might be a cuddly toy, for example).

The first step towards knowledge, then, is the one that passes through realistic projective identification (probably also accompanied by a bit of not-very-realistic projective identification) so, also considering knowledge as an event concerning the individual more than the group, but it is not a solitary event. This realistic projective identification is, in origin, that part of the first relationship with the breast in which the innate preconceptions of the infant encounter an external object, concretely real, which, (at least to a large extent) satisfies them, in the sense that an encounter occurs between "looking" and an findable object.

 It is worth trying to identify the difference between realistic projective identification and conscious expectations of the adult or the older child. This difference seems to lie in the belief, or faith, of the infant that the breast will really be like him if he prefigures it, and in the perception of the fact that the breast really "comes towards him", "reacts" to his projection. One may have an idea that is rather more connected with experiential data of what I mean by the term "realistic projective identification" by thinking about how the mother's milk may begin to flow at the moment when the child begins moving slightly in the crib, and is certainly still a long way from loudly demanding a feed. Conscious expectations do not necessarily have as their counterpart a complementary reaction, in the other or in the group, nor are they usually accompanied by a belief or a faith that this complementarity will come true.

In any case, however, adult human beings go on making use of projective identification, some more than others, and the "realistic" part of this means that our behaviours are never entirely without a relational component: we tend towards the other, or in some way we offer him something, even something immaterial like a thought or an idea, and we expect an answer. Of course, this discussion leaves aside the whole topic of non-realistic projective identifications, the excessive ones with which, in the end, as therapists we have greater familiarity. These might be at the basis of attacks of "stage fright", of "mutism" when we are asked questions or in an exam and so on. These are really, among other things, the basis of unconscious fears of finding oneself facing a hostile audience, fears that rarely find corroboration in reality.

The step towards knowledge is the one that leads us from the experience of "encounter" with something even only vaguely "waited for" at the stage of correlations and checks, that is, facing the single (or, more likely, repeated) experiential fact with his own inner common sense and that of the group. One might say that the individual cannot feel that he "knows" anything if he doesn't also feel supported by his own sense of appropriate inner correlation and the sense of being "in line" with the common sense of the group.

Knowing something, then, is not an exclusively individual matter: it almost needs the "approval" of the group, and this aspect is perhaps linked with what Bion says in *Cogitations*, about the fact that the individual feels he "possesses" a piece of knowledge as if he had become the owner of it. This involves, for the individual, the desire to feel that the group appreciates him appropriating a "piece of knowledge" and doesn't punish him for it. That the imminent presence of the group with regard to the question of the acquisition of knowledge may be felt as a problem of being human, may be deduced from the continued presence in our culture of various myths dealing with more group-related variations of the express theme of the tree of knowledge or that of the Tower of Babel: Prometheus, Pandora, to name only two. In these two myths, which are linked to one another, in the sense that when she was modelled by Hephaestus to be given as a bride to the brother of Prometheus, with the approval and "dowry" supplied by all the inhabitants of Olympus, we see what the group of the gods is like, and not only Jupiter, who is opposed to the acquisition of fire and also wants to provoke Pandora so that he can later punish her, and with her all of humanity, for having followed that same curiosity.

Learning, however, unlike knowledge of the extent to which it is clearly recognised as something that concerns an interaction between the individual and the outer world, poses other problems in terms of the relationship with the group: the social conventions connected with the roles of teacher and student are brought into play. The social conventions (all of them) owe their very great power both to their origin in the common sense of the group and to the fact that they are used as defences, experienced for millennia, and rather efficient, against the terror that the individual feels in the face of the group, because they supply a structuring of the group that is transmitted to it very easily from generation to generation. (Might that be why scholastic reforms in Italy are only possible every thirty years, at regular intervals?)

The advantage of this kind of defence against the terror of the group, socially acceptable, in fact, and promoted by society itself, is that it allows the individual not to have to take refuge in his own narcissism, since he cannot face up to the requests of the group, and thus encourages his social integration. This is advantageous both for the group which acquires a useful member and must not therefore take care of someone who has become psychologically disabled, narcissistically closed in on himself. (Might it perhaps be hypothesised that these mechanisms of terror of the group and narcissistic defence against this terror play a part in the emergence of some forms of infantile autism, and that they are recognisable in some autistic bulwarks in the adult?)

At any rate, the child, supplied with gymslip, tie, and lunchbox, facing the first formal lesson of her life, and the teacher imparting it to her, is coming to terms with:

> projective realistic identification;
>
> non-realistic projective identifications with attached unconscious fantasies;
>
> an unconscious threat without guilt about what may legitimately be known with the fear of going "off the track";
>
> the vital necessity to conform with the characteristics that the group has established as appropriate to social roles (student and teacher) that the two adopt;
>
> the common sense specific to each person is the common sense of the group, and then they have to learn and teach!

But what do these terms really mean, what do they imply in terms of mental dynamics?

The *oscillation* between the paranoid-schizoid and depressive positions is the base mental movement that is called into action for the purposes of learning. When we find ourselves faced with a problem of any kind, from the strictly personal one of managing our emotions to that of the blackboard on which signs are drawn for us, signs that at that moment have no meaning, the immediate emotional reaction is the sensation of persecution. It is only when we ourselves manage to pick up something that can act as a selected fact, or when someone else indicates one to us, that we can move along the arc of the oscillation towards the depressive position.

I do not mean by this that the individual who learns something moves from being paranoid-schizoid to being depressed (and vice versa, which I will come to shortly) within a very short interval, just long enough to "understand". I mean that he moves, he oscillates, between a sensation of not understanding, which is suffused with persecutory feelings, however faint, and a sensation of "having understood", which lacks those feelings. And he is not "depressed" at that point, quite the opposite, perhaps. Bion, in *Cogitations*, describes this state of mind as the necessary condition for the analyst to be able to formulate an interpretation, giving him the name of "positions" of a state of mind, which is to say that he participates in the appropriate emotions at both opposite poles without being either one or the other. At the moment when the child (or the analyst) has understood something, or a moment later, they cannot help realising that there are many other "things" that have remained outside his comprehension: the personal emotional problem, of which he had understood one aspect, and which he felt was almost "resolved", shows that it has many other facets that demand our attention as well: on the blackboard there are many other signs which are not like the ones why have just learned, which are "read" and "mean" Mama.

It is at this point that the "depression" emerges: the marvellous discovery is not the key to the understanding of the universe, it only serves to sort out a part of it. You have to start again with the next oscillation. If Bion was able to say that all infants are absolutely Kleinian, but then they forget, perhaps we might add that they all enjoy a good practical knowledge of the Hegelian dialectic.

But it is precisely at this point that I find a crossroads (between mental paths—or meanders?) and my problem with understanding of memory with regard to the term "epistemology" reappears. So the moment has also arrived to become part of the "marvellous discovery" that I made the last time I went to check the exact meaning of the term. I quote: "Epistemology: 'theory of knowledge' (1933 Italian Encyclopaedia, etc.), from Greek *episteme* (properly speaking 'that which is placed above', composed of, etc. ...). The term [and this was my most pleasing discovery] was coined by J. F. Ferrier, Institutes of Metaphysics (1854), along with agnoiology, the 'doctrine of ignorance'."

Now, a doctrine of ignorance is precisely what I lacked, precisely what I felt, more or less unconsciously, the need of, and I maintain that this term (almost unpronounceable to me) "agnoiology" is for me the selected fact that I as almost consciously seeking. In reality I am still blithely unaware of the contents of the unknown but meritorious Ferrier, and yet I will allow myself to borrow the word that he coined, imagining that it is a term indicating "the other side of the coin" of knowledge, the dark side of the moon, and maintaining that it is a complementary theory to epistemology.

It is entirely logical, above all for the analyst, to feel that we cannot produce a satisfying (and above all useful and functional) theory of knowledge without also taking into account how we *do not* know, how we do *not* find out, we do *not* learn, and also how that non-knowledge can exist.

But this is not the only facet of the problem of "not" knowing: there is also the aspect of the infinite "without form and void", the perception, sometimes vague and remove, and sometimes frighteningly imminent, of an unknown and omnipresent infinity, which we try to keep at bay with our small bits of knowledge. Perhaps it was precisely because, in spite of all the references to these problems in psychoanalytic theorisation starting with Klein, I lacked a name for a theory that could account for this side of things, because the term epistemology had never had a warm welcome in my theoretical baggage. (Now, in fact, I have the impression of having "understood" and thus "learned" it, "I have made it mine", as people say, which in Bion's terms is the equivalent of saying "I know".)

Among other things, the need for a theory to complement epistemological theories also seems to stress the aspect of reversed perspective which characterises, in quite a specific way, the analyst's observational ability: we must be able to pick up both sides of the caesura, pick up, as Sherlock Holmes would have said, even the meaning of the fact that the dog didn't bark.

Before I conclude, I would like to return to the title of this paper: knowing-understanding, learning, teaching: that last word has been left out a little. The situation of someone like himself who is speaking at a conference right now is not exactly that of a teacher in a the strict sense of the word: it is a little anomalous, I am not trying to teach something that I want you to learn, I am working at a more restrained level (can one say that? I always have a sense that in teaching there is a hint of aggression, in the very wish to mould the mind of another person, literally, to leave one's own mark). So, the pertinent level is more to "offer" some ideas, hoping simply that these ideas may stimulate your thought, but not mould it or make it the same as mine.

To the extent to which the presentation of one's own work has similarities with teaching the work of other people—whether it be psychoanalysis, mathematics or history, for example—it poses similar problems, and this is the reason why I have allowed myself an initial little digression into my emotions. How, for example, do we capture the attention of students or listeners? And then how do we keep it? What do we do if sometimes the attention is distracted? There are obviously answers on different levels, from the technique of standing on a podium or on a stage (production of the voice, movements, etc.) which are things that are normally taught on teacher training courses, but as analysts, or, and perhaps we must think that there are problems on deeper levels, which have to do with the psychology of the individual and that of the group.

If we refer to the pair of epistemology/agnoiology, we can see that one of the big obstacles that the teacher has to face is not so much that the students are ignorant—they are, almost by definition—but that they may be both have a terror of the unknown and not want to confront it, and have created a kind of defensive theory of praise of ignorance, perhaps entirely unconscious, which is very difficult to dismantle. These theories appear in the form of "up to this point" but not beyond, and in all forms of censorship, both inner and outer.

Certainly, it's a good thing for the teacher not to be boring, but even when he isn't, the reaction of boredom (which is sometimes expressed in somnolence, or in actual sleep), may often conceal an active defence against the fear of having to deal with the fact of not knowing something. We should always take into consideration the possibility that a child or an adult who seems to be presenting learning difficulties is simply overwhelmed by the terror of that which is unknown, and the unknown emerges overwhelmingly every time the individual moves towards the depressive position.

But what are things like from the point of view of the teacher who decides to deal with the possibility that his difficulties with his pupils might depend on him rather than on them? Can his position be considered similar to that of someone making a scientific communication? If we adopt this hypothesis, we must return to Bion's idea that the presence of a form of realistic projective identification is absolutely necessary not least where the teacher is concerned, and not only on the part of the students. This implies unconscious fantasies in the mind of the teacher about the fact that pupils want to learn, and are willing to act as containers for what the teacher wants to "cut into them" and therefore "stuff into their heads". It also implies that the teacher has an attitude of esteem with regard to the contents of his own mind, which he wants to "show, explain" to the pupils, without, however, feeling any excessive possessiveness towards his own mental contents. A patient of mine from many years ago, a secondary school teacher, risked losing her teaching position and had genuinely very poor relationships with both her classes and the pupils' parents, because of her oscillation between her absolutely unworthy, almost obscene, consideration of everything that her mind contained (which was why there was no point externalising it, in fact it would actually have been harmful to her pupils if she had done) and feeling that the ideas and information relating to her teaching materials were so beautiful and precious that she could in no way share them with others; to sum up, in her words, "filth before defenceless children" *and also* "pearls before swine". And the result of this mental attitude was that in essence she could not in fact teach while doing serious harm, as she acknowledged, to her classes. She couldn't teach, and she couldn't ask questions or give marks to written homework, because she could not contemplate the damage that she felt she had done to her pupils, or bear seeing her precious knowledge reflected in their minds. I must confess that I was almost stunned by the improvement in the professional abilities of this analysand following the analytic work which centred on these problems, analytic works which obviously also touched upon the deeper aspects of the problem of feeling unworthy, and of the opposite and complementary problem of the overvaluation, in practice an idealisation, of her material.

To conclude, then, I think I can affirm that for Bion the acquisition of knowledge and sharing it with others are always at root relational matters that have their root in the individual's primary relationship with the uterus and the breast.

But they rapidly become matters that call into account the relationship between the individual and his own internal group and with the external groups of reality. As John Donne rightly put it: "No man is an island, entire of itself; every man is a piece of the continent, a part of the main …", and we are not isolated even when it comes to the formation of something which seems initially as singular and particular to the individual as his own knowledge.

CHAPTER SIXTEEN

Bion's contribution to psychoanalysis (1996)*

Before I do anything else I would like to express my gratitude to Professor Pisani for this invitation, for which I feel very honoured, and I am also very happy to have the chance to come back to Rome, however fleetingly. I lived in Rome for ten years, and I feel a great affection towards the city.

I thought this evening that I would talk in the simplest possible way, not least because Bion is a very difficult writer, whose work branches off in different directions. I will try to give a sense of him as a person, because I maintain that for any psychoanalyst or anyone working in the field of the psyche or in the field of human relationships their primary tool is, in reality, themselves, as well as many theories, a great deal of knowledge and a great deal of study behind them. But the tool with which we put ourselves in contact with our patients is, to a large extent, our personality, so it seems to me that talking about a writer, a theorist in the field of psychoanalysis and totally leaving aside his personal story risks creating a kind of meaningless phenomenon in the void.

Bion was born in India in 1897, and to celebrate his centenary, the conference is being held next year, in Turin. He came from a family

---

*Transcribed from a lecture.

that was not strictly English; in fact, it was very non-English, in that his father was originally Swiss German, of a strong Protestant religious stamp, a non-conformist who worked as a civil engineer. He married a woman who was the daughter of a missionary, also non-conformist, and probably an Indian woman, which means that my grandmother was mixed race, so mixed race by mixed race there is a kind of Eurasian hybrid. A hybridity which turned out to be very important in the subsequent development of someone who was still a child; because Bion certainly absorbed a very great amount of Indian culture, much more than most of the, shall we say, colonialist children of the time did, precisely because of the work that his father did—he was a civil engineer who built some of the first railways in India and very long irrigation canals (1,600–1,700 kilometres) whose plotted course, like the railways, often passed through uninhabited areas (including the jungle).

So the family followed the construction site and moved month by month, as the construction site moved; practically a small European nucleus and a very large number of Indians so my father, when he was little, certainly for example spoke Hindustani fluently, something that he later forgot completely. A colleague from Bombay told me he heard Bion speaking in the last year of his life, giving a lecture in which he spoke about the *Bhagavad Gita*: speaking about sacred texts he had a very strong English accent, but when he quoted even a phrase of Hindustani he had no accent; so there was certainly a level, a stratification that had become entirely unconscious, of an Indo-European language that had been completely forgotten. This kind of biographical detail might seem completely irrelevant, were it not for the fact that in the last book he wrote there is a whole series of characters who are Bion himself at various times in his life; so with the idea of a single individual who has very many inner levels. In the book called *Cogitations* which was published recently by Armando, he states that for him the human being is a palimpsest in which one can see many stratifications almost like some Roma street, where one can find levels from the Etruscan, to the Roman, to the Baroque, to the Renaissance and the modern in a single blink of an eye; this was Bion's idea of a human being.

Like many children at the time, he was sent to school in England, and left school in 1917 to enlist in the Tank Corps. So he served during the last year of World War One, which was an atrocious experience for him, an experience of death, literally one of carnage and incomprehension; an experience in which he also encountered violence and stupidity, for example the stupidity of military chiefs. Tanks at the time were extremely heavy, much more so than today, they were practically steel boxes, more or less self-propelled, and they were sent to fight in certain zones of Flanders, boggy places where they sank calmly into the ground. One of the risks for the units was to die of drowning, not just to die at the hands of the Germans.

Eventually, however, he managed to survive this experience of war, of carnage and also the experience of being considered a hero, which he found incomprehensible, in the sense that he had the equivalent of the silver medal for valour for his behaviour in battle which he always said was dictated by cowardice and terror. He had sent the tank and made the crew get out and walk behind it, travelling at seven to eight kilometres an hour. So it was very slow, because it was clear that if they had stayed in the tank they would probably all have died because the Germans had managed to identify the position of the tank and were bombing it; obviously the tank could very easily have fallen into enemy hands, and that would have been quite disastrous because the Germans had no armed tanks. They were an English invention, so it would have been like putting a very expensive toy, ready for use, in the hands of the enemy; a little like giving someone a nuclear test for free nowadays. To their good fortune, the tank exploded and the crew managed to take a German machine-gun post. That was how they got this silver medal for valour, and Bion repeated for the rest of his life that it was really a medal for cowardice and stupidity. Bion had this idea of war and these big enterprises, and he was extremely disenchanted; all this at the age of twenty-one, very young, when perhaps he shouldn't have had experiences of this kind.

In fact I think he was a pacifist at heart. All his life, even though he wrote very little, almost nothing, about aggression, he went on buying books about wars, about the bellicosity of human beings, about the aggression that blurred into war until the year of his death. So it was clearly a problem that touched him deeply, and it continued to be a pertinent problem for him. Then came studies in history at Oxford University, and then medicine at London University, after which he became a psychotherapist at the Tavistock in the 1930s and in 1937, he began personal analysis with John Rickman. Rickman was a very interesting analyst who had spent many years in the Soviet Union and was enthusiastic about the Soviet system; I think that Rickman saw the best of the Soviet system because he came back to the west in the 1930s, I think;

and yet all of the development, the treatment of the social—the cure of the individual in society—is something that certainly had a big influence on Rickman, and probably through him influenced Bion as well. In fact, in *Experiences in Groups* we can glimpse an extremely strong social commitment, not only a patriotic one. It is certainly another text that was written in time of war, but against that very background, we feel the individual's efforts to make the group bearable, usable, and creative.

Then he had to finish his analysis with Rickman because they found themselves working together, both as military psychiatrists. In 1945, he resumed a training analysis with Melanie Klein. Training in an unusual manner, because at the time he was director of the Tavistock Clinic and had patients in treatment, and this was was not acceptable for a Candidate of the British Psychoanalytical Society. Bion refused to end the treatment of his patients, and the British Society reached a very English compromise: the record of the meeting of the training committee shows that they decided to consider Bion a Candidate in training.

Then, in 1951, he wrote his dissertation to become an Associate Member. After that, his career ascended steeply. He was already middle-aged (fifty-four at that point); he became a Member, and then a Training Analyst, within a few years. In the 1960s he had held various institutional roles, including that of President of the British Society and then in 1967 he was invited to California for two or three weeks to deliver his lectures. He decided to move to California in early 1968, where he had different institutional experiences. Some of the Californian analysts, on first hearing, were not very enthusiastic; The Californian institute in particular was not keen on Bion, considering him too subversive. He spent the last years of his life there, however. Bion returned to England in 1979, a few months before he died.

So, this gives an idea of his human journey, which is intimately bound up with his journey as an intellectual and a theorist. I would say that his work can be divided into two threads: the one which is very well-known, I think even to many of you, is the work on groups which in fact doesn't stop with the *Experiences in Groups*, even though he did not write other texts specifically dedicated to groups. They are found above all in the papers from 1970 onwards, from *Attention and Interpretation* to all the various clinical seminars (1977–1978), the Brazilian and the Rome lectures, *Cogitations*, which is a kind of collection of notes taken from the end of the 1950s through to the whole of the 1970s, and particularly in *A Memoir of the Future*. In these works, there are frequent references to groups and references to what may be considered the individual within the group, but also the group within the individual. A moment ago, when I said of Bion's idea that the human being is a kind of palimpsest I referred to this very idea of his of the individual as a group that can be almost unrolled; I do not know if you know those paintings by Klimt with Chinese or Korean vases unrolled as a background to the painting or as the woman's clothes, Bion's idea of an individual is a bit like that, so that if you look inside the individual you'll find a whole group of people.

This is a very interesting concept, which also has, in my view, very deep roots in English culture. I would say that the literary or artistic form that characterises English culture for me more than any other is in fact theatre, poetry, and theatre, in fact, which meet in the figure of Shakespeare. Theatre in England is still an extremely important form in England, an extremely important vehicle of social communication. In the 1950s—probably the situation is less rosy now—there were 500 theatres in London. Many social and pacifist movements, for example, had an important theatrical voice: you need only think of ... [it's impossible to make out the author's name in the recording] with regard to Irish politics. For us the theatre is significant as a form of social protest, of social denunciation, a description of society. I think Bion took much of his idea of the individual as a group from this idea of things that can be seen on a stage, that is, people talking among themselves and forming a coherent discussion between the different voices.

In fourteenth-century England, for example, as in modern European counties, plays were performed on the day of Corpus Domini, based on the Bible stories. But in England this developed in a way that it didn't, to my knowledge, in other countries: they didn't only tell the Bible stories, but also dramas called "morality" and "mystery" plays. The moralities are much more interesting because the characters on stage are characters like temperance, anger and modesty, that is, mental qualities which are given a voice and made to interact with each other. Today I think that Bion had this kind of thing very much in the back of his mind when he was writing *A Memoir of the Future*, which is a book of about 400–500 pages of text, of which the first seven chapters seem to consist of narrative. All the others are in dialogue form, some dialogues in which the characters are identified, others in which it is impossible to tell who is speaking, although they are still dialogues. For me this is something that Bion has done with various intentions and not just one, but one of these intentions was in fact to show how a single individual speaks with a multiplicity of voices, of which only a few can be heard at any one time, but almost always more than one. It is difficult for a person, not necessarily a patient, but anyone in interaction with others, to be totally univocal; we may take the example of a colleague of mine, also a pupil of Bion's, who is Meltzer. I have always been amused, in a friendly way, by the fact that when Meltzer speaks, he speaks with an American accent, but after living in England for many years his facial expressions and hand gestures are entirely English. Then I think that you will also be able to make similar comments about me, but this is also something it is important to be able to see in one's patients.

A patient tells us something, and perhaps in a sad way, but one might also have impression that at the same time they are giving a different message with their body, not necessarily a contradictory one, but still a message that adds dimensions to what the voice alone is saying. I think it is more or less the same kind of thing for any musician who might say: you believe that you are hearing a single note, but that note has many harmonies and we, as analysts, either with patients in individual analysis or in groups, must always try to catch the harmonies and hear these other collateral voices, or these other gestures or facial expressions or ways of sitting down or lying or whatever they are doing.

And this is something that was very close to Bion's heart. He needed to express this kind of concept in this very strange book. Because Bion's texts are subdivided into very clear periods of time: the first books, which are the driest, the most difficult, I would say, with the exception of *A Memoir of the Future*, which is not so, are the ones from the 1950s and the early 1960s. They are *Learning from Experience*, *Elements of Psycho-Analysis*, *Transformations*, and *Second Thoughts*, translated into Italian as *Analisi degli schizofrenici e metodo analitco* [Analyses of Schizophrenics and Analytic Method]. *Second Thoughts*, which might, as its title suggests, be seen as an afterthought, consists of a series of short papers with a final comment written several years after the first publication of the essays. All of these books are rather difficult to read not least because they were written at a time when the social pressures on Bion, as on other English analysts, were quite powerful. In England, psychoanalysis has never been looked upon very kindly. When Bion was at university, and already developing an interest in psychoanalysis, and very little Freud had been translated into English, and we are in the

1920s, they said to him, "what interest could you have in this business, it's all organised by Austrians, by Jews, forget it, it isn't English!" So there was a rather strong aversion against psychoanalysis, so much so that when I was at school, when the families of two of my schoolmates, and this was in the 1950s, found out that I was the daughter of a psychoanalyst, those two girls were forbidden to come to my house, because we were considered to be somehow infected. Such a situation in Italy today is absolutely inconceivable, not least because the Italians are more tolerant than the English in any case; but in England you felt that a lot, and inside the British Psychoanalytic Society you felt a lot of pressure to ensure that psychoanalysis was as scientific as possible.

If you look at *Cogitations*, which my stepmother decided to bring out in English in 1992, you will see that in the 1950s and 60s there are a lot of quite long passages which are extremely revealing. For example fairly incomprehensible concepts like α-elements, β-elements, contact barriers, α-functions, I do not think I could test them according to the facts. Many of these fragments are not dated, but I think they are fragments that Bion took from other essays and then decided to publish, and I think he cut them because they were very introspective fragments. In the fragment in which he really explains what an α-element means to him, he takes an example of a mental image that comes into his mind, and this was, for me at least, a revelation, because that was when I worked out what he meant by α-element, which I hadn't understood before. I think he cut those fragments out from texts he wrote in the 1960s because they were too personal and because he then felt the need to give at least a scientific appearance to psychoanalysis, but taking in my view an attitude not too far removed from later developments, every day we are less reluctant to discuss our mental processes, not least because there are scientists like ... [incomprehensible on audio recording] whom Bion quotes openly, and who was really writing in 1908.

They spoke about their emotional and mental experiences within scientific theorisation, thus giving a semblance of social acceptability to this kind of discourse that it lacked before.

Then Bion left England in 1968, and there was a kind of relaxation of this rigid, slightly dry aspect to his writing. The most legible essay of all is in fact *Attention and Interpretation: A Scientific Approach to Insight in Psycho-Analysis and Groups*, which he wrote when he was already in the United States. It is a text in which he explains very clearly what he means, and one in which he speaks of the difficulty of the mystic as he calls him in relation to the group, the mystic, the genius, that is, the individual who has new ideas and has to compare himself with the group, and who may also be excluded completely from the group, because the group does not like new ideas.

At the same time as the publication of *Attention and Interpretation*, Bion taught a great deal in Brazil and Argentina, where he found more people willing to be adventurous than he had in California. He was very struck by the celebration of the twentieth anniversary of Brasilia, to which he was invited, and he was also struck by the construction of Brasilia, which is an extremely curious city, artificial, if you like, because there was nothing there, but it is the expression of the ability of a man, the Brazilian President at the time, to put a dream into practice. Strangely, it was not a dream of his own, but a dream of Don Bosco who, almost a century before, had written to a missionary friend in Brazil, that one night he had dreamed that between the fifth and the twentieth parallel there would be a very large lake, and a city would emerge from it, and that was exactly what the Brazilian President did: he took Don Bosco's dream, they blocked the exit of a valley of that high plain, which was not particularly dry, but for thousands of square kilometres very high bushes grow, there's nothing, they made this artificial lake, there were four to five rivers that fed it, hence the possibility of electricity, and they built this extraordinary city.

Then I think Bion had the idea that Brazil was a country where you could have ideas and put them into practice, which was something he had been looking for, I think, for his whole life. In fact, the first publisher of *A Memoir of the Future*, of the first two volumes, was a Brazilian publisher from Rio. This text, which is the apogee of Bion's work, is once again very difficult to read for different reasons. When you try to read *A Memoir of the Future*, the first reaction after a few pages is that this is something very difficult to feel emotionally, because the other big foundation, the support, is Bion's awareness that most psychoanalytic texts are boring because they lack the emotion they should be discussing.

What he tried to do as a structure of the structure was to provoke emotion in the reader and then discuss it, but it isn't very pleasant to have someone continuously evoking your emotions. In fact it is a book which, having reached the eighth and ninth chapters, a Roman psychoanalyst of my acquaintance, a very respectable older woman, picked the book up and threw it to the other side of the room saying: I'm not going to look at it again, then picked it up and finished it. Why does it have this effect? It is a book that makes one despair, that makes one angry, that makes one cry, that makes one laugh a lot, it is a library that really tries to bring the human comedy to the mind of the reader, and then discusses it from the psychoanalytic point of view; so with the heuristic tools that a psychoanalyst may have at his disposal. But it is a book that makes very strong demands on the reader. It is not the kind of book that you can read calmly in the evening and then go to sleep, better not! In fact the best system for reading it is to find a group of friends or at least of people with whom one is not in very bad relations and read it out loud chapter by chapter, even taking the various parts and acting them out while one reads, and then discussing not so much what the book means but what has happened in it.

In his review of this book Lussana says that reading *A Memoir of the Future* is a little like changing your life, and that is why it is changing one's life at least from the point of view of psychoanalysis and psychoanalytic writing, because it is really a very subversive book. It is subversive like many of Bion's concepts that have not been passed over in silence because they are wrapped in rather unattractive paper. I think it is just after halfway through *Elements of Psycho-Analysis*, but I'm not sure, it might also be *Learning from Experience*, Bion calmly comments that his theory of α-elements, β-elements, and the α-function may adequately substitute for the Freudian theory of the primary process and the secondary process.

I suspect that the book was so difficult that none of his colleagues in the British Society reached that point, because otherwise he would have been thrown out of the Society rather than being made President; so in a sense he managed to save himself because the books are so unreadable. Today we can read them more easily, today we know more, we have greater familiarity with them, and his way of doing things no longer seems so strange to us. But at that time, in the 1960s it was simply unreadable. He was considered very subversive because certain approaches to Freudian theory, but he was also very Freudian, much more than he was Kleinian. Even though he made great use of the concept of projective identification, he developed it a great deal, also developing a hint of Klein, that is, there is a physiological form of projective identification and not only the pathological form. The physiological form is what allows the transmission of the capacity for thought from one generation to the next. This is a new development with regard to Freudian theories about thinking, about which Freud, among others, spoke very little. If you look at Laplanche and Pontalis's Dictionary, there is no heading either for "thinking" or for "thought", which are concepts that were really introduced into psychoanalytic thought by Bion, more than anyone else; certainly by Klein, Segal, and others of the British Kleinian group, with their work on symbolism—but even further by Bion (who, in my view, is not very Kleinian).

One other way in which Bion is very different from Freud, even if he is still close to him, is a kind of recuperation of Freudian theories about sexuality, not about the psycho-sexual development of the individual but more about the idea that there is a psycho-sexual foundation to the individual which is on the boundary, if we may put it like this, between the sexual soma and what becomes psyche. In *Cogitations*, there is a section that is called meta-theory,[1] which was written quite late in Bion's life, in which he speaks about interpretation in the form of a breast and interpretation in the form of a penis. It is difficult to understand, I have to admit, but in fact I think he is referring to an extremely primitive form of proto-thought that is very vulnerable to sexual impulses. I think it is something that happens, if I can put it like this, on this level which is very close to a brute physical impulse, to reproduce, if you like, which has very little to do with the mental. It causes problems because the person who brings this inside themselves feels at the mercy of a sexuality that they cannot in any way control.

Then I think that when Bion speaks about interpretation in the form of a breast or a penis he is talking about verbal mental formulation which has to do with this proto-mental level, which is once again the level that is below that of the base assumptions. These theoretical concepts describe what happens in a group when the group cannot function in an appropriate manner, using rational, conscious, thought thinking.

Bion was very interested, throughout his whole life, I think, in creating within the individual a kind of mental structure which allows thought that is made of sexuality, instincts, very strong emotions and rationality. For him, these things cannot in fact be separated, they are always mixed together, and are like a cable consisting of lots of wires and *A Memoir of the Future*, to return to this final text, is an attempt to reveal the threads that make up this cable and how they work.

---

[1] Found on p. 235 Volume XI of The Complete Works of W. R. Bion (2014). [Ed.].

For Bion, an individual with an internal group can never disregard the external group in which he finds himself: that is, what the individual is capable of doing or saying or thinking depends to a great extent on the wellbeing of the group. If the group allows him, he may have and express a new idea, whether the group allows him to or not. I think this is to a large extent one of the reasons why Bion chose to go and live in a place that was not England, where he felt that the group was too small; too rigidly Kleinian or Freudian or Winnicottian and he needed to be himself.

But this kind of discourse does not only concern this particular psychoanalyst at this particular historical moment, it also concerns all of us, it also concerns what we can say when we are not in the group, and this brings us back to the story of realistic projective identification. When a baby is born and put in its mother's arms it makes, because that is how it is made, realistic projective identifications, it cries because something is not right, and the mother says poor thing it's hungry and gives it the breast. Then with this repeated experience the baby begins to realise that there is a relationship between a state of terrible, catastrophic discomfort and a state of wellbeing. The interaction with another person begins, and this is true if the child is crying because it is soiled, because it needs to be burped or whatever. There is another human figure that says things, puts in words what is happening and does things to advance the situation, to change it, to put it in motion. This is realistic projective identification, the child projects into its mother an atrocious sensation and the mother says, "I'll do something about this".

We have realistic projective identifications as well. With regard to you, for example, I can think that you will listen to me, and in the end I feel that this has been confirmed by my experience so far. But we can also have non-realistic projective identifications. For example, being unable to speak in a group of people because we have unconscious fantasies about what the group will do if we try. There are situations in which these fantasies have also been validated by the behaviour of the group. We need only think of Savonarola, Giordano Bruno. Galileo got away, but many did not. So the individual is right to be afraid of the group because the group can tolerate him, but also not tolerate him. He may be a tolerable individual, but he might also be an individual who is not tolerable.

So it is very important for an analyst, whether he works only with single patients or works in a group always to keep in mind the fact that the individual has group pressures weighing upon him, and that the analyst too has group pressures upon him which come, as anyone who has worked with the relations of psychotics will be well aware, either from the social group of the patient or his own social groups.

The most atrocious thing that one can do to a psychoanalyst is to say, "But Freud didn't say that," when he comes out with a new idea, Freud didn't say it, I did, but not all groups will accept that. What I means is that Bion, as an analyst, was in my opinion very significant because he contextualised the individual much more than Freud or Klein did, but in a way that was perhaps similar to some of the analysts who went to the United States and some aspects of the first psychoanalysis, that is, the social aspects: the Berlin clinic, for example, and the London clinic of psychoanalysis.

This contextualisation of the individual is very important in contemporary psychoanalytic theorisation, because it also allows us to start talking about social groups that are not therapeutic groups. A lot of work has been done in England and in the United States through ... [audio recording incomprehensible] and the institutes ... [audio recording incomprehensible] in the United States about group behaviour and the individual in groups in industrial contexts, for example. A great deal of work has been done on union problems, for example using Bion's concepts: a ramification that is not strictly psychotherapeutic, but extremely important from the social point of view.

But Bion has also done important work on the development of thinking starting with the psychotics, but referring to less psychotic individuals. He divided psychotics into two classes, sane psychotics and insane psychotics, which is a very useful subdivision, in fact, because it allows us to talk about all of us without being misunderstood as Klein was misunderstood when she talked about paranoid-schizoid projections in small children, and everyone said but children aren't mad. But that wasn't what she was saying, and Bion was important not least because of the way he fought a great deal for the central importance of emotion in the life of the individual and in the individual's ability to think for thoughts that are fruitful and which can develop and I also hope to create a debate between us now.

GIAMPÀ: One question that often pops up in our weekly encounters, when the discussion turns to Bion, concerns without memory and without desire or without thought or oblivion of memory and thought, which I think is important to bring this meeting to a conclusion.

PARTHENOPE: Bion's chief idea was without memory and without desire, more than without thought, but without thought also seems to be a later justifiable development. This is something that is connected, I think, with Bion's childhood in India and with an encounter with a culture that was very different from our own, but which was also different from the English culture of the time. We have to bear in mind that the means of transport with which my father was most familiar as a child was the elephant; there were two elephants that belonged to the family, and they were so important that I even know their names, and they loaded everything onto those elephants including the little folding harmonium on which my grandmother played hymns every evening. So they were a family with a very religious inclination that was very respectful of Indian culture. I think that in the end, my grandfather had little patience with the English in general, but he became close friends with the head of the caste of untouchables who was in turn close friends with Gandhi, who is the only Indian whose name is mentioned in my family, and from whom my grandfather accepted a gift. Normally he never accepted anything, but he did accept a little silver cup from Gandhi for my father.

My grandfather became secretary of the National Congress Party in India, and I think he was the only white man ever to have worked with an Indian political party. My father had some knowledge of the Hindu religion and Hindu mysticism, and of the importance of knowing how to wait that is significant and important from this point of view.

Now I will say something that might seem irrelevant, but which is in fact very relevant indeed. Samuel Beckett underwent a course of psychotherapy with Bion in the 1930s, which Bion never talked about. Within the family, he told us about the times when Deirdre Bair, Beckett's biographer, had come to visit him and he hadn't told her anything. Beckett, on the other hand, talked about his experience of Bion in *Waiting for Godot* and his experience was one of waiting, a long wait in which something might have happened but then again might not, and this is the kind of concept for which Bion also drew to a large extent on the Christian mystics, of being able to wait until something appeared.

Also, if you read Proust, at the beginning of the novel there is that dramatic moment in the story of the little *madeleine*, there is an approach to this in which Proust is saying that memories cannot be forced. There is nothing to be done; you can't sit at your desk waiting for them to come. James Joyce (Ellmann, 1959) too talked a lot about epiphanies, when something is revealed in its essential nature.

These are all things that form a part of this Bion's concept of waiting without memory and without desire, that is without trying to remember in the silence of the session what the patient said the previous day, or what that dream was, or that idea that came to you during the night, or even how much I would like this patient to clear off or get better or for something else to happen. All of these thoughts, as well as the desire to try to understand what is happening in reality are very harmful because they do not allow you to see what's happening, and to see, or listen, or feel within yourself, or have reactions, even somatic ones, you need quiet and silence and a kind of mental quiet that is a kind of concentration on nothing in particular.

In reality, Bion said nothing different from Freud when he talked about evenly suspended attention. It's the same thing, but Bion went into greater detail and he said things that Freud wasn't able to say, not least because Freud had the big handicap of feeling he had to distance himself from religion, but religion is a very important part of the human being, and Bion, even though he was radically atheistic, says in *A Memoir of the Future*: "I would subscribe to this belief in the doctrine dogma of God incarnate if it were also understood to include belief in the Devil incarnate".

But he was capable of understanding the religious feeling in the need to wait, the need for faith, the need for hope. He felt these things too, but he didn't like to let them lead to any kind of God figure. But in his work he managed to use these concepts which normally, in Western culture, let's say, had until then been considered the prerogative of the religious. In fact we are witnessing a very important revolution in European culture, even thought sometimes we can seem stagnant, but we are realising in this century that aspects of human life or culture which for thousands of years have been the prerogative, for example, of a church, or a religion, or philosophy, or mathematics, are changing masters.

Some of these things are becoming the prerogative of psychoanalysis, which can say more about certain aspects of the human mind than religion, or mathematics, or music, or other major cultural areas have been able to do until now.

Then Bion once again, in this matter of without memory and without desire, introduced into psychoanalysis and illuminated through psychoanalysis the religious ide of the trusting religious expectation that something significant is going to happen. Certainly a religious person sees it within a different mental ambit, he sees it in the ambit of his relationship with the Godhead. Bion sees it in the ambit of his relationship with the patient's unknown and also with himself, with what will emerge from the session. But one can have this kind of mental attitude, which is fundamentally very scientific because it is concentrated on what is happening at this moment, only with certain conditions: those of not filling the mind with extraneous objects, extraneous sounds.

PISANI: I have two questions, one for clarification, one more out of curiosity. The clarification question, if you can tell us more about the concept of the α-element, β-element and α-function and how these concepts in Bion's hypotheses are substituted for the Freudian concept of primary and secondary process and how these concepts correlate with the other one of interpretation in the sense of breast and interpretation in the sense of penis. The second question is either curiosity or gossip. I would like to ask how it is that Bion and Foulkes, who have both dealt with analytic groups, both psychoanalysts, both members of the British Psychoanalytic Society, never actually met.

PARTHENOPE: Foulkes and Bion had quite a turbulent relationship, I think. I had a sense that Bion had the idea that Foulkes had made use of Bion and Rickman's ideas without acknowledging the work they had done. So there were really boring disputes about who had robbed from whom, the kind that happen in any academic environment. But the more substantial reason why they didn't meet afterwards was much more to do with both men's theories, because Bion wasn't interested in putting together a therapeutic group in which attention was paid to the problems of the single individual; he was only interested, when he used groups, in the group, in the internal dynamics of the group, and this is a radical difference. I think that was the reason why they never met afterwards, because they had completely different ideas of the kind of use that you can meaningfully make of a group.

Annoyingly, in reality the β-element precedes the α-element, which is a bit irritating from the point of view of the mental order. Bion needed to find terms to describe, without immediately saturating them with other thoughts, phenomena that he saw in psychotic patients. So he used two terms that meant nothing, β-element and α-element, with the intention of discovering the meaning of the contents of these two terms as he progressed.

This was his working project, and effectively he worked like this: the problem he faced existed because psychotic patients can apparently digest and use certain experiences and not others. What happens to those experiences? Why do some things become part of a dream and others not? That is, what has the mind done to these experiences? So his idea was that the human being experiences something, for example rain on the skin, a sensation of wetness, of cold, of damp, or something that comes from within—intestinal pain, liver pain, but not yet recognisable as such), a vague sense of something noticed at an unconscious level but not yet on a conscious level.

How many women know that they are about to menstruate or that they have become pregnant almost instantly, days before the menstruation or almost immediately the conception has occurred? A great many, probably because there are unconscious physical communications that are managed fairly adequately. I take this example because it comes more easily to me than other examples. Bion felt, maintained, and theorised that in fact all of our knowledge is based on the senses, all of it! There is no extra-sensory knowledge, because something that we call psyche or mind works on this rough material, which can indeed come from within or without.

But the psyche also works on unconscious emotions that in turn are presumably stimulated by what happens to us internally and externally. So Bion said that the first stage, the first stage is the β-element, the name he gave to rough sensory impressions, not mentally elaborated at any level, and he said that β-elements, that is, those rough sensory impressions, can be stored and used for projective identifications, that is, they can be violently expelled.

When I talked about the child who is wet or dirty, who is hungry, which are adult turns, what the child is doing is *waah*, a cry; with that cry it is expelling a discomfort: that is a β-element, or rather it is the kind of thing to which Bion gave the name β-element.

What does the mother do? She alphabetises! That is, she turns that β-element into an α-element, she internalises it, presumably makes an enormous series of procedures that I wouldn't try to start enumerating, and on the basis of her experience, the knowledge that she has of that child, and her memories, which are not entirely impossible for her to trace, in that they are memories of her own childhood, she says: this child is hungry! And she gives it the breast. That is, she has created an α-element, and probably, but not necessarily, a visible image of the mind of her own child, which would be fine if she gave it the breast.

The example that Bion gives of the α-element in *Cogitations* is very interesting and illuminating. It says more or less: a friend of mine asks me where I am going on holiday, and there comes to mind an image of a certain country town, of the church in a country town which is important because that's where the railway line stops, the nearest railway station. This thing that comes to my mind is what I call an α-element, that is, the image of the church, and it is the conclusion or stratified result of a very long series of emotional experiences to arrive in that particular bit of countryside by train, to disembark and go to the house. That is to say, the α-element is the visual image that that contains one or several emotional experiences, a real meaning at their base, which can be catalogued together, one might almost say. With α-elements, with these visual images that emerge from the unconscious, many things can be done because they can be used for conscious thought. Bion says that originally they are also used for unconscious daytime wakeful thinking and for conscious thought, and for the unconscious-conscious dream-thoughts. Alpha-elements are by and large subjects in the use for all processes of the primary process, including, and this is very important, considerations of representability. Knowing Bion I could say something more concerning my ideas about why a church had come into his mind and not the railway station. I think it is important to remain clear that the α-elements above all undergo a treatment in terms of displacement, of condensation, of reversal; but afterwards these things are used in conscious, rational thought. One example of this is Kekulé's dream of the benzene ring. He had the problem that he didn't know what the chemical formula was, and one night he dreamed of a snake biting its tail. This is what I would call an α-element, thinking of the dream the next morning he said to himself that's the form of the chemical formula, so he was using the α-element in rational thought.

CHAPTER SEVENTEEN

Bion: a Freudian innovator (1997)

One short essay by W. R. Bion constitutes a kind of crossroads or nodal point to help us understand many aspects of his work as a whole. In "Notes on memory and desire" (Bion, 1967), he describes a technical aspect at once Freudian and linked to a series of theories that make Bion one of the major Freudian psychoanalysts. I would like to use this essay as my reference point to show how Bion faithfully follows the main lines of Freud's thought and at the same time reveals himself to be an original thinker. His unprecedented thought was in every way oriented towards the service of *clinical psychoanalysis*, even at the peak of his theorisation and also when he was dreaming that one day scientists of other disciplines would pay attention to what psychoanalysts had to say (Bion, 1992).

"Notes on memory and desire" is a rare short essay, not more than three pages in length, which appeared in a Californian publication called *The Psychoanalytic Forum* in 1976. It was translated into Spanish and republished in Argentina (Bion, 1969), but until Elizabeth Bott Spillius published it in English in the second volume of *Melanie Klein Today* (Bott Spillius, 1988), it would have been hard to argue that it had enjoyed wide distribution in Europe (except among Spanish readers!). The original publication consists in three pages written by Bion, a series of critical observations to which he replies. Among the critics are: T. M. French, J. A. Lindon, A. L. Gonzalez, M. Brierley, and H. H. Herskovitz, and their comments range from favourable curiosity to actual rejection.

In short, in this essay Bion assumes an unusually peremptory tone to stress that analysts should deprive themselves of memory and desire to be able to observe correctly what happens in the consulting room. A correct observation is the basic point that makes analytic work possible. Bion profoundly condemns both memory, whose unconscious components falsify observation, and desire, which permits neither understanding nor cure. Luciana Nissim Momigliano maintains that the tone of this essay reminds her of ancient Hebrew prayers, which are severely prescriptive (Nissim Momigliano, 1981). And again when, not much later in 1976, Bion was asked an opinion about the mental attitude of the analyst and his interlocutor used the term "floating attention",[1] Bion replied: "It is as Freud described it; the best expression that I know" (Bion, 1987). Bion, in response to different topics raised by critics, referred to a passage in a letter from Freud to Lou Andreas Salomé, concerning "blinding himself artificially" in such a way as to concentrate all the light "on one dark spot", and admitted that he felt uneasy, as did Marjorie Brierley, if it was being insinuated that he was moving away from Freudian technique.

So what is Bion really saying in this essay? Is he simply amplifying a Freudian technique? Or is there something more "waiting in the wings" in this deceptive essay, formulated so categorically?

First of all it is worth nothing that this essay was written between *Transformations* (1965) and *Attention and Interpretation* (1970) and, leaving aside two book reviews (1966), it is the only text that Bion published that year, which also coincided with the upset of his first visit to California, to which he moved, and the start of his trips to South America to teach. Its style also seems to lie somewhere between the more abstract theoretical works of the 1960s and the more discursive—and hence the more legible—collections of clinical seminars from the 1970s. So we notice him moving towards simpler, more sober and colloquial writing: as Nissim Momigliano has stressed, Bion resumed a

---

[1] The correct translation of Freud's term, *gleichschwebende Aufmerksamkeit*, is "Evenly suspended attention". [Ed.]

discussion of the same topics in chapter five of *Attention and Interpretation*, using considerably more imperative terms.

These terms are less peremptory because they are expressed in the first person:

> To attain to the state of mind essential for the practice of psychoanalysis I avoid any exercise of memory; I make no notes. When I am tempted to remember the events of any particular session I resist the temptation.
>
> .... If I find that some half-memory is beginning to obtrude, I resist its recall no matter how pressing or desirable its recall may seem to be. A similar procedure is followed with regard to desires:

But at the end of the same paragraph about desires, all of a sudden Bion returns to a more incisive approach after a short "neutral" passage in which he asserts: "Introspection will show how widespread and frequent memories and desires are. They are constantly present in the mind and to follow the advice I am giving is a difficult discipline ..."

It may be observed that this is a particular technical discipline connected with the rest of Bion's work, even if it is hard to understand in what way it should be applied.

We might wonder how it is possible to try to abstain from one's own memories, even attempting to fight against them, and trying to do one's best not to desire even just the greatest benefit for one's own patient. Does behaving in this way not contrast with the fundamental principles of psychoanalysis? The answer can only be affirmative, provided that one chooses a specific psychoanalytic model that not only Bion refused (as we can tell from his two reviews: Eissler's *Medical Orthodoxy and Future of Psychoanalysis* and the first pages of the second chapter of *Attention and Interpretation*), but a model that even Freud did not fully accept, for example the medical one. Freud is quite categorical with regard to analysis, in fact for him psychoanalysis was much more than a therapy: the International Psychoanalytic Association also defines the term "psychoanalysis" in the same way. The reason to cling to a behaviour like that described in "Notes on memory and desire" is that this mental attitude increases the appreciation of the evolved aspects that Bion calls "O": "ultimate reality, the thing-in-itself, or truth" (Bion, 1970, p. 58), which is a fundamental necessity for health and mental growth.

But on a practical level, or what actually happens during the session, Bion refers to the state of mind that comes closest to α-elements. The latter, cited in *Cogitations* (Bion, 1992), have been described by Bion in various ways: as visual mental images (even though they are not necessarily visual, but can also be auditory fantasies, like a series of pieces of information collected by the mind, or a kind of specific sound, or an olfactory or tactile mental sensation) and possess a precise quality that Poincaré, often cited by Bion, attributes to a "selected fact". That means that they must link emotional and sensory experiences in the present with other fragments that have not "acquired a meaning" until that particular moment. It might be objected, and in the criticism was raised about "Notes on memory and desire", that it is difficult to distinguish an event, understood as such, from a memory, but a differentiation can be made, and that is what Bion does in his reply. He writes:

> I realise that it would be helpful if I could distinguish between two different phenomena that are both usually and indifferently called "memory". This I have tried to do by speaking of one as "evolution", by which I mean the experience where some idea or pictorial impression floats into the mind unbidden and as a whole. From this I wish to distinguish ideas that present themselves in response to a deliberate and conscious attempt at recall; for this last I reserve the term "memory". (Bott Spillius, 1988, p. 19)

It is interesting to note that Bion does not use the term α-element in "Notes on memory and desire", probably because he was more interested in looking for an approach that recalled the same concept through a more familiar language: in my view this is not especially useful to the reader, because it seems to eliminate that particular psychoanalytic technique from Bion's other theories, making a coherent overall understanding difficult. In a note in *Cogitations*, from around 1960, he states very clearly "Free-floating attention, regarded as necessary in analytic work, might then be described as that state of mind in which the analyst allows himself the conditions in which dream-work-α can operate for the production of α-elements."

It is not so easy to understand what Bion means by the term α-elements from the definition contained in *Learning from Experience* (Bion, 1962), in which the term appears for the first time. This is partly predictable, given his attitude of not always clearly referring to terms that he was thinking and writing about. At the start of Chapter Seventeen, for example, he says "… In the K activity on which I am engaged, namely in knowing, I have to be conscious of my emotional experience and able to abstract from it a statement that will represent this experience adequately." (At this point we might note that Bion's definition of "formulation" was sufficiently broad to include anything at all, including stammers, cf. Bion, 1963.) This abstract concept generates trust if, subsequently, it describes other unknown experiences when abstraction has already taken place. Hidden behind these phrases is the idea that the α-element is a jealously guarded pictorial emotional experience; to be clear, the K activity consists in a process of abstraction.

Below I shall repeat the second affirmation that I have quoted because it is relevant for the theme of *Nachträglichkeit*.

In any case, the understanding of the concepts of α-element and α-function was possible only when *Cogitations* was available. It was in fact possible to observe how Bion eliminated from his publications in the 1960s many of the fundamental thoughts that had led to the formulation of those concepts. Before the publication of *Cogitations*, the best description of what Bion means by the term "evolution" had been expressed by Proust (1954) in *Remembrance of Things Past*, in the long passage culminating in the episode of the fragrant tea-drenched *madeleines*, which brings the narrator back to the now forgotten memories of his childhood. Proust's description casts light on an implicit and important aspect of the theory of α-elements as two very clear factors in Bion's mind.

The implicit aspect is that the α-element tends to appear in response to some kind of stimulus. In the long passage in *Cogitations* in which Bion describes the appearance in his mind of the image of a church, this image arises in response to the question of a friend about where he intended to spend his holidays. To Bion's comments in this passage I should like to add that the "actual selection" of a selected fact, as if it were swimming (literally) into someone's mind, may always be connected with a specific emotional stimulus which emerges during the session. If it did not seem possible to return to the emotional stimulus during the session, we would have to suspect that the α-element has appeared as an alien aspect, a kind of defensive apparition that might be inserted in column two of the Grid. At this point, it is possible to identify the emotional stimulus that has produced a defensive rather than a constructive reaction. In any case, the α-element never appears without its emotional nucleus.

The other two aspects of Bion's theory which may be found in Proust's definitions are the "entirety" and "completeness" of the evolution (α-element)—which Bion elsewhere connects with the way in which a dream presents itself to the mind, either completely present or in a non-recollectable way—and the fact that the memory has its foundation in sensory impressions. This last point is what made Bion cautious about memory as an obstacle to the intuition of non-sensory mental phenomena during the session, but is also one of the aspects of his thought that bring him close to the theories of Freud and link him with the concept of primary ego, understood as the body-bound ego (Freud, 1923). In fact, one very important theme in Bion's work is the union between soma and psyche, and his clear questioning of the biological, material, and physical bases of mental phenomena. The fascinating hypothesis—which Bion defines as rational or fantastical conjectures—about sub-thalamic fear, described in a mysterious note in the key to the first volume of *A Memoir of the Future, The Dream*, represents a good example of it (Bion, 1975–79).

But to come back to Freud's "bodily ego", it may be objected that the ego goes on to "develop", and the fact that it is in origin a bodily ego must not in fact influence the relationship with adult patients. In *Cogitations*, however, Bion states: "I consider that the behaviour of the patient is a palimpsest in which I can detect a number of layers of conduct." Furthermore, in the next paragraph: "Winnicott says patients *need* to regress: Melanie Klein says they *must not*. I say they *are* regressed, and the regression should be observed and interpreted by the analyst..." (Bion, 1992). Bearing this in mind, Bion declares that certain basic functions do not change, in fact with psychological growth, and one of the aspects of mental life that falls within this category is fear of external reality—and of internal physical reality—perceived through the senses, which constitutes the whole of the basic information that we draw on in order to survive.

Bion calls this basic information β elements, and says that they can either remain in the mind in non-processed form—and in this case they can be used in projective identifications (or become part of the unconscious that Bion calls "inaccessible"), or, through the α-function, they can pass through a process of "alphabetisation" so as to be used in dreams and in unconscious wakeful thinking. Sometimes, however, in the right conditions, or in a state of reverie, these α-elements, as they are known, emerge and become available for conscious wakeful thinking. This is what Bion means by the "evolution" of an α-element that can be used as a basis on which to build a thought and can then in turn become an interpretation if the analyst chooses. But at this point, we must abandon the realms of unconscious thought and seek more conscious levels on which to use the tools that rational thought makes available to us.

The tool that Bion calls the "Grid" falls within this category. Now, how can something as rational and restricted as the Grid be connected with the ideas contained in "Notes on memory and desire"? The two states of mind, one appropriate to reverie and the other for the use of the Grid, may at first sight appear quite incompatible. But this is not in fact the case, because a mind instructed to flee memory and desire waits quietly for the appearance of a selected fact/α-element, in a state of profound concentration addressed to nothing in particular. It is not a mind that has abandoned all complex thoughts, but remains external to the session. The Grid is used to reflect on the session, almost playing with the information that has emerged, making hypothetical interpretations that are different from the ones really given, like a child trying different ways to climb a wall. In the first layout of the Grid (1963)[2] Bion unequivocally states that not only the patient's accounts but also those of the analyst must be inserted in the categories of the Grid to observe the route undertaken, something that has been done with the material, if defence mechanisms have been used by both partners, either alternately if an evolutionary turn has taken place, or towards a greater falsification in the thought processes (moving towards the bottom) or towards a wider range of uses (moving across).

The Grid is supposed to be used as a frame of reference both for the thoughts that have emerged in the session and for meditating upon them. This supplies a strong mental approach, or internal container, which constitutes a necessary complement to floating attention, useful within the session. The Grid is also an extreme synthesis of all of Bion's theories about thinking. When the Grid is used it must be taken as read that its categories refer to the processes and progress of the mental activity from the bases to the highest levels of sophistication, and in spite of the fact

---

[2] Bion (1963). Bion also wrote a second essay with the same title in 1971, taken from a speech given at the Psychoanalytic Society of Los Angeles, which was subsequently published in 1977 (two essays, *The Grid and Caesura*).

that thinking may seem like a personal activity, the Grid is used against the background of a two-person relationship. There are different points in Bion's writings in which it is deduced that for him thought may not be considered as an individual activity. I would like to clarify this aspect.

It already seems apparent from the essay *A Theory of Thinking* (Bion, 1962) that for Bion the beginning of the processes of thinking or at least, of the processes that may lead back to thinking, is firmly based on the dynamic of the mother–child dyad. What may not appear so obvious is that for the whole life of every individual his thought processes make use of internal dynamic relations, substantially the passage Ps ⇌ D, but also of relations between the various parts of the personality and above all between one series of containers and contents. Although at a macroscopic level we are referring to a thinking person, in a psychoanalytic context it is useful to conceptualise thought processes as if they were the result of internal relations between a multitude of objects and internal parts.

Bion's hypothesis on the use of the model of a group to describe the inner world (set out most clearly in the third volume of *A Memoir of the Future*) is one of the aspects of this conceptualisation. A psychoanalysis in itself is obviously an example of thought processes that advance thanks to the presence of two individuals, but Bion's insistence on the couple, as a fundamental human unit, makes me wonder about the fact that he did not really think about thinking as always, because he was convinced of the necessity of a dyadic relationship at the end of an advancement.

Returning to the Grid and its explanation of the elements of Bion's theory of thinking, apart from the basic state of reverie whose existence is taken for granted in the Grid, there is one important aspect that is not made clearly explicit: the thinking of the group, or "common sense". In a few words we might say that this element is implicit in the idea of a deductive scientific system that obviously requires homologation on the part of the group, but is not exactly clarified by the way in which the grid is constituted.

In any case, the Grid acts as an external reference point to clarify and deepen the events of the session and as a kind of fortress of rational thought to which the analyst may return, perhaps with a feeling of relief after abandoning the positions Ps and D during the session. In the Grid we may find almost all the key words which, taken together, form a network through Bion's theories of mental functioning: the α- and β-elements, dream thoughts, dreams, myths, preconceptions, conceptions and concepts, the deductive scientific system and algebraic calculation, and also, on the horizontal axes, defining hypotheses, the degree of intensity, annotation, attention, inquiry and action. The Grid itself makes Bion look a long way from Freud, but in fact he has taken at least seven elements from Freud's theories, which he uses with original meanings.

At this point I should like to take a step back and enlarge upon two details that I hinted at above: how the concept of *Nachträglichkeit* is linked to that of the α-element, and why we should use a halo almost of mystery or fear with regard to eschewing memory and desire—Nissim Momigliano has captured the good emotional climate in her observations.

First of all, returning to this last point, when an analyst is in a state of mind tending towards reverie, trying to keep memory and desire at bay as much as possible, it means that they find themselves in a state in which they are more receptive to their own observations about the patient, but that they are also more open both to projective identifications coming from the patient and to the emergence, on a conscious level, of "evolutions" in their own α-elements (and other unconscious mental activities, including more complex thoughts). As the result of this greater permeability of certain particular contact-barriers—to return to a broader Freudian use of the term (Freud, 1895)—or, greater contact and smaller barrier between conscious and unconscious, the analyst has less defence against attacks on his or her mental stability, whether these come from inside or outside (the patient).

To put it more plainly, the analyst is more at the mercy of unconscious thought, which is not always a merciful companion. St. Paul, in his discussion of charity in his first epistle to the Corinthians, is well aware of how unconscious thought can be ruthless, and how its "lack of charity" can spoil the best conscious intentions.[3]

Perhaps while we are quoting St. Paul it is not inopportune, in this context, to try to understand why working without memory and desire would seem to evoke an almost religious aura. I think that this phenomenon has something to do with two main areas.

The first consists in the fact that meditation has been, and remains, associated more than anything with religious practices, and also, in a specific way, with a monastic austere lifestyle, so that perhaps there is

---

[3] "Though I speak in the tongues of men and of angels and have not charity, I am become as sounding brass, a tinkling cymbal." (1 Cor. 13, 1.)

an almost automatic association between the profound state of reverie, which is a fundamental prerequisite for the mental discipline of avoiding memory and desire, and religious practices. The association, however, does not have to be convincing: it can be fake, or a kind of false trail. Perhaps it is closer to the truth to suggest that both religious meditation and psychoanalytic reverie are closely connected with a fundamental human need.

The other aspect that must be connected with religious feelings, at least as discussed by Bion in *Experiences in Groups* (Bion, 1961), is that of the sensation of being dependent which, unlike the state of reverie, can be very strong. The analyst and the patient are in fact interdependent, they are like mother and child, and each more of the pair must be as satisfied as possible in the role that he or she is interpreting.

This aspect of interdependency takes us to the "dangerous" side of reverie, which is intimately connected to the individual's relationship with himself when he is in a "paranoid-schizoid" state or on the Ps side of the oscillation Ps $\rightleftharpoons$ D. If he can endure the feeling of fragmentation and bear it until something clearer emerges, having acquired a talent for negative capability, he is using his mind in the way that Bion calls "healthily psychotic": but, at such moments, he is also particularly vulnerable because it only takes a small push in one direction or another to knock him off balance. I am referring to phenomena in which the analyst (or the patient) is falling asleep, or, as Alexander describes, the analyst is suffering almost unbearable sleepiness (Alexander, 1981). This could be seen as a defence mechanism activated by a sense of excessive vulnerability to the patient's hostile projective identifications, but I think it may also be a defence against the awareness of frightening thoughts coming from the unconscious of the analyst himself, including a perception of imminent pain when the depressive position is reached. This is a mental area in which the bond that one has with oneself becomes extremely important. The ideal state is closer to an L link rather than a K, because the meditation of a state Ps suffused with love (or charity) is more bearable, and therefore has a greater chance of lasting—so it can be more productive. A K-link with oneself, at that particular moment, is a defence that goes beyond "fact and reason",[4] and does not contribute to the observation of events. And this immediately brings us back to avoiding memory and desire.

---

[4] Letter from Keats to his brother, quoted in Bion, 1970.

Having at this point closed the circle, and hoping that its circumference has been sufficiently broad for the meaningful experience of a journey along it, as Bion describes in his 1963 essay on *The Grid*, I would like to return to the concept of *Nachträglichkeit* that I mentioned above.

Bion asserted that one important element of abstraction, which happens when the emotional experience is subjected to a particular *process*, consists in the fact that it generates trust if it represents other unknown ideas when the abstraction has been effected. By saying this Bion meant that that an α-element, a pictorial image, should be sufficiently saturated in appearance to be useful on successive occasions, its significance growing as it does so. To quote an example of what I'm saying from Bion's works, we might say of "not knowing", as for a boy on a boat trip with his teacher and his other schoolmates on the Broads, how significant the word "Norfolk" might be—the toponym itself is an abstraction—and how it may grow in the course of his life: in fact Bion was referring to the church in Cromer in the passage on α-elements that I quoted above, written almost fifty years later. Going back, we may imagine how his visits to Norfolk as an adult, with his first wife and then with his second wife and his family, acquired different meanings in the course of his life, and gave a greater significance to his "first experience" in adolescence. However, we may say that additions of a later meaning to the already existing α-element constitute the nucleus of *Nachträglichkeit* and this concept plays an important part in the construction of *A Memoir of the Future*, even though Bion does not quote it in this way.

A new approach to Freudian and Kleinian concepts, which Bion calls "vertices", is actually a particularity of Bion's, and the concept of the vertex per se accurately illustrates the way in which he was a Freudian and at the same time not Freudian. Overall, it is right to assert that Bion accepted most of Freud's theories—with the adjustments that we have seen—as a basis of thought for a correct "psychoanalytic" method. However it seems that beyond the original concepts a kind of subtle, epoch-making change occurred: "Notes on memory and desire" does not recall the technical essay in which Freud quotes "floating attention" (Freud, 1912), or the relevant chapter of *Attention and Interpretation*. I maintain that this is the result of a twofold shift of emphasis: first of all, the object has changed from a predominant interest in the emotional aspect of mental life, which is a neurotic problem, to the aspect of mental life that deals with thinking and thought processes.

It is true that it might be an impossible task to unravel the skein completely and, specifically, take into consideration the fact that for Bion the most abstract part of thinking is scattered with emotion, pervaded by it, and has an emotional nucleus per se, but it is also true that Laplanche and Pontalis's dictionary (1967) does not contain the headings for thinking or thought, which are certainly key words in Bion's writings. Another change has also occurred between Freud and Bion, collected by Klein, which consists in the object of the analyst's attention.

If it is true to maintain that when reading Freud we identify and suffer with his patients, and that Klein's work casts light on the relational aspect of human life, it must also be admitted that Bion seems to have directed the spotlight more towards the analyst. The change in style between "Notes on memory and desire" and the fifth chapter of *Attention and Interpretation* is pertinent in this context. It looks as if Bion has moved from an impersonal to a person approach. That could have exposed him to criticism of being excessively introspective and consequently somewhat unscientific—in fact I strongly suspect that many of the passages on the α-function in *Cogitations*, written during the 1960s, were omitted in the publications at that time to avoid and forestall that kind of accusation. What might have provoked a similar change of position?

It is rather unlikely that with the passing of time he became less concerned with the scientific status of psychoanalysis. My idea is that his letters on scientific philosophy and on the philosophy of mathematics, during the 1960s, allowed him to broaden his concept of science and to decide that a really scientific discussion of psychoanalysis would need to turn its attention to "the thinker" as much as "the object of thought". He felt he had to turn his won attention to the more complex situation, during the session: the patient, the analyst and the relationship between them, but to do this adequately he had to study the main tool that he was using, his mind, as much as that of the patient. This is why he maintains the use of the Grid to follow the moments of the thinking of both, a little like a sauce that goes with both duck and gosling. His position was not substantially different from that of a physicist who wants to know exactly how the tools he is using work, from the simplest thermometer to the most complex particle accelerator.

This new vertex, or psychoanalysis from the point of view of the psychoanalyst as a part of the psychoanalytic process, is a distant cry from the main vertex of Freud directed towards the patient. Perhaps it is this aspect that chiefly confers a different flavour to Bion's writings from the 1970s, a sense of freedom and novelty. And yet …

And yet, Bion's psychoanalysis is still recognisable as psychoanalysis as understood by Freud, with the fundamental reference to the dominion of the unconscious and the conviction of the active existence of the transference.

Perhaps we might say that Bion introduced another small Copernican revolution in the way of studying ourselves and the world in which we live, but the planets, the stars, the constellations and the galaxies, the object of study, have remained the same as before. Not entirely, but almost. I recently made a discovery that rather amused me: Bion is often seen as an epistemologist, and as I was doing a little research into this field of thought, I encountered the fact that the English philosopher Ferrier who coined the term Epistemology in 1854 also, at the same time, coined another term at the same time that might be seen more or less as its opposite, agnoiology: the study of ignorance and what we do not know (Ferrier, 1854). The idea of Bion as an agnoioloist rather than an epistemologist attracts me, because it places the emphasis on our lack of knowledge, and how we do not know. So perhaps his revolution, like that of Copernicus, is completed with a new and later incision into the central position of man as omnipotent and omniscient.

So we might say that Bion's new vertex on Freud's theory casts light on our ignorance and our lack of knowledge, not only as patients but also as analysts, and this represents the radical detachment from the image of the analyst as a person who "knows". With Bion, the experiences of "knowing", "not knowing", "being", and "understanding" have become a matter of team work, and the analyst is no longer alone, but has become a member of a psychoanalytic couple.

CHAPTER EIGHTEEN

Dreams (1998)

Let's begin with "blinding ourselves" so that we can see better.

Bion never actually wrote anything specific or systematic about dreaming. After the 1960s, he wrote little that was apparently systematic. The famous "trilogy" is not in fact a systematisation, even though it may draw a great deal on his previous thought. But in this "trilogy" one of the clear things, which he drops eventually, allows us to see that Bion's ideas on dreams were different from Freud's. I am quoting from the second volume of *A Memoir of the Future*:

> "'I won't wish you sweet dreams,' says Alice, 'because as P. A.'—the Psychoanalyst, another of the characters—'would say, the dreams are always sweet by the time we have verbalised them.' Then the Psychoanalyst who is Bion replies: 'Not I—Freud.' That is, Freud's idea of the dream was that once we have managed to verbalise the dream we have sweetened it, some with sugar, some with a more artificial sweetener, but at any rate we make it relatively nice. Bion says that this is something that Freud says, not he, and it is from here that we derive the idea of what a dream is, what the function of the dream is and how it works.

For Freud dreams had two main functions: one was that of safeguarding the dream. The idea was that the dream allows us to remain asleep, because otherwise we would be woken by an excessive influx of anxiety that would make us wake up; and sometimes there are anxious dreams from which we awaken with a start that is usually extremely disagreeable. The other function that Freud ascribed to dreams was that of managing, digesting (I would say, more in Bion's terms) childhood sexual desires—which had been repressed because they were inacceptable. Freud said that at the core of every dream there was a repressed childhood desire. Then he had to do a lot of acrobatics to come to terms with dreams that are extremely unpleasant, anxious dreams that seem to have nothing to do with either sexual or infantile desires. In some cases of these which he relates in the *Interpretation of Dreams*, he succeeds in making an adjustment that is tolerable enough on the logical plane, but in reality not in others. The Freudian theory of 1900 already, in my view, shows cracks, lacunae that Freud was very good at making look as if things were going well when in fact they were not.

Bion approached the problem of dreams from different directions at the same time, as a psychoanalyst and before that. He was treating patients who were in borderline or frankly psychotic states, and whose dreams presented abnormal situations compared to those of Freud's patients—which were more often accompanied by associations. Very often Bion found that his psychotic patients did not associate, and he says categorically, "you can't interpret a dream if there are no associations". The reason for this is obvious in reality. The dream cannot be explained by its mental context, but this brings us to one of Bion's ideas, that the dream is effectively always part of a mental context, it is never a thing on its own, it is never something sent by the gods, for example. It is always part of the mental life of the individual, and here Bion is picking up an idea that Freud expresses *en passant* I think, in the sixth chapter of *The Interpretation of Dreams*. Freud speaks of the dream as something that is part of night-time thinking, and in the same context, he also talks about unconscious wakeful thinking. For Bion the idea of unconscious wakeful thinking was a very important idea because it allowed one to think of what James Joyce, in *Ulysses* and later in many other texts, describes as a "stream of consciousness" (Ellmann, 1959).

Bion had the idea of a stream of consciousness, not in the sense of being unconscious, but in the sense of not being aware. There are some children who give the impression of having a stream of unconsciousness, in the other sense of the term, but that need not concern us. In fact, for Bion, the dream was always part of the individual's unconscious thought! Twenty-four hours a day! If we take this as our starting point, we might say that we are always dreaming, but we are not always aware of our dreams. Parts of our dreams peep out like mountain peaks in the middle of a cloudy day, or like an iceberg in the sea: a large part is submerged and the peaks can be seen. They are dreams. Logically speaking, we should say that we can also dream during the day and perhaps sometimes even be aware of our dreams. I think this is something that actually happens in psychoanalysis, and I think it also happens during group analysis; not necessarily only in the mind of the analyst or the leader of the group, but also in the minds of the patients, above all when they have more experience of therapeutic work, usually when they are advanced in years.

Bion has theorised a concept that derives from a French term, the "reverie" or thought that wanders but doesn't think about anything in particular. He used this concept connecting with the idea of the state of mind, I would say almost a state of grace, of the nursing mother, in which the mother is not aware of everything that is happening, but allows herself to relax a lot and have a stream of thoughts part of which she is aware of and part not. Bion took this idea and imported it into psychoanalysis with a view to working without memory or desire.

In fact, this concept means allowing oneself to be in a mental state, and also in a physical state, in which one is very relaxed. For that reason it is also important to have a comfortable couch, on which one can rest and allow one's own thoughts to flow without obstructing them, without forcing them, and if possible without interrupting them. This allows the analyst to spot an unconscious thought of his own which comes quite close to the surface, because the physical state is more similar to the physical state that we have when we sleep and the state of mind is also more similar to what we have when we are sleeping. I do not know how similar because I think one would have to make a whole series of tests, as are done on sleep, on people who are preferably experts in analytic work, in a state of reverie. It would be very interesting to do the various electroencephalograms and the other studies that are done on sleeping people in this situation. However, they were not done, and for the time being, this is science fiction. What did Bion say happens when we are in a state of reverie or a state of unconscious wakeful thinking? He said that thoughts form above all, mostly in the form of what he calls α-elements, or mosaic tiles; in reality, more complex than mosaic tiles because they are already formed thoughts. Very often the α-element is a visual image, most times and for most people, but it is not always so, because sometimes it may be the sensation of a sound, the idea of a sound, the idea of a perfume, of a smell, the idea of a tactile sensation. But there are things that pass through the memories of our senses and in all likelihood, I think we can say, always based on a previous sensory experience that, however, has nothing to do with the situation at hand.

The prime example of this in literature is the one in Proust of dunking the biscuit, the little *madeleine*, in the cup of lime tea, and the flavour of the biscuit, a mixture of almonds and lime blossom, suddenly summons to the young man's memory his whole childhood, all ten volumes of it. No—but an image of this city, an image of his aunt and it's from there that the whole rest of his search for lost time emerges. It is interesting to see that from this somatic and sensory memory, which then becomes thinkable, Proust derives a whole book, a vast book, the whole of his life. This is interesting because in reality we do not stop our thought process when we reach the level of having caught an α-element, an idea, a visual image that has come to our mind. It is here that rational thinking begins, we start to judge, we say to ourselves: "Is this thing that has come to my mind now telling me something about the patient, and did it for example catch the atmosphere of the session?" And then we can perhaps compare the previous session with the one in which he told a dream up to that absolutely uninterpretable point. And if we are lucky, we can use all the various processes of the procedures of logical thought to produce an interpretation in the end. So there is a sort of continuum from unconscious thought, through the formation of the α-element to even more sophisticated levels, if you like, of more abstract thought such as a mathematization, for example of the situation in the session. Even if it's rare, it does happen.

This is part of an operation that Bion carried out on Freud's work, which would have caused a scandal if anyone had noticed; but luckily no one did because Bion wrote this piece in 1963, I think. By now Bion had been accepted as a member of the Pantheon, which was why he stopped causing a scandal, perhaps because people still do not read very much. The potentially scandalous aspect of what Bion said is that his theory of the α-function, that is, the ability to create α-elements and then use them to think, can safely stand in for the Freudian theory of the primary process and the secondary process. Freud says that what applies in the unconscious is the primary process which uses certain kinds of mental behaviour; condensation, in which two or more things are superimposed or become a single thing, as for example in a dream when the patient says: "Oh, yeah! The person who was with me in the train was a little girl, she was young, pretty and nice, but then she turned into my friend who's an arsehole." There is a superimposition between those two figures; it's a kind of condensation, in the bastard friend who is also a little girl. Interpreting the dream, we see that I'm there too, and so is my mother, and a whole series of other people who he thinks are bad towards him. Freud also talks about displacement, which is to say that something rather than being here is there and vice versa, and various other things.

In the sixth and seventh chapters of *The Interpretation of Dreams*, Freud presents a whole series of considerations about how unconscious thought works in dreams, and then goes on to say that there is a secondary process which is that of logical thought—mathematical, artistic, more thought-out, more rational. What Bion says is that in reality this difference does not exist, there is no need to hypothesise two different systems that have trouble touching one another, we need only think of this continuum as something which turns the handle that makes contact, in a sense, that this α-function, which makes the α-elements things that can be used to think consciously. The implication of this is that for Bion, in fact, the dream is simply a part of normal mental processes, and hence can be used to resolve problems; that is to say, problems are resolved during the dream.

Problems of a certain kind, because the problem that is resolved is an emotional problem, an emotion that may have arisen in the course of the day, even Bion does not swear to this. Freud is more precise: a dream must contain the day's residues. There is not always a residue of the day just past, sometimes we have days" residues from some time previously in dreams, or there are none, or they are not recognisable as such. But the α-element is always something that has its own emotional core. We are fundamentally lazy, I mean mentally, and we do not take the necessary trouble or effort to construct an α-element if it is not emotionally significant; which means that there is a core of emotion in every α-element. So what Bion says, broadly, is that dreams serve to resolve problems that have an important emotional component. If we look at this, it is not very different from what Freud said about the fact that dreams serve to manage repressed infantile sexual desires. In fact these are particular cases, a particular class of the more general condition that Bion suggests. I think that Bion was suggesting this more general thing for various motifs: one was certainly his experience with patients, but the other was his reading of the book by Poincaré, a French mathematician, written in 1908, called *Science and Method*, which is very interesting. It is a book in various volumes, one of which is *Science and Method*. In this particular volume Poincaré, who was a highly esteemed mathematician, who had read almost nothing of Freud (perhaps he hadn't read anything, not least because in 1908 there wasn't much to read), he asserts that dreams helped him to resolve mathematical problems, and gives various examples of this. Poincaré himself, who was the first to coin the phrase "the selected fact" says that when you find yourself faced with a mass of information you do not know where to go, you feel lost, confused, you have a mess in your head, eventually one of the facts you have in front of you gives all the others form and significance and makes the situation thinkable.

Bion very gladly adopted, with both hands, this idea of the "selected fact". He always quotes the same passage from Poincaré. But I think he was also influenced by the rest of the book that contains those dreams. In them Poincaré explains how he resolved these mathematical problems not through mathematics, but through visual images similar to Kekulé's famous dream about the benzene ring. Kekulé could not understand what the chemical formula for the benzene ring might be; then, one night, he dreamed about a snake eating its tail and understood that the formula had a formula like that rather than a linear one. So dreams are useful, very useful, when it comes to managing emotional problems, but also managing intellectual problems that probably have strong emotional components. I think we can see that Freud had good reasons for thinking that dreams always had something to do with sexuality, for the good reason that a high proportion of our mental activity deals with sexuality, which is—for a mammal, possibly not for amoeba, but certainly for a mammal—one of the most important things that exist, if not the most important, whether we like it or not! Consequently it was easy for Freud to limit what he saw in dreams, even taking into account his "patient pool", to use a horrible term, which consisted to a large extent of hysterics, women, particularly in 1898. So I think it is very possible that most of the dreams that these people presented were dreams with a strong sexual component.

But the interesting thing is that in *The Interpretation of Dreams* Freud, out of fairness to his patients, does not talk about his patients" dreams, he talks about his own dreams, which are often made specific; which makes us think of him as a man with a great sense of honesty and great candour. We must also remember that it is also a book which, published in six hundred copies, sold two hundred of the first print run. People didn't like it! In fact, it is an absolutely fascinating book; it is beautiful to see how Freud manages the interpretation of his own dreams and the associations and all the rest. In my view, however, the idea of the dream as a system for resolving problems is not just a Bion's or just a Freudian idea. If you think of Kurosawa's film *Dreams*, I have a sense that in this film we can see that Kurosawa had a very similar idea. If it is applied to some of the dreams of your patients or yours, or indeed ours, we may see how we tend to finish the dream at the moment when in some way we have a sense that a problem has been solved. If I am not mistaken, in the first dream in the film there is a child who has to apologise to a fox because he has seen the fox's wedding, so he has to go to the end of the rainbow. In fact this dream ends with the child suddenly in a flower-covered valley where the rainbow ends—it finishes at the moment when there is no need to go any further. I think this is an important element in the formation of dreams; we dream because we need to, and we stop when we have nothing more. Then the problem arises of why we remember certain dreams and not others. Another problem arises and I will ask your help in a moment. I think that some are remembered, and many dreams are not remembered, if it is true that we always dream when we are in the REM phase; logic tells us that we dream every night. Now some doubts have recently been expressed about the question of whether we dream in the REM phase, and I must say that I have some patients who tend to dream at a particular point during the night, just before they wake up; which does not seem compatible with the idea that it is an REM phase, not least because they are people who wake up spontaneously and not with an alarm. If they were woken by an alarm one would say, "the alarm rang while they were in the REM phase", but they are people who do not as a rule use an alarm, and I have also heard it said by someone much more expert than I am, I think it was Mancia, but perhaps in fact we dream in phases that are not REM phases. But if it is true that we dream in the REM phase, this leaves out a lot of dreams that we never remember, and my idea, not Bion's idea, is that perhaps these are dreams that manage to do their work properly, that is, they do not need to emerge into consciousness so that we can work on them later on because they have already done what they were supposed to do, they have already done their duty, we might say in a sense.

That is to say, a dream that works well is a dream that we do not remember. Just as we aren't aware of our liver, our kidneys or anything else when they are working correctly. Then we find ourselves in a situation in which there are probably lots of dreams that are part of nocturnal and diurnal unconscious thought that remains unconscious. We have some things that we call dreams that emerge during the night so that we remember them during the day and have proto-dreams, α-elements, that may emerge when we are working with our patients and which we can use in our work with our patients.

What happens when a patient dreams and brings a dream to analysis? One of the things that Bion says is that if the dream is not interpreted, the lack of interpretation is an extremely important factor in the production of acting out: that is, if the patient and the analyst together are unable to unravel that particular dream later on, the patient will be in a sense obliged to act out the dream. This is something that happens quite often, it is not a rarity; many dreams, I could not say how man, ten or twenty per cent, told at the start of a session seem to be a kind of plan for how the session will develop in the patient's mind. It is not always easy for patients, even at very advanced points in the analysis, to tolerate their own dreams, particularly if they are anxious and one can actually see the function of the analyst in being there as another mind that can verbalise something that was not—even if it was thought—verbalisable.

It takes two people for many dreams, it takes someone to dream and someone to receive and bear to thank them.

Discussion

GIAMPÀ: A book was published, in 1976, written by Julian Jaynes, psychology professor at Princeton University, entitled *The Collapse of the Bicameral Mind and the Origin of Consciousness*. He maintains that originally the right hemisphere was inhabited by "voices of the gods", while the left was dominated by conscious life. In the days of the Assyro-Babylonians, they still thought with the left hemisphere and with the right they had waking dreams (the voices of the gods). Many years ago when neurophysiologists began to study dreams, and they woke people while they were dreaming (to ask them the contents of their dreams), those people started to have dreams whose contents were filled with aggression towards the observers, so in some way the dream must also protect sleep.

PARTHENOPE: Certainly, that's right. What you're saying is very interesting. I'm reading a bit about Australia at the moment, and it seems that the Australian aborigines have this idea of a primordial time that was the dream time.

QUESTION: I would like some clarification concerning what you have said about dreams that we don't remember, are those the ones that satisfy us more than the others?

PARTHENOPE: We don't generally claim to do more work than is necessary; this is what produces swiftness, but I think the mind and the body both work like this: that is, when things are going well we are unaware of it, when we are well oiled, when everything is going "according to plan". We go to the doctor when something goes wrong. I would say that what I said is entirely theoretical but it seems logical to me because if it's true that we always dream in the REM phase why don't we remember all our dreams? We should remember much more, why do we only remember some of them? Why are not all the dreams we remember so terrifyingly unpleasant?

QUESTION: It occurred to me that these dreams are the dreams that don't manage to get to the ... [recording incomprehensible].

PARTHENOPE: This is an equally valid hypothesis, I think. It's true that sometimes we have dreams that don't ... [recording incomprehensible] well and later that same night we find ourselves waking up and then dreaming the same dream until we reach a better conclusion; this is a reasonably common experience, but since this possibility exists, I still think that there are also dreams that fulfil their task. In fact, our unconscious thought remains unconscious; I think we are aware or conscious of a very small part of our mental process. I think there are many,

many things that we do habitually, which we don't think about, gestures that are automated and yet definitely unconscious.

QUESTION: [barely comprehensible recording about dream as content]

PARTHENOPE: I don't really see it like that, because it seems to me that the dream is self-referential. Just as Gertrude Stein said, "A rose is a rose is a rose", a dream is a dream is a dream. In the sense of container and contained, there is always the idea of a certain tension between the two terms, they are not necessarily in opposition, but they can be and they can be in a very violent way, while I have the impression that the dream is something more like a monocellular animal, something that is born as container and contained. It functions as a whole, without that demarcation line that the two terms imply. I'm not comfortable with the idea of a dream in terms of container-contained; it has more to do with the schizo-paranoid-depressive process—with that oscillation—in which the various pieces are brought together not least through the choice of the selected fact to create a dream; but I am not at ease with this idea, I wouldn't like to say what Bion thought about it because I don't know, I can't think of a single instance in which he connected these two types of concept.

QUESTION: [incomprehensible on the recording, about dream as content]

PARTHENOPE: But what you're saying about narrative is very pertinent to the discussion. Because Bion says—I don't remember where, I don't think it's in *Cogitations* but in one of the clinical seminars, it is difficult to trace since I don't have the reference—that the narration of a dream in which things apparently come in sequence is sometimes what the patient imposes on material that is not in fact sequential. But the narration forms a kind of mortar that sticks together the different little pieces. Sometimes I've told a patient that I had a sense that he was relating a dream as if it were a story, when in fact it was, let's say, three different scenes relating the same thing on different levels of the mind, or with regard to different aspects of the patient's life, and hence the narrative form was in fact, in a sense, a fake one. But we tend to prefer narrative to anything else. It is true that in the twentieth century this is changing, we are getting used to things that don't necessarily tell a story, so I am a little worried, it's too much! In short, I'm a bit doubtful about the influence of "narratology" in psychoanalysis and in psychoanalytic interpretations because I have a sense that we are making a big mistake, that we are privileging, as if it were something important, something that is only a habit of our way of thinking.

PISANI: I wanted to ask you if I'd understood correctly how important the analyst's attitude toward the patient is, the attitude of reverie which is essentially one of extreme receptivity that allows you, through immediate intuitions, while you are pursuing your own thoughts, to find one which is the keystone to the meaning of the dream. I think this is Bion's new element compared to Freud, but as regards contents, the contents to do with infantile sexuality and with the primary mother–child relationship, I wonder if the Freudian contents do not remain much more important.

PARTHENOPE: Absolutely, they are extremely important, but our way of approaching those contents is very different. For example Freud, in his interpretation of dreams, leaves a lot of room for symbolism—as if symbols can be eternal, fixed, immutable, and universally valid! We don't think that way any more.

PISANI: In my view, it is a great error if there is no meeting point between the different psychoanalytic trends, and amongst other things, it contradicts the spirit of analysis. Kekulé's dream, the one about the benzene and the snake—I wonder once again how much it might have in common with Jungian archetypes, and whether these come very close to Bion's β elements or the protomental.

PARTHENOPE: I fully agree that analysts should speak to everyone; in fact in Turin there are Adlerians with whom we had a little conference last year. Together we are producing a publication on depression because we think that we all have things to say to each other, and that it's only by bringing our forces together that we can produce new ideas. I know that my father, at the end of his days, was reading Jung again, with reference to archetypes. Because he was very taken with the idea that they were a kind of thought that was familiar to him, and that sat well with his way of thinking.

QUESTION: [recording not entirely comprehensible] I wonder if in the narration with the patient its language is really referential to the extent that the narration of a discourse can be made through learned, conditioned emotions, and hence ...

PARTHENOPE: Yes, I was probably wrong to use the term referential. What I meant is that I just wanted to give the impression of a dream as an internally coherent unity; it may not be coherent with other conscious thoughts that the patient has, it may not be acceptable to the patient. I think that it is only through deep analytic work with patients that we arrive at an answer that is different for every patient. We all use what we find in front of us with which to construct our thoughts, our dreams, and it is clear that an individual with a richer emotional, intellectual or cultural life will have dreams that are probably more significant. I don't know if we can take the example of the dream of Anna Freud as a child who had indigestion from strawberries and during the night she talked in her sleep and said "strawberries, strawberries, strawberries", a very primitive dream, in many respects unformed.

QUESTION: [incomprehensible in the recording]

PARTHENOPE: Yes, but Wittgenstein didn't have patients in analysis and he knew nothing about projective identification (clinical case material omitted). So the verbal is extremely important, but it is a point of arrival in a process that is absolutely non-verbal when it begins, and which can be broadened, fed, as a process of many other things that are not verbal.

QUESTION: [incomprehensible in the recording]

PARTHENOPE: Psychoanalysts mustn't read only psychoanalysis, they mustn't only read each other, they must also read academics like the ones in Palo Alto. There's a very interesting book by Eric Berne, "What do you say after you say hello?", which describes some sessions filmed at high speed keeping the video camera on the people's faces, and in which the micro-movements of the faces are then decoded and catalogued. I think a high proportion of projective identifications are effectively conveyed by changes in physical positions and visual expressions so fast that we don't pick them up consciously, but perceive them unconsciously and react in consequence.

These are not verbal and will never be verbal; if you saw them for a hundred years, you would be able to say what they said with their face. They have communications that are extraordinary. Recently at the Centre in Turin two paediatricians came in who were part of the Piedmont campaign for breastfeeding, and they explained to us all the various hormonal changes that take place when the infant is breastfed and it was clear that a large part of a fundamental communication is physical and we tend to pretend that we are not physical.

CHAPTER NINETEEN

From formless to form (1998)*

Ps ⇌ D to public-ation

Public-ation is an essential of scientific method ... If [common sense] is inoperative for any reason, the individual in whom it is inoperative cannot publish, and unpublished work is unscientific work (Bion, 1992).

During a conference on psychoanalysis I liked the idea of having a "trans-disciplinary dialogue", given that it is in the very nature of psychoanalysis to be a "trans-disciplinary" subject: it is impossible to have a "pure" psychoanalysis because it would be like trying to establish a link between non-objects or mental objects. Bion says he reached this situation only in the case of a severely ill patient (Bion, 1967; see also Bion, 1965). Fundamentally, psychoanalysis refers to every single human activity, which passes through the mind before or when it manifests itself, or without manifesting itself, as for example premonition (Bion, 1967); something similar happens with smooth muscle tissue in cases of colitis, ulcers, and tachycardia.

---

*A slightly different version of this essay (Bion, 1973–1974) was presented at the Sociedade Brasileira de Psicanalise of Sao Paulo, III Biennial Meeting, Hotel Melia, Sao Paulo 16–17 November 1996: "Dialogo Trandisciplinar". I am indebted to the Brazilian translator, Paulo Cesar Sandler, for the many improvements made to the text and for the notes added in this version.

In this context I shall move from the general to the particular, perhaps also following a chronological line, from the experience of formlessness, which all human beings feel at a certain moment in their lives (from birth onwards), and which some instantly escape, to the technical implications for a psychoanalyst who understands the passage from "formless" to "form", to the particular clinical case in which the patient's thoughts tend to be particularly stuck.

The unconscious contents of the human mind in the course of becoming partially conscious, have been expressed in a myriad of different ways, not only through art, literature, music, through mathematics, the engineering involved in building bridges, discoveries in physics and chemistry, but also through myths and countless religions, whether private or public, and so on. Perhaps it is worth noting that in the context of the move from "formless" to form, from Ps to D, that the recent winner of the Nobel Prize for physics has linked his research into a unifying form of force, and his profound conviction of its existence, being an active believer in a monotheistic religion.[1]

So I will begin my discussion of the move from "formless" to "form" by using some examples taken from literature or certain writers, using them to highlight Bion's theories on the oscillation Ps ⇌ D which I think applies to the examples and clarifies them.

There are many descriptions in literature, or in many different kinds of religious writing, of the sensation that is felt inwardly in contact with the "formless", before being capable of producing a work of art (or a scientific communication, cf. Bion, 1967b).

It is possible to use as one of the many possible examples, to describe the deep sense of anxiety, connected with the force necessary to "win" something from the "void and formless infinite", a quotation from Milton of which Bion was very fond. Milton continued in the same vein:

> ... With other notes than to th'Orphean lyre
> I sung of Chaos and eternal Night
> Taught by the heav'nly Muse to venture down
> The dark Descent, and up to re-ascend,
> Though hard and rare ...[2]

---

[1] Abdus Salam, Nobel Prize for Physics, 1979.
[2] John Milton (1688, Book III, lines 17–21).

With the idea of descent into his own mind Milton indicates a relevant, I would say central, aspect inherent to the personal experience of creation; this is one of the main aspects of the elevation of anxiety present in every creative act, not only of those which attain a final result, but also those that we try to deny or from which we try to escape. Our own creativity is an elevation of anxiety, whether we be artists, psychoanalysts, parents, wives or whoever we prefer, and a kind of empirical test les in the fact that there are few human beings who dare to "sing" the "Chaos and eternal Night", and very few people over the centuries who have been capable of investigating this area, or who have felt a pressing need to do so. But in fact this is a problem that all psychoanalysts have to confront eventually, perhaps at a given moment in every analysis, or at various points of one or two of them, when we are becoming capable of confronting not only the intimate chaos of the patient, but also our own, *at that precise moment*, in such a way as to be capable of elaborating the painful interpretation, a flicker in the dark depths.

In psychoanalytic terms, like those used by Bion, it might be suggested, without moving very far from the beaten track, and wandering in the marshy realms of psycho-biography, that these words of Milton's can be used, out of context, as an illuminating description of the first creative phase, rich in sensations of inner chaos and something "that has not yet acquired a meaning". The key word here is "yet": the artist trusts that one day he will emerge from the extreme and painful torment, and will therefore be capable of bearing it; that is, he is capable of tolerating, and even dwelling within it, a mental area suffused by paranoid-schizoid fragmentation, taking courage from the belief that he will "overcome it". Presumably some poets are capable of accepting the contemplation of their chaotic process of artistic creation, with great serenity towards Milton and Shakespeare who, in a less tormented way, writes the following lines, which seem to belong to one of them:

> And as imagination bodies forth
> The form of things unknown, the poet's pen
> Turns them to shapes and gives to airy nothing
> A local habitation and a name.[3]

---

[3] W. Shakespeare, *Midsummer Night's Dream*, Act V, Scene I.

The following nod to Shakespeare's thought (and dreaming in thinking, or thinking in the dream):

> We are such stuff
> As dreams are made of, and our little life
> Is rounded by a sleep.[4]

may provide us with the idea that Shakespeare perceived himself as having a very lively inner mental life, populated by friendly and productive dream-thoughts that germinated almost effortlessly. This impression is particularly interesting from the psychoanalytic point of view because (returning to the first quotation) Shakespeare seems in fact to begin a step ahead of Milton with the sense that his imagination "*bodies* forth the *form* of things unknown", which is to say that it seems to be a direct—or unconscious?—passage from the sensation of already having the potentially concrete forms in mind, without the anxiety of having to battle against formlessness.

And yet, with all due respect to Shakespeare, the two juxtaposed quotations could be used as the description of a creative act that is born unconsciously in sleep and dreams, and then becomes apparently conscious only at the level of the formation of visible/α-elements, the step that follows the contemplation of the inner chaos that seems to take place in dreams or in the state of half-sleep of which the writer is never aware.

It is quite apparent from his choice of words, in the first quotation, that Shakespeare is thinking of his work as a dramatist, and this provides an illuminating perception of the way in which his characters assume shape and substance entirely through their (or his?) words.

This example taken from Shakespeare shows a more serene approach through a specific medium, that of words; perhaps the greater serenity that does not bring him every time to the burning abyss that blinded Milton, may be linked to his remarkable production. Hegel, in his *Aesthetics*, a work that is fundamentally a description of the ways in which the Spirit expresses, over the millennia, its own development through the evolution of human art, from the most material (sculpture) to the most pure and spiritual (poetry), refers to the way in which painters

---

[4] W. Shakespeare, *The Tempest*, Act IV, Scene I.

(what would be, in his mind, the art of the future), would use only *colour* to create a figure.

> The figure is composed of shadow and light ... light, in fact, as we have seen, does not exist without a relationship with something different from itself, and in particular with darkness. (...) Light so disturbed and obscured in turn penetrates and illuminates the darkness and forms the principle of colour, which is the actual material of painting (...). Form, distance, the delimitation of spaces, plenitude, in short, all the spatial relationships and all the shades of the manifestations of space are produced through colour in painting ....[5]

From our point of view, through his theory that during the evolution of the Spirit the technique (probably similar to that of Botticelli) of the use of lines to emphasise a figure is eliminated, Hegel seems to be theorising (in 1826–27) something that would become the base of "divisionism", a theory of painting that would come into being forty years later, and certainly not very far removed from many schools of modern art. In any case, he is plainly emphasising they idea that a single medium is enough to "give form" to something that was previously in the mind.

It is not enough to maintain that "painters depict life", as if that eliminated the passage through the mind of the individual, since, above all, painters have to be capable of "seeing" through what I call "the painter's eye", something that can be mentally elaborated and expressed through colour, before it is done in reality. Also pertinent to my discussion is the fact that Hegel specifies that light can be seen only through, and in contrast with, its opposite: darkness. We might suspect that this contains more than a nod to the "void and formless infinite" that the painter feels he has to illuminate, and to which he seeks to give a form.

So we find ourselves in a situation in which great poets and a great philosopher tend to be in fundamental agreement about the fact that there is something in creativity that it is truly difficult to confront, something that is in origin formless, obscure, dark and difficult to unravel, but which fights to emerge (for Hegel, this is the Spirit).

---

[5] From: Hegel's *Lectures on Aesthetics*. Translated for this edition.

The experience of confronting this darkness and inner chaos, to put it very briefly and neatly, is exactly what Bion means by the idea of *contemplation* of the paranoid-schizoid position, without memory, desire or immediate comprehension. This formulation is based on the concept of the maternal reverie, which makes the mother capable of tolerating and elaborating the infant's projective identifications, even thought his maternal function is entirely unconscious, while the analyst's reverie is more conscious and certainly more intentional. Probably the artist's reverie and that of the scientist come from that part situated between the mother's reverie and the analyst's, with the same degree of absorbed awareness. What is certain is that a kind of reverie is a necessary passage through the production of a genuine thought on any subject.

The analyst and, I think, the artist, in order to exercise their own faculty for reverie without "irritable reaching after fact and reason"[6] must summon personal characteristics like, for example, the "negative capability" which in *Attention and Interpretation* (Bion, 1970) is immediately linked by Bion to the concepts of "patience" and "security" which are, from the analyst's point of view, the non-pathological analogy of paranoid-schizoid and depressive positions.

Being able to bear remaining in the paranoid-schizoid position, however, does not represent the end of the difficulties of the human being who becomes aware of the urgency of carrying a thought forward, in any form: Bion's theory treats depression as a consequence of creativity, just as paranoid-schizoid anxiety is its precursor, and both are indeed also the inescapable components of the act of greatest artistic success. Success does not completely eliminate post-partum depression, real or metaphorical, although it can alleviate it considerably. It is important to compare Bion's long description and the detailed discussion in *Meditations* about the results (in a psychotic patient) of synthesising a selected fact, which contains within itself the synthesis of the lethal super-ego,[7] with the quotation that will follow below.

The Italian author Giovanni Verga wrote, in a letter to his writer friend Luigi Capuana, with an extraordinarily clear description, his feelings (certainly far from Bion's normal neurotic patients) almost as if he were comparing with Capuana information about something that he felt was common to both of them: the "public" communication

---

[6] John Keats, Letter to George and Thomas Keats, 21 December 1817.
[7] Cf. Bion (1992) for a complex discussion of the synthesis of the intolerable super-ego.

of a Ps ⇌ D experience would seem in fact to followed by subsequent instances of Ps ⇌ D.

Verga's words, written following the publication in February 1881 of *I Malavoglia* (The House by the Medlar Tree), which is considered his masterpiece and a milestone in Italian literature, may be used as the expression of a change of vertex, observing the situation from a different perspective: no longer observing the storms of anxiety and depression that precede the creative act, but on the contrary the depression and disappointment perceived at the end of the creative process when the poet's pen has transformed the "form of things unknown" into forms with a name and a place:

> To give you an idea of the pleasure I felt when I read your comments on my work, I will tell you of my sensations during and after the final reading and corrections. I felt as if I could have said things in a better way and in a hundred different ways, and I was worried about all those things. [In the next sentence he speaks of the difficult relationship with his editor, which was never satisfied.] I have run up against a whole host of problems trying to get away from the preoccupations of Treves, which always leave him unsatisfied and out of the picture, exactly similar the effect that provokes in us any kind of work that leaves us discontented and unsatisfied, the natural result of the shrinkage, I would say, that the work of the imagination undergoes when it loses everything vague and luminous in its concept to assume precision of colour and form.[8]

Here we may certainly observe the vivid description of the persistent depression and unease that Verga was trying to conceptualise following the completion of a work of art, comparable with the idea that Bion had of the depression accumulating after the passage from Ps to D was accomplished successfully. But one of the fascinating aspects of the description that Verga gives of himself at the end of the letter to Capuana—"I started work on *Mastro Don Gesualdo*, the plot of which I still like a great deal ..."—leaves us with the idea that he had started work on the structure of a second novella in the cycle of *I Vinti* while he was still finishing the first one. In some way this relieved his

---

[8] Quoted in G. Cattaneo, *Verga*, UTET, Turin 1963.

post-partum depression, the sense that the composition of a work so close to the first novella stimulated a perception of depression about "other writings that still had to be composed, or the concrete realisation of the selected fact represented by *I Malavoglia* led Vergo, who was going through a state of moderate depression caused by his perception of a later paranoid-schizoid phase to the formation and growth of a new selected facts, which at that moment was becoming *Mastro Don Gesualdo*.

But there are writers, and I suppose other artists, who do not consider themselves capable of accepting the challenge of verbalisation (or painting or any other artistic form), seen as a very profound aesthetic experience, as Lawrence of Arabia wrote in *The Seven Pillars of Wisdom*: "Air and light [...] The colours of cliffs and trees were so pure, so vivid, that we ached for real contact with them, and at our tethered inability to carry any of them away."[9]

These feelings of frustration and incapacity can either stimulate the author to bear them for a moment before moving on, as if he had "discovered" a selected fact, or discourage him to the extent described by Lawrence. What he says in conclusion is an admission of his perception about the existence of something that is outside of him which he cannot appropriate for himself in a way that would allow him to know his own internal objects, elaborated and finally expressed—an object of public-ation, in Bion's terminology. He could perceive the difficulty present in his sensation that beauty might not be expressed in words, but might need some medium that he does not feel competent about.

In the quotation from *Cogitations* with which I opened this paper, Bion speaks of the "public-ation" of a scientific, not an artistic work, in connection with the relationship between the individual and the group and with his need to take into consideration the "common sense" of the group itself. I think there is not too much difference, from the point of view of the relationship of the individual with the group, if the achievement of "public-ation" is perceived as artistic or scientific, from the moment when the creative journey, the passage from darkness to light, follows the same course in both cases. The perception of the existence of an internal knowledge of "nothing", sufficiently sophisticated to be expressible, implies that a long preliminary work has taken place, which has led to

---

[9] T. E. Lawrence, The Seven Pillars of Wisdom, Ch 71.

the sensation of having "an inner common sense", which amounts to saying the convergence of a significant number of paths all leading to the same result. In *Cogitations*, to illustrate this concept, Bion speaks of the sensation of fur, which must be picked up by a person's other senses, other than sight, to be capable of asserting that there is a living animal present. These other senses might for example be hearing and smell, once no sounds or smells are apparent there might in the end be a teddy bear on the floor.

But Bion also says that there is a group common sense which functions more or less following the lines of the common sense within the individual, with correlation and validation, "acceptance" or (refusal) of the new idea, depicted by the group itself as a poem or a thought. This implies that the presentation of new ideas to the group may become, or be perceived as, a hazardous enterprise. This almost always needs the "permission" of the group and must perhaps be connected with what Bion asserts in *Cogitations* about the fact that the individual feels as if he "possesses" a piece of knowledge, or an idea, etc. as if he had made it his own. It follows that the individual desire to perceive that the group is satisfied both by his offer of a new piece of knowledge, a poem, etc., and by the fact of having picked up an idea from the group, allows him not to be penalised for either.

As I said above, it seems to me that what Bion indicates as a necessity to make public someone's thoughts is equally valid when those thoughts represent an artistic rather than a scientific expression. Chiefly there is a slight difference between artistic and scientific creativity, apart from the fact that it is more common among artists to express their own experience of personal research rather than for scientists, as if they felt less obstructed by the group in which they live (perhaps because artists, rather than scientists, "birds of a feather", will follow each other, like Verga and Capuana?). Bion seems also to be aware of the difficulty in making someone's introspective work public, given the various sections of *Cogitations* (about which he had little to say) which deal with the formation and appearance of α-elements as if they were emerging from his own unconscious, evoked, for example, by a question from a friend.

These sections of *Cogitations*, made available by Francesca Bion, whose long and meticulous work on this text, in particular, as well as on others, deserves all our gratitude, were made public only (unfairly?) thirty years after Bion had published complex texts like *Elements of*

Psycho-Analysis and *Learning from Experience*. My impression is that these first theoretical works would have been notably improved by the addition of descriptive and illustrative sections, now published in *Cogitations*, and I suspect that they were part of the original aforementioned work that Bion did not want to publish. We might rightly say that the social climate, not only of the psychoanalytic group in itself, but of society taken as a whole, would certainly be hostile to the introduction of something that seemed really unscientific, such as introspection, were it not supported by similar experiences of other people (Bion's "group common sense", once again!), and that Bion wanted to keep the controversy at a level that would give his works some slight chance of survival.

Not least for this reason, the first books do not enjoy a wide public, at least until the next generation of analysts, and now, paradoxically thanks in part to his ideas, the climate has changed to such an extent that we would read them with more pleasure with greater understanding, if only we could read the author's thought processes, as they developed in his mind or, if Bion had allowed, rather than eliminating, his perception of the more personal mental processes that supported his theories, along with his clinical work. Not least at the moment of publication, this would not have been a completely impossible line to pursue, even thought Bion wanted to produce an indubitably *scientific* book, as Poincaré had shown as long ago as 1908 with his *Science and Method*, so often quoted by Bion. But the latter very much needed his message to reach his colleagues, without causing too much disturbance.

But let us abandon conjecture and return to our profession: what the analyst does in practice, during the session, once he has decided that these theories of Bion's "give a meaning" to his own analytic experiences, so he has absorbed them as an integral part of his theoretical baggage, acknowledged in the fact that he perceives it as "part of himself"? This is to say that the analyst must not constantly return to this in a corner of his mind to make certain that it is still there, or rather, understand that if he still knows, and has no need to run through the experience, familiar to any student, of that hasty rustle of mental pages that may almost be heard somewhere in his own mind, as if he were asking himself, "What did Freud, Klein, Bion—or some such—say about ..."

The answer to the question of how theories concerning the oscillation from formless to form, $Ps \leftrightarrows D$, of reverie and normal and excessive projective identification, seems to fall within the area of discussion about the analyst's capacity to "feel", "listen", "see", and "look", in short to "perceive" what is happening during the session, so as to "guess" it. At the same time, it is always important for the analyst to keep somewhere in his mind the concept of the social groups of the patient (and the analyst himself). Suppose we find ourselves in a situation in which we have absorbed Bion's teachings to the point that we can try to put them into practice, even though that might require a period of rigorous discipline before we began to feel at ease. If we decide that the patient's symptoms and his personal history, as thy are, appear predominantly psychotic or normal-neurotic, in any case we are always forced to take into consideration the characteristics which are not currently at the surface: we must listen to the *dog that didn't bark*.[10] (This is another aspect of the theory of "reversible perspective"). It means that we are preparing to face the session in a relaxed reverie, contemplating the α-elements as they emerge, evoked perhaps, from the patient or from ourselves. When a verbalisation or something similar produces an α-element, the first thing we must try to resolve is whether it is endogenous (really concerning ourselves, or whether it is the visible tip of the iceberg of an unusual and unconscious counter-transference) or whether it is something evoked by the patient, to which we have to pay greater attention, noting its appearance, because one day—not necessarily in the same session—it might link with something that the patient has said or done, or with the emergence of another personal α-element. Events can be represented with a structure similar to the original, and if they can in turn be linked to others, after a series of similar configurations they can be used as a basis for interpretation.

But what sort of mental state do we need to be in to be able to do all this, how can it be described in terms that are not simply a repetition of the word "reverie"? It is certainly a state that depends on the analyst's inner capacity for "common sense". The analyst's ability to use his own common sense and work in this way depends in a sense on his availability to entrust himself to his unconscious elaboration of the material that comes from the senses. This is not always easy if he has, for example, an altered sense of smell because he has a cold or a particular atrophy of one sense or another.

Above I spoke of the "painter's eye", and when I was a child I remember thinking that some of my father's colleagues had a "psychoanalyst's eye", although what I meant by the phrase does not coincide with what I know now. However, it had something to do with

---

[10] A. Conan Doyle, the Sherlock Holmes story "Silver Blaze".

the perception of a look that was benevolent, not judgemental, but penetrating. As I grew up I realised that I had come across something real and significant, inherent to the analyst's way of "sitting behind his own eyes", without being immediately reactive. Now I know that, in spite of the apparent "absence of mind", he is really capable of picking up even the smallest change in appearance, the position assumed on the couch, the way of walking, and so on, so that analytic observation, even if effected in a semi-relaxed unconscious way, is almost a task in itself.

This must be linked to the use of the "psychoanalyst's ear", as a truly particular listening technique, with a range that is broader but also refined. An analyst, in my view, must "listen polyphonically", even if there is a patient in the room with him who seems particularly "monotonous". We must broaden our own predisposition to pick up all kinds of sound, including the ones which, in a well-mannered society, a lady or a gentleman could avoid noticing and listening too, such as various instances of flatulence, sobbing, and so on. But we also need to pay attention to extracts from other notes that might be present in the monotonous drone—even if they are not as pleasing as Tartini's "third sound", the harmonic that musicians listen to in order to tune their own instruments. When a patient says something that comes from his own mind, far from the work being done during the session, it reaches the ear like a dissonant chord. The daily complaints about the husband, the wife, the daughter the son and life in general have another undertone that can alert the analyst to the fact that the inner emotional situation has changed even though the patient is doing everything to keep the analyst from noticing this change. There is also the pressing need to be able to listen to what one would prefer not to hear: stories of violence, pain, shame, despair. The analyst must sometimes make a conscious effort not to "turn off" his receptive apparatus, but he must listen serenely to the pain-filled words that are so hard to bear; then he must wonder what else the patient is communicating to him, and hope for the presence of a visual or olfactory clue that might help him.

Little has been written about the use that the analyst makes of the sense of smell, perhaps because there is a sort of embarrassment about what is noticed as an "uncivil" sense, but also perhaps because that sense seems to have atrophied over the years, and is not strong in many of us. At this point, a problem arises: what exactly does "atrophied" mean? If the problem is connected to the olfactory nerve itself, perhaps we cannot add anything else, but if it concerns the ability to be able to pick up molecular messages carried on the air, perhaps a kind of psychological atrophy is implied, one which is worthy of investigation. After all, human beings are influenced by pheromones, without "being able" to perceive them: certainly, we react physically to a gas leak, feeling ill or fainting, even though we are not aware of its smell. Might this imply that we can be struck by molecular messages coming from the patient without being able to identify them precisely? The end of Patrick Susskind's novel *Perfume* implies a possible trail to follow. What I am trying to suggest is that, even if we make little use of touch and even less of taste in our analytic work, we must accept that we are non-selective receivers of information supplied by the other three senses, in so far as we can hear when no sound has been emitted, to see even if the patient has not modified his position, to inhale even when we are aware that the wind is carrying something that we cannot consciously pick up: for this reason, the practice of reverie leads to the condition in which we are not intensely concentrated on anything in particular. After all, how can we think that projective identification, or perhaps some aspects of projections, are channelled from one person to another, even if they are not explicitly verbalised? It seems to me to be a valid reason to explore the hypotheses that may exist of micro-communications based on a slight change in appearance, of position, of tone and volume of voice, of odour emitted, all used as means to channel projective identifications, all unconscious, and unconsciously picked up by other people's antennae. Perhaps it would be opportune to examine this topic in greater depth.

But how is it possible to connect this technical, not to say hypothetical, discussion about the mental state of the analyst with the first part of my paper? And how is it possible to obtain from this theoretical thought a brief clinical vignette, with which I hope to conclude?

My brief discussion of writers and poets was intended to underline how the ability to contemplate the paranoid-schizoid state of mind (looking towards the abyss and being capable of staying there briefly, without too many harmful effects, in spite of fear and anxiety for our mental state—Bion speaks of it as of a hazardous undertaking) and as the consequences of the Ps ⇌ D oscillations both depend on our ability to maintain a state of reveries. But if this observational activity—in which all the senses are harmonised to check the information—must generate useful results and the production of selected facts, the "α-elements" which can be used for creative thought, must successively be made public. In the case of an artist or a scientist this happens when he shows his work to at least one other person, while in the case of the analyst, it happens primarily by giving the patient a significant interpretation, and secondly, discussing his own work with colleagues who are not too prejudiced towards him. This last aspect of the publication means reviewing a number of times the whole series of encounters (as if transcribing a case, or preparing an essay) not once, but various times, even though perhaps a small part of the work has already been carried out with the patient in question.[11]

By way of conclusion, let us briefly re-examine the journey that we have taken from the oscillation Ps ⇌ D to public-ation and "making public". The steps following on from the public-ation of something that is presented primarily in the form of Chaos, without form, and of the dark inner abyss, include the contemplation by the patient of paranoid-schizoid areas of someone's mind, the appearance of a selected fact > "α-element", the ability to make use of it, even if it is equally likely that it is not entirely conscious, the look upon the "post-partum depression" and emergence from it. This inner process must be re-elaborated, in a more conscious way, through a logic more Aristotelian than symmetrical (Matte Blanco, 1976), and then presented in public. This last passage implies, as demonstrated by the brief story of Professor V., that excessive projective identifications must be eliminated from more realistic ones, along with fantasies of becoming an open book for one's own interlocutor. The teacher, orator, artist, scientist, analyst or whoever else, must bring order to his expectations about how he will be received, in such a way as to face the group in a reasonably realistic state of mind.

Thus we can see how creative processes and the production of thoughts, which are fundamentally the same thing, improve relations with others. If the first passages (Ps ⇌ D) can be interpreted as essentially private matters for the individual himself, they all have their origin, in every case, in his childhood, within the exchange of excessive and realistic projective identifications, between him and the person who took care of them. This more private passage becomes in sequence a question chiefly concerning the relationship between the individual and his inner group, his inner "common sense", and subsequently the relationship with his external group, which will accept, or not, through the "common sense" of the group, what the individual has said, done or produced; including psychoanalytic essays!

---

[11] We have omitted, for reasons of privacy, a brief clinical insert, which is not in our opinion indispensable for the understanding of the paper as a whole (Ed.).

CHAPTER TWENTY

Laying low and saying (almost) nothing (1998)

> The Tar-baby said nothing, and Brer Fox, he lay low.
> Don't jump to conclusions, Griselda.

Perhaps I ought to start with a very brief introductory note on my use of language: one of my friends noticed, quite a few years ago, that when speaking in public about W. R. Bion I tend to oscillate (rather disconcertingly, I gather) between referring to him as "Bion" and referring to him as "my father". At the time we rather laughed it off and went on to more serious matters. But I have done a little thinking about it since then, and have come to the conclusion that this is not so much an indication of a serious, pathological, "split" as a natural outcrop from whichever field of thought it is that I am engaged on at the time. By this I mean that if I am thinking of him as I remember him personally—and when I was a child, he was just "Daddy", and in fact was not yet a psychoanalyst anyway—I tend to use a more familiar term, but if I am thinking about his theoretical or clinical writings, then I tend to refer to him as "Bion", which seems to me to be normal in a scientific paper. Since today I *do* intend to speak about his theoretical work, but approaching it via memories from a long time ago, I will no doubt move from one usage to another. You have been warned!

The two quotations that I have chosen as a starting point come from children's books that my father either read to me as a rather small child, or gave to me when I was a little older. They were the first things that came into my mind while I was rather idly wondering whether there might be traces in his private, personal life, which would show some sort of coherence with his later writing; things which perhaps illuminate his character, a certain type of philosophical attitude towards life in general, which could have merged in with his later rigorous thinking. In Italian we say "*Il buon giorno si vede dal mattino*" (Good beginnings bode well). I am not really talking about extra-analytical sources for his thinking, which was in any case most firmly rooted in Freud, because at the moment I am more interested in trying to capture something of the over-all flavour of his personality as it emerges from a glance at some of his general reading. Reading was a very important part of our family life, as my father read to us children in the evenings at weekends, as Francesca did during the week, and we were almost all rather precocious and dedicated readers, having complete access to the "library" (which really meant books in cases all over the house). Nemesis has in any case caught up with the only one of us who could have been said to be a slightly less enthusiastic reader (in the sense that when called or searched for she wasn't absolutely *necessarily* reading, but sometimes did other things too) since my sister Nicola now works as an editor at Oxford University Press.

So, after this digression, back to work! As to Bion's writings that I have in mind as the base camp, so to say, for my brief paper today, "Notes on memory and desire" (1967) as well as some later comments on the same ideas in *Cogitations*, are the main ones—though in fact you can find references to his clinical technique, as well as the theorisation on this subject, scattered through many of the clinical seminars held in different countries. There is a very great difference between the style of "Notes on memory and desire" and the later seminars, but, although the latter are much more discursive, they are only apparently less rigorous, and the main ideas remain the same. These can be briefly summarised: the analyst should rid his mind (perhaps, for the sake of political correctness, I ought to say "its mind", but this seems to be going rather too far with analytical neutrality) of extraneous, permeating thoughts and emotional states. He should actively try to get rid of conscious searching for memories of the patient such as "what on earth was the dream that this person told me in the last session, and to which he is now referring without giving me any clue about the contents?" as he should also rid himself of desires, of whatever sort, such as wishing for the end of the session or week, or hoping that the patient will get cured, or even *desiring to understand*.

I will come back to these points later.

The first quotation comes from one of the Uncle Remus stories (Pritchard, 1925), The Wonderful Tar-Baby Story, which is part of the saga of the unending struggle between Brer Rabbit and Brer Fox, who was his sworn enemy. In this particular story, Brer Fox makes a sort of statue of tar mixed with turpentine and sets it in the road along which the rabbit will be passing. The tar-baby, of course, does not reply to Brer Rabbit's polite greeting—so Brer rabbit, punches, kicks, and butts it with his head, to teach it a lesson in good manners, getting completely stuck in it, all four paws and his head too, while Brer Fox lies low, and the tar-baby goes on saying nothing. As a matter of fact, the two lively characters in the story must also have "run" together somewhat in my mind, as I remember my father misquoting it as "Brer Fox, he lay low and he said … Nothing". Naturally, I may be wrong about its being his misquotation (although he frequently did so, just slightly, adopting and adapting phrases to his own need) and it may simply be mine. The pertinent aspect of this, in any case, is that I now tend to think of Bion as an analyst partaking a little of the characteristics of all three figures, the fox, the tar-baby, and the rabbit. (This might be said to be a sub-set of his internal group!)

For example, his comments on α-elements in *Cogitations* make it quite clear that there really were moments when he felt "stuck", like the rabbit, and that he was only able to get clear of the morass by thinking very deeply about his own emotional reactions to the atmosphere in the consulting room. (Not to be confused with the idea of using one's countertransference, which he liquidates rather scathingly in *Bion in New York and São Paulo, 1977–1978*.) Furthermore, one gets the impression from several people who had been in analysis with him that he must, at times, have seemed rather like the tar-baby, too, saying almost nothing, or perhaps nothing at all. And as for the fox? Well, from my childhood memories of him, I can imagine my father "laying back" in the rocking-chair in his consulting room and just waiting to see and to feel his way through what was about to happen—although not with the malicious intentions of the story-tale fox.

The complex concept of working without memory or desire links up, in fact, with the idea of trying to purify your mind, letting what is inessential sediment somewhere and drain away, so that you could have the "laying low" without the sneaky or violent element ... although it is interesting to note that analysands with paranoid streaks frequently comment that they cannot stand the analyst's silence precisely because it does feel malicious and threatening to them, as though they were being spied on with evil intent. Another aspect of laying low can be seen in the firm decision not to fall in with the analysand's unconscious ploy of seducing the analyst away from the present moment, for example, as I said earlier, by mentioning a previous dream while being very careful not to give him even the slightest of hints about its contents. This can be dealt with on the spot, to my mind, by interpreting—or simply mentioning—the fact that the analysand seems to be desirous of distracting attention from what is going on now. One may also be fortunate enough to be able to detect the dominant emotion which is suffusing this way of speaking, as the analysand may have already given hints through other phrases, or his behaviour, as to which emotion is the principal one. It is sometimes possible to tell whether he is feeling envious of the analyst, or reluctant to "come into" the session at all—he might have been late—or whether he is just trying out the analyst's capacity to remember him and not get him muddled with someone else. This latter attitude, then, might come either from doubts lying behind feelings of omnipotence (You couldn't possibly forget *me*!—or could you?) or else from despair at ever being able to make any sort of impact on anyone. This possibility was brought home to me by a very depressed patient who was absolutely amazed on discovering that I actually did remember things that had been said to me even years back, without any muddling with other patients. From the patient's point of view, it was a question of discovering in my mind a vital container, whereas from mine, it was α-elements again, working as selected facts to illuminate a whole series of events in such a way that they make "new sense".

The other points that arise in connection with "laying low" include simply sitting and waiting, with the negative capability involved in this stance, not striving after answers of any sort. It is interesting that Bion mentions understanding as being one of the things which one must not actively seek, as well as the "cure" of the patient. To his mind, *any* extraneous desire was damaging to the analyst's capacity to concentrate on the present situation, but I would add that these two in particular are perhaps worse than others, since they open the flood-gates of the analyst's own anxiety about his ability, and anxiety is not a useful companion in the consulting room, unless it arises from the reception of conscious or unconscious communications from the patient.

The second quotation comes from a book (Molesworth, 1877) about a little girl staying in a strange house full of all sorts of curiosities, through which she is accompanied on nocturnal explorations by the cuckoo from the cuckoo-clock, who tries to persuade her to stop making logical (or illogical) leaps in her reasoning processes. This, I feel, is a particularly strange quotation to have come into my mind in this context, and I might have thrown it out as not being relevant, were it not for the fact that intuition in a session (and not only the analyst's) has to be backed up by hard rational thinking. So though one's intuitive flash—the spontaneous presentation to one's conscious mind of an α-element—may seem perfectly correct, it is not enough, on its own, to serve as an interpretation, although it will probably merge with other things, including a private (to the analyst) process of reasoning about the other parts of the mosaic of fragments that this α-element "makes sense of", to form the *base* for an interpretation.

The other side to this quotation is naturally Griselda's curiosity about the enticing things in the house, which the cuckoo tried to keep "open" and "alive" by not coming to precipitous conclusions, encouraging the little girl to go on observing. This seems to me to tie up with Bion's ideas on the stifling of curiosity by premature answers, as in the quotation from Maurice Blanchard which was "bestowed" on him by André Green, and as exemplified by the second column of the grid. This particular column sometimes seems rather less useful as an idea against which to check your own interpretations as well as the analysand's remarks, but in fact the attacks on the furthering of the thinking-feeling process are a fundamental aspect of analytical exchange, and the possibility of their subtle occurrence should always be kept in mind. In my early days as an analyst, I coined the phrase (in my own private language for thinking about my work in): "stop it" interpretations. This referred to those which made the patient suddenly "dry up", in an unpleasant fashion as though they had been shamed or bullied into silence, and I think that they had a lot to do with my own unconscious counter-transference. Analytical practice and attempts at putting into practice the discipline advocated by Bion "without memory and desire" have greatly improved this slight tendency on my part, which was certainly an attack on both the patient's and my own curiosity.

Speaking of curiosity, it is noticeable how Bion's treatment of the subject has moved slightly from the Freudian-Kleinian base of almost exclusive concentration on the Oedipal contents to a greater interest in the mechanisms and uses of curiosity (and misuses) of curiosity itself.

In any case, I feel that these two quotations, together with the backgrounds of the stories from which they come, can give us an inkling about Bion's general philosophical attitude to life—not so much his real philosophical leanings, which were neo-Kantian as much as anything else, but in the sense of his way of taking things. This attitude certainly included a capacity for "not jumping to conclusions" which he developed more as he grew older, even reaching the point of eliminating conclusions altogether, as towards the end of his life he spoke of interpretations themselves as being not only transient—staging posts on the way somewhere else—but also as being in a certain sense "too late". By the time the analyst reaches the point of formulating an interpretation, which indicates the conclusion of a process of thought which has come about between analyst and analysand, he is talking about a state which is *already past*; the analytical couple has already moved on. So no interpretation can be a conclusion, and I may add that my father didn't think much of death as indicating one, either—it was merely an end. *His* idea of a suitable epitaph for his tomb was "Snuffed out", but none of us in the family quite felt that we agreed.

In fact, the very lively and numerous attendance at this Conference itself seems certainly to belie his having been "snuffed out", although for some years after his death, about ten, I would say, very little notice was taken of his work at all.

Conclusions

Bion's writings on technique are aimed at helping analysts to be free of preconceptions and so freer to think. Although in various ways all his discussions of this topic suggest that we discipline ourselves to be patient, and not leap to conclusions, not to stifle our imagination and our curiosity. The general idea is expressed in papers which sometimes strike the reader as unpleasantly prescriptive and even frustrating, but it is simply that we should try to provide ourselves with the best possible conditions for thinking, because as analysts and analysands, run-of-the-mill human beings, we realise that these conditions constitute a fundamental need. This is one of the fundamental, rigorous convictions of Bion's thought, and in his way of being, but it is still true that he also used it to encourage his children (in a very mild way) to familiarise themselves with these concepts from a tender age.

REFERENCES

Alexander, R. (1981). On the analyst's "sleep" during the psychoanalytic session. In: J. Grotstein (Ed.), *Do I Dare Disturb the Universe?* Beverly Hills, CA: Caesura.

Aristotle. *The Nicomachean Ethics.* J. A. K. Thompson (Trans). Harmondsworth: Penguin, 2004.

Asimov, I. (1982). *Foundation's Edge.* New York, NY: Doubleday.

Astor, J. (2005, p. 74). *The Journal of the British Association of Psychotherapists,* Volume 43, Issue 1, pages 74–87, January 2005.

Bion, W. R. (1940). The "war of nerves". In: Mawson, C. (Ed.), *The Complete Works of W. R. Bion. Volume IV.* London: Karnac, 2014.

Bion, W. R. (1948). Psychiatry at a time of crisis. Cogitations. In: Mawson, C. (Ed.), *The Complete Works of W. R. Bion. Volume XI.* London: Karnac, 2014.

Bion, W. R. (1959). Attacks on linking. Second thoughts: selected papers on psycho-analysis. In: Mawson, C. (Ed.), *The Complete Works of W. R. Bion. Volume VI.* London: Karnac, 2014.

Bion, W. R. (1961). Experiences in groups and other papers. In: Mawson, C. (Ed.), *The Complete Works of W. R. Bion. Volume IV.* London: Karnac, 2014.

Bion, W. R. (1962a). A theory of thinking. Second thoughts: selected papers on psycho-analysis. In: Mawson, C. (Ed.), *The Complete Works of W. R. Bion. Volume VI.* London: Karnac, 2014.

Bion, W. R. (1962b). Learning from experience. In: C. Mawson (Ed.), *The Complete Works of W. R. Bion. Volume IV*. London: Karnac, 2014.
Bion, W. R. (1963). Elements of Psycho-Analysis. In: Mawson, C. (Ed.), *The Complete Works of W. R. Bion. Volume V*. London: Karnac, 2014.
Bion, W. R. (1965). Transformations: change from learning to growth. In: Mawson, C. (Ed.), *The Complete Works of W. R. Bion. Volume V*. London: Karnac, 2014.
Bion, W. R. (1966). Book reviews. In: Mawson, C. (Ed.), *The Complete Works of W. R. Bion. Volume VI*. London: Karnac, 2014.
Bion, W. R. (1967). Notes on memory and desire. Cogitations. In: Mawson, C. (Ed.), *The Complete Works of W. R. Bion. Volume XI*. London: Karnac, 2014.
Bion, W. R. (1970). Attention and interpretation: a scientific approach to insight in psycho-analysis and groups. In: Mawson, C. (Ed.), *The Complete Works of W. R. Bion. Volume VI*. London: Karnac, 2014.
Bion, W. R. (1973–1974). Brazilian lectures. In: Mawson, C. (Ed.), *The Complete Works of W. R. Bion. Volume VII*. London: Karnac, 2014.
Bion, W. R. (1975–1979). A memoir of the future. In: Mawson, C. (Ed.), *The Complete Works of W. R. Bion. Volumes XII–XIV*. London: Karnac, 2014.
Bion, W. R. (1976). Emotional turbulence. In: Mawson, C. (Ed.), *The Complete Works of W. R. Bion. Volume X*. London: Karnac, 2014.
Bion, W. R. (1977). Two papers: The grid (1971) and Caesura (1975). In: Mawson, C. (Ed.), *The Complete Works of W. R. Bion. Volume X*. London: Karnac, 2014.
Bion, W. R. (1977–1978). Bion in New York and São Paulo. In: Mawson, C. (Ed.), *The Complete Works of W. R. Bion. Volume VIII*. London: Karnac, 2014.
Bion, W. R. (1978). Clinical seminars. In: Mawson, C. (Ed.), *The Complete Works of W. R. Bion. Volume VIII*. London: Karnac, 2014.
Bion, W. R. (1994). Cogitations. In: Mawson, C. (Ed.), *The Complete Works of W. R. Bion. Volume XI*. London: Karnac, 2014.
Bott Spillius, E. (1988). *Melanie Klein Today*. London: Routledge.
Bromberg, P. M. (1998–2001). *Standing in the Spaces: Essays on Clinical Process, Trauma and Dissociation*. New York, NY: Analytic Press.
Cattaneo, G. (1963). *Giovanni Verga*. Turin: U.T.E.T.
Corrao, F. (1977). Per una topologia analitica. *Rivista di Psicoanalisi, XXIII*, 1.
Cremerius, J. (1985). *Il Mestiere dell'Analista*. Turin: Boringhieri.
De Masi, F. (Ed.) (1989). *L'emozione e la Regola. I Gruppi Creative in Europa Dal 1850 al 1950*. Laterza: Bari.
Dearmer, P. (Ed.) (1986). *Songs of Praise*. Oxford: Oxford University Press.
Ellmann, R. (1959). *James Joyce*. Oxford: Oxford University Press.
Ferrier, J. F. (1854). *Institutes of Metaphysics*. Edinburgh: Blackwoods.

Ferro, A. (1992). *La Tecnica nella Psicoanalisi Infantile*. Milan: Raffaello Cortina.
Ferro, A. (2004). *Seeds of Illness, Seeds of Recovery*. London: Routledge, p. 125.
Fornari, R. (1981). Da Freud a Bion. *Rivista di Psicoanalisi, XXVII*, 3: 4.
Freud, S. (1900a). *The Interpretation of Dreams*. S. E., 4–5. London: Hogarth.
Freud, S. (1908d). "Civilised" sexual morality and modern nervous illness. S. E., 9: 179. London: Hogarth.
Freud, S. (1912e). Recommendations to physicians practising psychoanalysis. S. E., 12: 111. London: Hogarth.
Freud, S. (1915c). Instincts and their vicissitudes. S. E., 14, London: Hogarth.
Freud, S. (1921c). *Group Psychology and the Analysis of the Ego*. S. E., 18: 69. London: Hogarth.
Freud, S. (1927c). *The Future of an Illusion*. S. E., 21: 3. London: Hogarth.
Freud, S. (1927–1939). *The letters of Sigmund Freud and Arnold Zweig*. New York, NY: Harcourt, 1971.
Freud, S. (1930a). *Civilisation and its Discontents*. S. E., 21: 59. London: Hogarth.
Freud, S. (1933a). *New Introductory Lectures on Psycho-Analysis*. S. E., 22: 3. London: Hogarth.
Freud, S. (1933b). *Why War?* S. E., 22: 197. London: Hogarth.
Freud, S. (1937c). Analysis terminable and interminable. S. E., 23: 211. London: Hogarth.
Freud, S. (1939a). *Moses and Monotheism*. S. E., 23: 3. London: Hogarth.
Hume, D. (1739). *A Treatise on Human Nature*. Harmondsworth: Penguin, 1985.
Homer. The Iliad. E. V. Rieu (Trans). Harmondsworth: Penguin, 2003.
Isnenghi, M. (1989). *Le Guerre degli Italiani*. Milan: Mondadori.
Jacoby, R. (1983). *The Repression of Psychoanalysis. Otto Fenichel and the Freudians*. Chicago: University Of Chicago Press.
Jones, E. (1953–1957). *Sigmund Freud: Life and Work. Volumes 1–3*. London: Hogarth.
Kant, I. (1781). *Critique Of Pure Reason*. Cambridge: Cambridge University Press, 1999.
Laplanche, J., & Pontalis, J. -B. (1967). *The Language of Psychoanalysis*. London: Karnac, 1988.
Lonsdale, R. (Ed.) (1989). *Eighteenth Century Women Poets*. Oxford: Clarendon.
Matte Blanco, I. (1980). *The Unconscious as Infinite Sets: An Essay in Bi-logic*. London: Karnac.
Meltzer, D. (1970). Positive and negative forms. In: *Sincerity and Other Works: The Collected Papers of Donald Meltzer*. London: Karnac, 1994.
Meltzer, D. (1978). *The Kleinian Development*. London: Karnac, 2008.

Molesworth, M. L. (1877). *The Cuckoo Clock*. North Hollywood, CA: Aegypan, 2008.
Money-Kyrle, R. (1931). The remote consequences of psychoanalysis on individual, social and instinctive behaviour. In: *The Collected Papers of Roger Money-Kyrle*. London: Clunie, 1978.
Nissim Momigliano, L. (1981). Memory and desire. *Rivista di Psicoanalisi, XXVII*: 546–557.
Plato. The Republic. D. Lee (Trans). Harmondsworth: Penguin, 2007.
Poincaré, H. (1902). *Science and Hypothesis*. London: Walter Scott, 1905.
Popp, W. (1988). Le Attività della Scuola per la Pace. In: *Educazione e Cultura della Pace*. Rome: Riuniti.
Pritchard, F. H. (1925). *Fifty Stories from Uncle Remus*. London: Harrap, 1958.
Proust, M. (1954). *Du Côté de Chez Swann*. Paris: Gallimard.
Reeves, M., & Gould, W. (1987). *Joachim of Fiore and the Myth of the Eternal Evangel in the Nineteenth Century*. Oxford: Clarendon.
Rousseau, J. -J. *The Social Contract*. Q. Hoare (Trans). Harmondsworth: Penguin, 2012.
Thucydides. *The Peloponnesian War*. R. Warner (Trans). Harmondsworth: Penguin, 2000.
Turquet, P. (1975). Threats to identity in the large group. In: L. Kreeger (Ed.), *The Large Group*. London: Karnac.
Winnicott, D. (1953). Transitional objects and transitional phenomena. *International Journal of Psychoanalysis, 34*: 89–97.

FURTHER READING

Bettelheim, B. (1983). *Freud and Man's Soul*. New York, NY: Knopf.
Bion, W. R. (1946). The leaderless group project. In: Mawson, C. (Ed.) *The Complete Works of W. R. Bion. Volume IV*. London: Karnac, 2014.
Bion, W. R. (1954). Notes on the theory of schizophrenia. Second thoughts: selected papers on psycho-analysis. In: Mawson, C. (Ed.), *The Complete Works of W. R. Bion. Volume VI*. London: Karnac, 2014.
Bion, W. R. (1966). Catastrophic change. In: Mawson, C. (Ed.), *The Complete Works of W. R. Bion. Volume VI*. London: Karnac, 2014.
Bion, W. R. (1967). The development of schizophrenic thought. Second thoughts: selected papers on psycho-analysis. In: Mawson, C. (Ed.), *The Complete Works of W. R. Bion. Volume VI*. London: Karnac, 2014.
Bion, W. R. (1976). Four discussions. In: Mawson, C. (Ed.), *The Complete Works of W. R. Bion. Volume X*. London: Karnac, 2014.
Bion, W. R. (1977). The Italian seminars. In: Mawson, C. (Ed.), *The Complete Works of W. R. Bion. Volume IX*. London: Karnac, 2014.
Bion, W. R. (1982). The long weekend: 1897–1919 (part of a life). In: Mawson, C. (Ed.), *The Complete Works of W. R. Bion. Volume I*. London: Karnac, 2014.
Bion, W. R. (1985). All my sins remembered: another part of a life. The other side of genius: family letters. In: Mawson, C. (Ed.), *The Complete Works of W. R. Bion. Volume II*. London: Karnac, 2014.

Freud, S. (1887a). Review of Averbeck's "Die Akute Neurasthenie". *S. E.*, 1: 35. London: Hogarth.
Freud, S. (1889a). Review of August Forel's "Hypnotism". *S. E.*, 1: 91. London: Hogarth.
Freud, S. (1895d). *Studies on Hysteria*. *S. E.*, 2. London: Hogarth.
Freud, S. (1905). *Fragment of an analysis of a case of hysteria*. *S. E.*, 7: 1. London: Hogarth.
Freud, S. (1910). The future prospects of psycho-analytic therapy. *S. E.*, 11: 141. London: Hogarth.
Freud, S. (1915b). Thoughts for the times on war and death. *S. E.*, 14: 275. London: Hogarth.
Freud, S. (1923a). Two encyclopaedia articles. *S. E.*, 18: 235. London: Hogarth.
Freud, S. (1923b). *The Ego and the Id*. *S. E.*, 19: 3. London: Hogarth.
Freud, S. (1926d). *Inhibitions, Symptoms and Anxiety*. *S. E.*, 20: 77. London: Hogarth.
Freud, S. (1937d). Constructions in analysis. *S. E.*, 23: 257. London: Hogarth.
Freud, S. (1941f). Findings, ideas, problems. *S. E.*, 23: 299. London: Hogarth.
Freud, S. (1950a). A project for a scientific psychology. *S. E.*, 1: 175. London: Hogarth.
Galtung, J. (1996). *Peace by Peaceful Means: Peace and conflict, Development and civilization*. Oslo. PRIO.
Klein, M. (1929). Infantile anxiety situations reflected in a work of art and in the creative impulse. In: *Love, Guilt and Reparation and other works 1921–1945*. London: Vintage, 1998.
Klein, M. (1931). A contribution to the theory of intellectual inhibition. In: *Love, Guilt and Reparation and other works 1921–1945*. London: Vintage, 1998.
Klein, M. (1946). Notes on some schizoid mechanisms. In: *Envy and Gratitude and other works 1946–1963*. London: Vintage, 1997.
Klein, M. (1952). Some theoretical conclusions regarding the emotional life of the infant. In: *Envy and Gratitude and other works 1946–1963*. London: Vintage, 1997.
Klein, M. (1955). On identification. In: *Envy and Gratitude and other works 1946–1963*. London: Vintage, 1997.
Mandelbrot, B. B. (1977). *Fractals: Form, Chance and Dimension*. London: Freeman.
McPhee, J. (1985). *La Place de la Concorde Suisse*. London: Faber.
Meotti, A. (1981). A Bionian Hypothesis on the Origin of Thought. Rivista Psicoanal., 27:425–435.
Milner, M. (1950). *Disegno e Creatività*. Florence: La Nuova Italia, 1968.
Resnik, S. (1995). *Mental Space*. London: Karnac.

Schonberg, H. C. (1970). *The Lives of the Great Composers*. New York: Norton.
Steinberg, S. H. (1967). *Historical Tables 58 BC–AD 1965*. London: Macmillan.
Trist, E. (1985). Working with Bion in the 1940s: the group decade. In: M. Pines (Ed.), *Bion and Group Psychotherapy*. London: Routledge, 1992.
Tustin, F. (1981). *Autistic States in Children*. London: Routledge.
Tustin, F. (1986). *Autistic Barriers in Neurotic Patients*. London: Karnac.

INDEX

"acceptance" 233
α-element 18, 109–111, 114–116, 122, 124–125, 129–130, 140, 144, 153–154, 157, 207, 214, 218, 235, 238
    "evolution" of 203
α-function 109, 129, 144, 152–153, 156
    construction of thoughts 114–115
    dream-work-α 122–123
    of analyst 115–116
    relation with α-elements 115, 129–130
    relationship with oblivion/sleep 109, 113–114, 124
    structure and mental functioning 109, 113–116
aggressiveness 23, 58
Alexander, R. 206
Analysis Terminable and Interminable 13
analyst
    fee 94
    Freud's rule for 119
    α-function of 115–116
analytic objects 162
analytic work, visualisation of 86–90
anamnesis 132
Anschluss 40, 93
anxiety 144, 161–162
    task as defence against 29–37
Aristotle 13, 23
Asimov, I. 139
assunto di base 98
aspect of interdependency 206
Astor, J. 77
Attacks on Linking 159
Attention 99–100
Attention and Interpretation 7, 91, 157, 182, 185–186, 198–199, 207–208, 230

Balint group 32
Barbusse, H. 40
basic assumption group 65–66
basic assumptions 51, 56, 59, 65, 155
    and projective identification 97–99
    disturbance caused by 53
    of dependence 67, 92
    own 52
Battle Song: Julia Ward Howe 60
beautiful interpretation 78
β-elements 18–19, 108, 122, 195, 204
bellicosity
    and symbolic wars 66
    attitude of modern states towards 50
    definition of 50
    education for peace and 67–71
    group, characteristics of 54–56
    group, conscious manipulations of 65–67
    unconscious systems for control of 57–65
    visible traces in society 56–57
Bion, W. R. 1–7, 12, 33, 91, 93–95, 97, 109, 161, 163–164, 197–198, 200–202, 204, 206, 225, 230, 239
    advice to eliminate Memory and Desire 4
    after First World War 5
    aspects of writing 1–3
    began course of analysis with Rickman 5–6
    "Intra-group tensions in therapy," 1943 6–7
    move to California in 1968 6
    mystic 3
    "The Grid," 1971 7
    theories of mental functioning 204
    Training Committee by 6
    undertake course of psychotherapy with Hadfield at Tavistock 5
Bion's Grid, model of 75
"blinding ourselves" 211
Bornstein, B. 41
Bott Spillius, E. 197, 200
British Psychoanalytical Society 182

caesura 159–165
    analytic objects and 162
    and anxiety 161–162
    and connection of anxiety with reversible perspective 163
    definition of 161
    myriad of 160
    omnipotence and 163–164
    polyphonic listening and 160
    reversible perspective and links 159
    in synthesis 164–165
    types of 160
Cattaneo, G. 231
Civilisation and its Discontents 41, 43
"*Civilised*" *Sexual Morality and Modern Nervous Illness* 41
clinical psychoanalysis 197
Cogitations 94, 96, 98, 100, 107, 113, 120–122, 136–137, 143, 155–156, 163, 171–172, 180, 182, 185, 188, 195, 200–201, 220, 232
α-elements in 241
α-function in 208
Collapse of the Bicameral Mind and the Origin of Consciousness, The 218
common sense 144–145
    of individual links with group 145
    object of attacks and 146

socialism/narcissism and
    146–149
communicate 169
conscious manipulations, of group
    bellicosity 65–67
Copernican revolution 209
Corrao, F. 103
counter-transference 15, 30, 73, 112
creative processes 238
Cremerius, J. 4
Cuore 64

de Amicis, E. 64
Dearmer, P. 63
deductive scientific system 204
De Masi, F. 52
depressive positions 18–19, 94, 136,
    174
desires 11
"divisionism" 229
Doyle, C. 14
"draft-dodgers," 67
Dream, The 103, 106, 109, 202
dream-work-α 117–130
    α-elements and 122, 124–125,
        128–130
    α-function and 122–124, 129–130
    inner wakefulness and 125
    interpretation of dream 127–128
    mental assimilation and 121–122
    structure and mental functioning
        106–108, 111–112

education for peace 67–71
    advertising and 68–69
    awareness of child's own
        individuality and 69–70
    confronting children and 69
    difficulties in 70
epistemology 209
    vs. agnoiology 167
ego 4, 49–50, 53, 66, 110, 151

civilised 58
defence from changes in analysis
    13–14
function 110
individual 22
nuclear war and 28
relation with sexuality 150–151
ego-functions 27
ego instincts 150–151
Einstein, A. 48
Elements of Psycho-Analysis 18, 184,
    187, 233–234
Ellmann, R. 192, 212
emotional weight 105
"*en passant*" 24
ephemeral mental model. *See* mental
    model
"epistemology" 175
Eternal Gospel, The 53
Experiences in Groups 6, 91–101, 106,
    155, 157, 159, 163, 169, 206
extra-economic sources 94

Ferrier, J. F. 209
Ferro, A. 138, 142
Fornari, R. 5
free-floating attention 117–130
Freud, S. 39–47, 75, 116, 202, 205, 207
Freud's theories 205, 209
Freud-Einstein correspondence
    39–48
    Freudian text 43–44
    Freud's letter 40
    Freud's "sociological" texts 44–45
    social psychoanalysis, role of
        41–43
    writing to Arnold Zweig 41
Freudian technique 198
Freudian theory of the primary
    process 187
Freudian theory of the second
    process 187

256 INDEX

Friedlander, K. 41
furor sanandi 132
Future of an Illusion, The 43

galactic map 140
Gero, G. 41
Gould, W. 52
Grid, The 207
group
  development of small 31–32
group bellicosity
  characteristics of 54–56
  conscious manipulations of 65–67
group-dynamic attitude 30–31
group dynamics 33, 36, 47, 93–94
group psychoanalysis 50–54
groups 91–101
  awareness of importance of 92
  bellicosity 54–56, 65–67
  cohesive power in small 92–93
  dynamics of 93–94
  large 33–36
  non-therapeutic 29–37
  of projective identification 97–99
  size of 93–94
  social 92
Gyomroy, E. 41

"healthily psychotic" 206
historical truth 135
holy terror 4
homo homini lupus 157
Hume, D. 13, 23
hybridity 180
hypothetical interpretations 203

id 22, 27, 49–50, 110
idea of sound 214
Iliad 23
inner alertness 80
inner wakefulness 125

inside and outside transference 131–142
  double history 135
  patient's history, application of 131–133
  psychoanalysis or psychotherapy 139–141
  relations between mental objects 137–139
  selected facts 137
  tiles of mosaic 133–135
  topology 135–137
in statu nascendi 139
Institutes of Metaphysics 175
International Psychoanalytic Association 199
Interpretation of Dreams, The 116, 212, 215, 217
intra-psychical envy 50–51
ipso facto 105
Isnenghi, M. 54, 56, 67

Jacobson, E. 41
Jacoby, R. 42
Jerusalem: William Blake 62
Jones, E. 41, 43
Joseph, B. 4, 13
Jungian Collective Unconscious 51

Kant, I. 140
Kekulé's dream 221
Kim 64
Klein, M. 18
Kleinian Development, The 18
Krieg, W. 39

"lack of charity" 205
Lancet, The 6
Lantos, B. 41
Laplanche, J. 188, 208
Learning from Experience 93, 184, 187, 200, 233–234

Levi, P. 25–26
Leviathan 53, 57
linguae 104
linguaggi 104
Lonsdale, R. 59

maternal reverie 84–85
Matte Blanco, I. 136, 238
Medical Orthodoxy and Future of Psychoanalysis 199
Meditations 230
Meltzer, D. 18, 76, 89,1 84
Memoir of the Future, A 3, 17, 95, 100–101, 103, 106, 109, 111–112, 116–117, 183–184, 186–187, 192, 202, 204, 207, 211
memory 11
mental armour 124
mental attitude 4
mental boundaries 89–90
mental models
　analyses of borderline patients 80
　beautiful in analysis 77–79
　emotional configuration 81
　fishing tackle 79–86
　interpretation of dream 83–86
　maternal reverie 84–85
　mental boundaries 89–90
　mental levels 87–88
　mental movement, concept of 74–75
　overview 73–74
　represented by images 79–83
　sense of growth 84
　vision in analysis 75–77
　visualisation of analytic work and 86–90
mental movement 74–75
Meotti, A. 81
Miller, E. 1
Molesworth, M. L. 243

Money-Kyrle, R. 41
"morality" 183
Moses and Monotheism 43
mother–infant relationship 25
"mystery" 183
myth
　eternal gospel 52–53
　racial 152–154

Nachträglichkeit 104
narcissism
　and socialism 149–151
　definition of 146–147
　primary 148, 151
　relationship with common sense 146–149
narrativisation 135
narrativise psychoanalysis 133
"narratology" 221
National Congress Party 191
Nebbiosi, G. 103
Neuroses in War 91
Nissim Momigliano, L. 2, 198
non-therapeutic group 29–37
　development of small group 31–32
　group-dynamic attitude 30–31
　hospital structure and 35
　large groups 33–36
　overview 29–31
　psychodynamics of 30
　thinks about itself 32–33
"Notes on memory and desire" 7, 10, 100, 197, 200, 203, 207, 240
nuclear war 21–28
　aggressiveness and 23
　concentration camp 26
　extermination camps 25–26
　individual ego and 22–23
　limitations of nuclear weapons 27
　problem with 22
　unthinkability of 21–28

258   INDEX

Oedipus myth 153–156
omnipotence 163–164
Onward, Christian soldiers! S. Baring-
    Gould 61
opinion-makers 71
oscillation 18, 174
Oxford University Press 240

palaeo-Christian sign 87, 127
palaeo mental zone 84
palimpsest 100
paranoid-schizoid fragmentation
    227
paranoid-schizoid position 18–19,
    94, 136
paranoid-schizoid projections 190
Past Presented, The 110
Paulo, S. 160
Peloponnesian War, The 23
Perfume 237
personality cult 67
"piece of knowledge" 172
Pizzi, N. 16
Plato 13, 23
Poincaré, H. 18, 153
Pontalis's Dictionary 188
Pontalis, J. -B. 24, 188, 208
Popp, W. 68
premature regimentation 69
Primavera 16
Pritchard, F. H. 241
process of "alphabetisation" 202
projective identification 30, 46, 73, 90,
    111, 114, 124
    basic assumptions and 97
    group of 97–99
    Kleinian theories of 94
    primordial 33
    realistic 33, 97–98
    receivers of 97
proto-dreams 218
Proust, M. 16, 201

Ps⇌D operation 17–19
    concept of triangle 19
    dispersed β-elements 18–19
    "reification" in 18–19
Psychiatry at a Time of Crisis, The
    91, 94
psychoanalysis 139–141, 199
    Bion's experience of 13–14
    Bion's mental attitude and
        12–15
    concepts and theories of 50–54
    fractal geometry 78
    group 50–54
    medical attitude in 12
    memory and desire exercise
        10–12
    narrativise 133
    psychoanalytic observation 10
    stories and 14–15
Psycho-Analysis and Groups 185
"psychoanalyst's ear" 236
psychoanalytic conceptualisation 89
"psychoanalytic" method 207
Psychoanalytic Forum, The 197
psychoanalytic interpretations 221
psychoanalytic observation 10
psychoanalytic process 208–209
psychotherapy 139–141
public-ation 225

Question of a Weltanschauun, The 42

racial myth 152–154
realistic projective identification
    33, 97–98
reasoning processes 243
Recessional: Rudyard Kipling 64
*Recommendations to
    Physicians Practising
    Psychoanalysis* 117
Reeves, M. 52
regression 98, 110–111

Reich, A. 41
reification 18
REM phases 217
Remembrance of Things Past 16, 201
Res Publica 53
"reverie" 213
reversible perspective 163–164
Rousseau, J. -J. 13, 23

Science and Method 153, 216, 234
Scientific Deductive System (SDS) 153
SDS. *See* Scientific Deductive System (SDS)
Second Thoughts 17, 107, 120, 184
Segal, H. 26
self-analysis 86
sense of frustration 25
Seven Pillars of Wisdom, The 232
Shakespeare's thought 228
socialism 146–147
    common sense and 148
    narcissism and 149–151
Soviet Union 181
specific emotional weight 104–105
Springtime 16
"stream of consciousness" 212
structure and mental functioning 103–116
    dream-work-α 106–108, 111–112
    α-elements 108–110, 113–115
    α-function 109, 113–116
    theories of 105–107, 112
super-ego 22, 27, 49–50, 110
    delinquent 110, 146
    function 110
    premature 157

Survival in Auschwitz 26
symbolic wars 66

Tavistock Clinic 182
"theory of knowledge" 175
theory of painting 229
theory of "reversible perspective" 235
Theory of Thinking, A 33, 93–95, 97–98, 169, 204
Threats to Identity in the Large Group 170
Thucydides 23
Tower of Babel, The 152–154
"trans-disciplinary dialogue" 225
transference 30
    inside and outside 131–142
transferential interpretations 88
Transformations 184, 198
"trilogy" 211

unconscious 89
unconscious memory 120
unconscious systems, for control of bellicosity 57–65

vertex 10

Waiting for Godot 191
Watts, A. 143
What do you say after you say hello? 223
Why War 48
Winnicott, D. 6, 98, 202
working group 31

Zweig, A. 41